The Critical Reception of James Baldwin, 1963–2010

Studies in American Literature and Culture:
Literary Criticism in Perspective

Brian Yothers, Series Editor
(*El Paso, Texas*)

About *Literary Criticism in Perspective*

Books in the series *Literary Criticism in Perspective* trace literary scholarship and criticism on major and neglected writers alike, or on a single major work, a group of writers, a literary school or movement. In so doing the authors—authorities on the topic in question who are also well-versed in the principles and history of literary criticism—address a readership consisting of scholars, students of literature at the graduate and undergraduate level, and the general reader. One of the primary purposes of the series is to illuminate the nature of literary criticism itself, to gauge the influence of social and historic currents on aesthetic judgments once thought objective and normative.

The Critical Reception of James Baldwin, 1963–2010

"An Honest Man and a Good Writer"

Conseula Francis

CAMDEN HOUSE
Rochester, New York

Copyright © 2014 Conseula Francis

All Rights Reserved. Except as permitted under current legislation, no part of this work may be photocopied, stored in a retrieval system, published, performed in public, adapted, broadcast, transmitted, recorded, or reproduced in any form or by any means, without the prior permission of the copyright owner.

First published 2014 by Camden House
Reprinted in paperback 2016

Camden House is an imprint of Boydell & Brewer Inc.
668 Mt. Hope Avenue, Rochester, NY 14620, USA
www.camden-house.com
and of Boydell & Brewer Limited
PO Box 9, Woodbridge, Suffolk IP12 3DF, UK
www.boydellandbrewer.com

Paperback ISBN-13: 978-1-57113-968-9
Paperback ISBN-10: 1-57113-968-0
ISBN-13: 978-1-57113-325-0
ISBN-10: 1-57113-325-9

Library of Congress Cataloging-in-Publication Data

Francis, Conseula.
 The Critical Reception of James Baldwin, 1962–2010: "An Honest Man and a Good Writer" / Conseula Francis.
   pages cm. — (Literary Criticism in Perspective) (Studies in American literature and culture)
 Includes bibliographical references and index.
 ISBN-13: 978-1-57113-325-0 (hardcover: acid-free paper)
 ISBN-10: 1-57113-325-9 (hardcover: acid-free paper)
  1. Baldwin, James, 1924–1987—Criticism and interpretation. I. Title.
PS3552.A45Z657 2014
818'.5409—dc23

2013046724

This publication is printed on acid-free paper.
Printed in the United States of America.

Contents

Acknowledgments	vii
Introduction	1

Part I

1:	Judging James Baldwin: 1963–73	7
2:	Canonizing James Baldwin: 1974–87	35
3:	Retheorizing James Baldwin: 1988–2000	59

Part II

4:	The Critical Reception of "Sonny's Blues"	81
5:	James Baldwin and the Popular Reviews	97

Part III

6:	Baldwin Studies Now	125
List of Full-Length Works by James Baldwin		145
Works Cited		147
Index		161

Acknowledgments

Any book owes its existence to many more people than the name that appears on the front cover, and this book is no different.

This book simply would not exist without the scarily efficient assistance of my graduate student Ed Lenahan.

Emmanuel Nelson proved an incomparable source of knowledge of all things Baldwin.

I could not have navigated the byzantine manuscript-to-book process without the patience and guidance of Jim Walker.

Scott Peeples, an editor and colleague par excellence, was a model of encouragement and camaraderie.

Claire Curtis and Alison Piepmeier, two-thirds of Super Ninja Writing Force, held my hand through every stage of the writing process and the book is better for it.

Frances and Cate, the Girls, were relentless in their efforts to derail the entire project at the exact same time as they were my biggest cheerleaders.

And Brian kept me supplied with comic books, purple pens, and endless debates about the minutiae of *Star Wars*, as every good husband should.

Introduction

> *All art is a kind of confession, more or less oblique. All artists, if they are to survive, are forced, at last, to tell the whole story, to vomit the anguish up.*
>
> —James Baldwin, "Northern Protestant"

IT IS DIFFICULT TO CONSIDER a survey of African American literature or the development of black intellectual thought in the twentieth century without some mention of James Baldwin. His short story "Sonny's Blues" remains a perennial favorite in literature anthologies and all of Baldwin's essay collections and novels remain in print. His first essay collection, *Notes of a Native Son*, is a seminal work that led a new generation of African American writers out from under the shadow of Richard Wright. *The Fire Next Time* is one of the most profound and accurate articulations of black consciousness during the civil rights movement. Readers and critics alike, for the past sixty years, generally agree that James Baldwin is a major African American writer. What they do not agree on is why. As a result, the reception of James Baldwin has been equal parts critical devotion and critical neglect.

Writing in *Black Women in the Fiction of James Baldwin* (1985), Trudier Harris laments that despite being "one of America's best-known writers, and certainly one of its best-known black writers, [Baldwin] has not attained a more substantial place in the scholarship on Afro-American writers" (3–4). Craig Werner asserts that "the general silence [on Baldwin's work in African American literary criticism] suggests that the larger changes in intellectual fashion have influenced the internal dynamics of discourse on Afro-American culture" ("The Economic Evolution of James Baldwin," 107). For example, the teacher's guide that accompanied the first edition of the *Norton Anthology of African American Literature*, which includes a number of Baldwin's selections, failed to include James Baldwin in its list of major authors who "have an undeniable genius or panache that uniquely distills the best [the] tradition has to offer." Manning Marable's 2003 collection of political black writing, *Let Nobody Turn Us Around: Voices on Resistance, Reform, and Renewal*, a collection Henry Louis Gates, Jr. calls "a broad compilation of the signal primary sources through which black people articulated both their always shifting and always various definitions of what, precisely, a black identity is, as well as the most efficacious methods through which to achieve our freedom," fails to mention Baldwin at all (quote from back cover).

This book is an examination of the paradox of how Baldwin is both significant to our understanding of the African American literary tradition yet remains on the periphery of that tradition. This seeming marginality, I contend, arises, ironically, from the widespread critical "availability" of Baldwin's work. The work of writers like Toni Morrison, Zora Neale Hurston, Richard Wright, and Ralph Ellison (to name but a few) commands sustained, focused critical attention, wherein critics generally agree on the most significant critical issues. No such agreement exists in Baldwin criticism. Baldwin's work speaks to, validates, and challenges a variety of critical sensibilities, resulting in his central-yet-still-marginal status in African American letters. He writes openly of homosexuality in his fiction, but seemed reluctant in his life to accept that identity as defining of his experience. He drew heavily for imagery and symbolism from the black church, but never shied from criticizing that church. He is unrelenting in his criticism of America and American institutions, yet always spoke as one of its most committed citizens. Because of this artistic and intellectual complexity, Baldwin's work resists easy categorization and, consequently, Baldwin scholarship spans the critical horizon. In this book I examine the major divisions in Baldwin criticism, paying particular attention to the way each critical period defines Baldwin and his work for its own purposes.

Writing on the critical reception of James Baldwin is difficult for a number of reasons. First, Baldwin was a widely reviewed, widely studied, prolific author. He published twenty-two full-length works in his lifetime, in addition to many essays, reviews, introductions, and interviews. In addition, his career was quite long. He made his mark on the literary scene in 1949 with his essay "Everybody's Protest Novel" and published a long essay on the Atlanta child murders and a retrospective collection of his essays in 1985. As a result of this long and prolific career, Baldwin's work experiences numerous waves of being in and out of vogue, making it difficult to ascertain which critical trends are significant in Baldwin scholarship and which are merely the result of critical fashion.

Another difficulty in studying the critical reception of Baldwin is that so many critical, political, ideological, and identity groups lay claim to him that it is almost impossible to find a critical center in Baldwin scholarship. Studying the last fifty years of Baldwin scholarship means engaging feminist and queer theory; it means considering the critical backlash against black nationalist politics; it means looking at the tradition of black American writing both inside and outside the United States; it means wading into a critical pool that is as interested in his sexuality as it is his gender and nationality and religion and taste in film. Yet it is for all these reasons that taking stocking of half a century of Baldwin criticism is also a very exciting task. Making sense of the contradictions, accounting for the absences, shedding light on the controversies, and taking stock of the trends allows us to consider Baldwin's work in a new light.

I used the following rationale when choosing which articles and reviews to discuss in this book: I included no dissertations and no articles in languages other than English, although a good case can be made for a book-length study of the critical reception of Baldwin in languages other than English and in places other than Europe and America. Rosa Bobia, *The Critical Reception of James Baldwin in France* (1997), is a notable work. I paid particular attention to articles that stand out because of quality, because they are touchstones or landmarks in Baldwin criticism, or because they are representative of a particular trend or theme. Space would not allow a discussion of every single piece of criticism ever published on Baldwin or his work and I have tried to avoid repetition where possible. While some works, particularly collections of critical essays like those edited by Fred Standley, Keith Kinnamon, and Dwight A. McBride, have critical overviews in their introductions and often provide detailed lists of reviews and criticism, what this book does is try to give an overview of the critical trends in Baldwin scholarship to put them into larger historical and critical context. In this way this book aims to provide what we don't yet have in Baldwin scholarship: a picture of that scholarship that has both breadth and depth.

The book proceeds chronologically in part 1, breaking up the criticism into three stages. I begin with the years 1963–73, the height of Baldwin's fame and influence. Chapter 1 looks primarily at essays published by Irving Howe, Eldridge Cleaver, and Robert Bone and considers not only how they articulate the most prevalent critical concerns during this period (questions around Baldwin's authenticity, his ability and right to speak for black America, whether his fame diluted his art, whether Baldwin was a good replacement for Wright), but also how they cast a shadow over Baldwin scholarship until after his death. Chapter 2 takes up the years 1974–87, the years leading up to Baldwin's death in which he continued to publish (in fact, he was quite prolific during this time), but also a period in which many reviewers and critics labeled him as out of touch, old-fashioned, and irrelevant. Despite this claim of irrelevancy by some, this is the period of canonization in Baldwin scholarship, the years in which critics take to the task of close reading and attempt to determine what Baldwin's legacy will be. The final chapter in part 1 looks at the years 1988–2000, the years following Baldwin's death, in which there was a reassessment of Baldwin's place in American literary history and in the African American literary canon, primarily because of the burgeoning field of queer studies.

Part 2 proceeds a little differently. In chapter 4 I look at the criticism of Baldwin's most famous and most anthologized short story,

"Sonny's Blues." The critical conversation around this story stands almost wholly apart from the rest of Baldwin scholarship and warrants a discussion of its own. Chapter 5 looks at the popular reviews of all twenty-two of Baldwin's full-length works. As I argue in that chapter, looking at only academic criticism allows us to talk about only five, maybe six, of Baldwin's books. The popular reviews give us a fuller picture of Baldwin's entire career and also help to flesh out the conversation taking place in the criticism. Finally, in part 3, I end with a consideration of the current state of Baldwin scholarship, the scholarship that has been published since 2000. While literary criticism is, ultimately, always an exercise in the selective perception of a single critical mind, this final chapter is particularly selective. Without the benefit of hindsight to assist in assessing the most significant work published on Baldwin during this period, I instead consider criticism that seems to chart new territory in Baldwin studies.

James Baldwin wrote about the triumphs and failings of American democracy, about the church and families, about love and sex and identity, about American history and American amnesia, about the world shaping and shaped by the Negro. He seemed endlessly interested in all facets of human experience and endeavor. And because this interest played out in his work, critics from a wide range of critical schools—feminist, queer theory, reader response, poststructuralist, ethnic and multicultural, Marxist, psychoanalytic, new critical—find that his work resonates. This book, then, is as much about idiosyncratic critics and criticism as it is about Baldwin and his work. The nature of a work like this one, which spans nearly fifty years of criticism, demands that we account for changing tastes and practices in literary criticism, as well as account for how that criticism treats Baldwin's work. In the case of this book, we find tremendous changes in literary criticism (we are in the era when theory becomes Theory), and Baldwin's work often serves as a critical Rorschach test, especially where African American literature is concerned. With *The Critical Reception of James Baldwin* I hope to shed some light on these trends and detail the many rich and varied voices that comprise Baldwin studies.

Part I

1: Judging James Baldwin: 1963–73

JAMES BALDWIN PUBLISHED his third novel, *Another Country*, in 1962. The story of Rufus Scott and his intimate circle of friends, featuring numerous and constantly shifting heterosexual, homosexual, and interracial couplings, *Another Country* was greeted by critics with, at best, mixed reviews and, at worst, disgust. (It did, however, become a best-seller.) The author of the beautiful, lyrical *Go Tell It on the Mountain* (1953) and the piercing, soulful essays of *Notes of a Native Son* (1955) and *Nobody Knows My Name* (1961) had seemingly betrayed his audience's trust. The homosexual themes of *Giovanni's Room* (1956) turned out not to be an aberration. The critical uproar was almost deafening.

Therefore, we can well imagine, there was more than the usual anticipation with the publication of *The Fire Next Time* in 1963. Here was a chance for Baldwin to redeem himself, and the prospects looked good, as he returned to the form and content he had built his reputation on—essays on the American racial drama. But what Baldwin delivered, rather than a gut-wrenching confessional that carried the promise of reconciliation and healing, was a prophecy of apocalypse: "God gave Noah the rainbow sign, No more water, the fire next time!"

While critics and readers were decidedly uncomfortable with *The Fire Next Time* (if the reviews are any indication), especially the sympathy he expresses for Elijah Muhammad's Black Muslim movement, this book nonetheless sold extremely well and catapulted Baldwin to a new level of celebrity. Whereas before *The Fire Next Time* Baldwin's reputation and fame didn't reach very far outside literary circles, after *The Fire Next Time* he became a staple of mainstream public media. In 1963 alone he embarked on a lecture tour for the Congress on Racial Equality (CORE). He lectured widely throughout the South and made numerous appearances on TV and radio. He appeared on the cover of *Time* and as part of a photo story in *Life* in May. Along with Dr. Kenneth Clark, Lorraine Hansberry, Clarence B. Jones, Jerome Smith, Lena Horne, Edwin C. Berry, Harry Belafonte, Rip Torn, and Henry Morgenthau, he met with then attorney general Robert Kennedy to urge the Kennedy administration to more forceful action in the fight for civil rights. He participated in the march on Washington and worked with the Student Non-violent Coordination Committee (SNCC) in a voter registration drive in Selma, Alabama.

Baldwin's popularity, his sudden leap to the cultural forefront, can be explained, I think, by the seeming prophecy of *The Fire Next Time*. The

1963 bombing of the 16th Street Baptist Church in Birmingham (known to many in the civil rights movement as "Bombingham"), which resulted in the deaths of four black girls, the murder of Medgar Evers in Mississippi, the assassination of John F. Kennedy, and the increasingly violent response to civil rights protests seemed to be Baldwin's "fire" realized.

Baldwin's popularity can also be attributed to shifting literary tastes concerning African American literature. Richard Wright's publication of *Native Son* in 1940 "shifted the paradigm of African American writing" (Dickson-Carr, 8–9). Noel Schraufnagel's *From Apology to Protest: The Black American Novel* (1973) credits *Native Son* with the birth of the modern novel. Schraufnagel goes on to say that *Native Son* makes such an impression because "most novels of black Americans either avoided racial issues or were in the apologetic tradition, which portrayed Negro characters who were physically victimized by white racists. Wright began a new trend in protest literature by presenting a character who is psychologically thwarted by racism" (ix). The impact of *Native Son* created a particular set of expectations of African American literature in the minds of readers. They came to expect psychological realism, social commentary, and "protest" from black writers. The period in which Wright reigned supreme as America's premier black writer (the 1940s to mid-1950s) was even termed the "protest era" (though many writers of this era don't fit comfortably in the Wright school or urban realism, including Dorothy West, Ann Petry, Gwendolyn Brooks, Margaret Walker, Ralph Ellison, and James Baldwin). But while Wright may have commanded a new audience for African American literature, "protest" was never taken quite seriously as art.

Ralph Ellison's 1952 novel *Invisible Man* "elicited a new respect for black authorship" (Dickson-Carr, 9) and raised expectations for the aesthetic quality of African American literature. Many critics read his work, as well as that of Baldwin's, as the "major challenge to protest literature." The "high-minded critics" (as Irving Howe calls them in his "Black Boys and Native Sons") had, by 1963, grown unimpressed and frustrated with African American protest literature and seemed eager to pass the proverbial torch on to the next generation of black writers who they saw as eager to abandon Wright's brand of literary naturalism. In addition, perhaps in reaction to the upheaval of political and social protest movements of the time, the reading public seemed eager for African American literature that didn't shout so loudly.

This chapter considers the critical reception of Baldwin's work at the height of his career, from 1963, the year Baldwin published *The Fire Next Time* and appeared on the cover of *Time*, to 1973, the year *Time* declared Baldwin too passé to publish an interview with him. During this period, critics seem interested, more than anything else, in appraising Baldwin's work and career. They seem to be asking whether Baldwin has earned or deserves his newfound celebrity. While few of the essays and articles discussed in this chapter explicitly mention debates over protest in African American literature, they are nonetheless informed by this critical conversation. And while many of the critics do explicitly take on Baldwin's increasing celebrity and popularity as a topic, they fail to recognize how that celebrity unfairly colors their perception of Baldwin's work. This is especially true of the three essays that anchor this period as touchstones of Baldwin scholarship: Irving Howe, "Black Boys and Native Sons" (1963); Robert Bone, "The Novels of James Baldwin" (1965); and Eldridge Cleaver, "Notes on a Native Son" (1968). While contemporary scholarship invokes these essays primarily to challenge the assertions made about Baldwin and his work, the fact that over forty years later critics still feel it necessary to engage their arguments speaks to the critical sway Howe, Bone, and Cleaver have held over Baldwin scholarship.

In the Shadow of Richard Wright

Before we begin a thorough discussion of these essays, however, it is imperative to return to the figure of Richard Wright, particularly the assumption informing the essays of Howe, Bone, and Cleaver (and many other critics)—namely, that Wright is the epitome of the black male artist as spokesman and that his vision of black America is true. In one way or another, Howe, Bone, and Cleaver, in assessing Baldwin and his career, are asking if Baldwin is worthy or capable of taking Wright's place in the American imagination.

Ralph Ellison, in the 1945 essay "Richard Wright's Blues" (an essay also notable for Ellison's famous definition of the blues), defines the role of black male artist-as-spokesman that Wright occupies: "to discover and depict the meaning of Negro experience, and to reveal to both Negroes and whites those problems of a psychological and emotional nature which arise between them when they strive for mutual understanding" (128). Wright occupied this role for many years. *Native Son* was the first novel by an African American to be named a main selection by the Book of the Month Club. The novel, along with his autobiography *Black Boy* (1945), secured Wright a prominent spot on the American literary landscape. These works also paint a grim portrait of African American life that would become fixed in the American imagination. In *Black Boy*, Wright writes:

> After I had outlived the shocks of childhood, after the habit of reflection had been born in me, I used to mull over the strange absence of real kindness in Negroes, how unstable was our tenderness, how lacking in genuine passion we were, how void of great hope, how timid our joy, how bare our traditions, how hollow our memories, how lacking we were in those intangible sentiments that bind man

to man, and how shallow was even our despair. After I had learned other ways of life I used to brood upon the unconscious irony of those who felt that Negroes led so passional [*sic*] an existence! I saw that what had been taken for emotional strength was our negative confusions, our flights, our fears, our frenzy under pressure." (37)

This vision of a people so damaged by American racism that they lived only the shallowest of emotional lives is one that held much sway with the American public, especially with the critics considered in this chapter. Howe and Bone, and to some extent Cleaver, in their criticism of Baldwin, all seek to defend Wright's vision, or, at the very least, his legacy. Writers like Baldwin and Ellison are viewed as pretenders to the throne, though Baldwin certainly bears most of the criticism.

Part of the problem is the way Baldwin views himself in the world. In the "Autobiographical Notes" that begin *Notes of a Native Son* (1955), he writes:

I do not like people who like me because I am a Negro; neither do I like people who find in the same accident grounds for contempt. I love America more than any other country in the world, and, exactly for this reason, I insist on the right to criticize her perpetually. I think all theories are suspect, that the finest principles may have to be modified, or may even be pulverized by the demands of life, and that one must find, therefore, one's moral center and move through the world hoping that this center will guide one aright. I consider that I have many responsibilities, but none greater than this: to last, as Hemingway says, and get my work done.

I want to be an honest man and a good writer.[1]

The above quote is deceptively straightforward, a simple (though beautifully evocative) statement of purpose. Of course, Baldwin isn't simply, humbly, offering us insights drawn from the view from his "moral center." Baldwin, here, seeks to define for himself the kind of writer he will be, a luxury not granted African American writers in the 1950s. He doesn't want to be Richard Wright. He wants to be an "honest man and a good writer." This goal of honesty and goodness, perhaps more than any other statement Baldwin will make, informs much of the criticism of this period. Coupled with his famous criticism of *Native Son* in "Everybody's Protest Novel" (and in "Many Thousands Gone"), Baldwin's goal of becoming an "honest man and a good writer" reads almost like a manifesto, like drawing a line in the sand on the other side of which stands Richard Wright and his legacy. At the very least, critics from this period seem to read it this way.

In repeatedly invoking the figure of Wright in their essays, Howe, Bone, and Cleaver challenge us to measure Baldwin by the standards he sets for himself, and force us to consider the expectations we have for black male artists. Howe, the founding editor of *Dissent* and famed New York intellectual, published "Black Boys and Native Sons" in *Dissent* in Autumn 1963, shortly after the publication of *The Fire Next Time*. To Howe's credit, I think he genuinely intends to do the work of the critic—assess the aesthetic value and accomplishment of Baldwin's (and, to a lesser extent, Ralph Ellison's) work. The first paragraph gives a fairly accurate summary of Baldwin on Wright and it seems as if Howe is going to engage Baldwin's ideas about the "failure of the protest novel." While generally dismissive of Baldwin's criticism of protest, likening it to the "attacks launched by young writers against their famous fathers" as "a kind of announcement of [their] intentions" ("Black Boys and Native Sons," 254), Howe nonetheless makes a good point.

> If it is true, as Baldwin said in "Everybody's Protest Novel," that "literature and sociology are not one and the same," it is equally true that such statements hardly begin to cope with the problem of how a writer's own experience affects his desire to represent human affairs in a work of fiction. Baldwin's formula evades, through rhetorical sweep, the genuinely difficult issue of the relationship between social experience and literature. (255)

Perhaps Baldwin doesn't, in fact, allow that it is difficult to keep one's experience from shaping one's art, or relatedly, that Wright's experience could have resulted in nothing other than Bigger Thomas. Perhaps, Howe seems to imply here, Wright's "social experience" of Mississippi is different from Baldwin's experience of Harlem, and we can't easily dismiss those differences in experience when studying the literature they give rise to. But the reader expects further explication of this idea, and expects that Howe will provide a new defense of the Wright school of protest literature. Instead, we get a definition of art that forgives the black writer for producing bad books and a backhanded compliment for Baldwin's work.

Howe clearly thinks of Wright as the epitome of the black spokesman, by which he means the black writer who translates the black experience for white America. His greatest strength as a writer, at least according to Howe, is his willingness to embrace the rage engendered by the black male existence (*Native Son* is, by all accounts, a violent, angry novel). Howe writes:

> In all its crudeness, melodrama and claustrophobia of vision, Richard Wright's novel brought out into the open, as no one ever had before, the hatred, fear and violence that have crippled and may yet destroy our culture.... Wright forced his readers to acknowledge his anger, and in that way, if none other, he wrested for himself a sense of dignity, as a man (256).

Howe assumes that Baldwin and Ellison fail to see the dignity of Wright's anger and views this rejection of Wright's form of protest, literary naturalism, as a betrayal. These two "native sons" fail as spokesmen, according to Howe, when they reject the "black boy" that is Wright.

Howe goes on to say, "If such younger novelists as Baldwin and Ralph Ellison were able to move beyond Wright's harsh naturalism and toward more supple modes of fiction, that was possible only because Wright had been there first, courageous enough to release the full weight of his anger" (256). And while Howe acknowledges that Baldwin may have a point about the burden of the "full weight of anger," he nevertheless defends the role of spokesman: "All one can ask, by way of reply, is whether the refusal to struggle may not exact a still greater price" (262). And it is this sympathy for the struggle that ultimately leads Howe, despite his criticisms, to defend Baldwin against charges that his tone, with the publication of *The Fire Next Time*, had become too strident.

Howe asserts that Baldwin, by 1963, had finally, if belatedly, given in to the "blackness" of his experience, which he can't help but express in Wright-like terms.

> He wanted to move, as Wright had not been able to, beyond the burden or bravado of his stigma; he wanted to enter the world of freedom, grace, and self-creation. One would need a heart of stone, or to be a brutal moralist, to feel anything but sympathy for this desire. But we do not make our circumstances; we can, at best, try to remake them. And all the recent writing of Baldwin indicates that the wishes of youth could not be realized, not in this country. The sentiments of humanity which had made him rebel against Richard Wright have now driven him back to a position close to Wright's rebellion. (268)

According to Howe, evidence of this rebellion can be seen in *The Fire Next Time* and Baldwin's essays on Harlem and the South, essays that "gain at least some of their resonance from the tone of unrelenting protest in which they are written, from the very anger, even the violence Baldwin had begun by rejecting.... Like Richard Wright before him, Baldwin has discovered that to assert his humanity he must release his rage" (270). Here Howe suggests that if Baldwin (and, to some extent, Ellison) actually did move African American literature in a new direction, it was only to find that the old path, the path of Wrightian protest, is the most useful in writing about black life.

To prove his point, Howe has praise for Baldwin the novelist as well. Whereas he dismisses Baldwin's widely acknowledged masterpiece *Go Tell It on the Mountain* as an "enticing but minor work" (263), he champions the much-maligned *Another Country*, calling it a protest novel.

> The narrative voice is a voice of anger, rasping and thrusting, not at all "literary" in the somewhat lacquered way the earlier Baldwin was able to achieve. And what that voice says, *no longer held back by the proprieties of literature*, is that the nightmare of the history we have made allows us no immediate escape. Even if all the visible tokens of injustices were erased, the Negroes would retain their hatred and the whites their fear and guilt. Forgiveness cannot be speedily willed, if willed at all, and before it can even be imagined there will have to be a fuller discharge of those violent feelings that have so long been suppressed. (268–69, my emphasis)

It is important to note here that Howe's praise rests on the assumption that *Another Country* is not as "literary" as Baldwin's other work. Freed from the "proprieties of literature," Baldwin, like Wright before him, is able to unleash an authentic (angry, unforgiving) black voice. Howe implies a definition of literature that must be put aside when dealing with work by black writers. Good literature seems to require emotional and intellectual distance (what Baldwin tries to achieve early in his career, what Wright recognizes as impossible), yet the power of African American literature lies in the inseparability of the writer and the work. These two assumptions of Howe's allow him to forgive what he perceives as poor aesthetic quality in African American literature. They allow Baldwin to be a failed writer and *Native Son* to be a failed novel, yet both remain important.

For all the praise he heaps on Wright and *Native Son*, Howe seems to have very little respect for the novel as a work of art.

> That *Native Son* has grave faults anyone can see. The language is often coarse, flat in rhythm, syntactically overburdened, heavy with journalistic slag. Apart from Bigger, who seems more a brute energy than a particularized figure, the characters have little reality, the Negroes being mere stock accessories and the whites either "agit-prop" villains or heroic Communists whom Wright finds it easier to admire from a distance than establish from the inside. (258)

But Wright is forgiven these "grave faults" because "Negro existence" is so harsh that objective distance, a requirement of good art, is impossible. Howe writes:

> A certain amount of obsession may be necessary for the valid portrayal—writers devoted to themes of desperation cannot keep themselves morally intact. And when we come to a writer like Richard Wright, who deals with the most degraded and inarticulate sector of the Negro world, the distinction between objective rendering and subjective immersion becomes still more difficult, perhaps even impossible. For a novelist who has lived through the searing

> experiences that Wright has there cannot be much possibility of approaching his subject with the "mature" poise recommended by the high-minded critics. (260)

And it is these high-minded critics, those criticizing Baldwin and *The Fire Next Time*, whom Howe has in mind in this essay. Though he clearly has a bone to pick with Baldwin and Ellison, and he clearly is seeking to preserve Wright's legacy, Howe seems most interested in defending African American literature, defined for Howe as protest literature. Howe understands that we should be wary of praising or encouraging the kind of violence we see in *Native Son*. Seemingly conceding to the literary culture of the time, he acknowledges that we should caution against a too "subjective immersion" into one's subject matter. Yet, he maintains, African American literature, particularly protest fiction, is too powerful and important to dismiss, despite these faults: "To say this is not to propose the condescension of exempting Negro writers from moral judgment, but to suggest the terms of understanding, and still more, the terms of hesitation for making a judgment" (260).

Howe's essay remains significant for a couple of reasons. First, it occasions a very famous response from Ralph Ellison, in the essay "The World and the Jug," who says that Howe sees in the black man "not a human being but an abstract embodiment of living hell" (159). Second, it is one of the first in a flurry of critical essays during this era examining the so-called Wright-Baldwin debate. This debate, consisting of three essays by Baldwin ("Everybody's Protest Novel," "Many Thousands Gone" in 1951, and "Alas, Poor Richard" in 1961) and a few comments by Wright, was rehashed by numerous critics at this time, in part because, like Howe, they are reacting to Wright's death in 1960. They want to determine whether the new kid on the block, Baldwin, is worthy of taking Wright's place.

The best of these critical essays is Maurice Charney's "James Baldwin's Quarrel with Richard Wright" (1963).[2] Rather than using the "quarrel" to stake a (usually black nationalist) ideological position or to write off the issue as simply an instance of literary patricide, Charney attempts to get at the heart of the difference between the two writers.

> Baldwin's quarrel with Wright, then, centers on the large issues of the intention and aim and values of the writer. Although both feel the inevitable rage of being a Negro in the United States, their ways of dealing with this rage are radically different. One makes fiction out of the rage itself, brutal, pure, violent and unconstrained, while the other tries to penetrate and analyze that rage and convert it into a recognizable human emotion. (66)

While Charney will spend most of the essay discussing Baldwin's work, it is important to note here that he doesn't judge Wright's work harshly.

Unlike Howe, who perceives only one way for the black male writer to speak to white America, Charney seems to see a multitude of ways and identifies this as the ultimate quarrel between Wright and Baldwin. Baldwin's "attack on the protest novel," Charney says, "is really an attack on the assumptions of naturalism" (74). And here is where Charney is at his most insightful. Rather than taking Baldwin to task for failing to live up to Wright's example, or criticizing Baldwin for giving into "protest" despite his earlier disdain (as other essays examining this quarrel tend to do), Charney takes Baldwin at his word. Baldwin says he wants to be an "honest man and a good writer" and Charney tries to get at what Baldwin wants to be honest about. He concludes that Baldwin sees that "the Negro problem is part of a more general injustice of man to man, perhaps a reflection of the capacity for evil in the nature of things that the innocently optimistic American refuses to see" (72). Baldwin, then, acknowledges the specificity of American racial drama (Baldwin insists that we remain ever cognizant of the historical circumstances of the current American racial drama), but he also says that the pain of this drama is not new. If the innocent American has to accept that he is, as a human, capable of evil, then the black American must also acknowledge that his suffering is not unique, even though his situation may be.

That Baldwin comes to these kinds of conclusions puts him at odds with the growing black nationalist movement of the 1960s. Many blacks, both inside and outside the mainstream civil rights movement, grew frustrated with the violent response to nonviolent resistance. They also became disenchanted with the idea of integration, arguing, among other things, that the black community possessed everything it needed to sustain itself and that middle (white) America offered little of value to black people. For those of this ideological bent, Baldwin was an anathema.[3]

Among Baldwin's harshest critics was Eldridge Cleaver, arguably the most visible and virulent spokesman of black power. Cleaver gained notoriety as the author of *Soul on Ice* (1968), an essay collection he wrote while serving a prison sentence for attempted murder and as minister of information for the Black Panther Party. An essay in *Soul on Ice*, "Notes on a Native Son," is famous for its outrageous homophobic attack on Baldwin.[4] Indeed, this essay becomes a touchstone for queer theory scholars who take up Baldwin's work after his death. The essay starts off innocently enough with Cleaver praising Baldwin's genius (a familiar move in Baldwin criticism of this period):

> After reading a couple of James Baldwin's books, I began experiencing that continuous delight one feels upon discovering a fascinating, brilliant talent on the scene, a talent capable of penetrating so profoundly into one's own little world that one knows oneself to have been unalterably changed and *liberated*, liberated from the

frustrating grasp of whatever devils happen to possess one (*Soul on Ice*, 97).

This clever rhetorical move makes the rest of the essay that much more damning. Cleaver is nothing short of reverent in this passage, so we are sympathetic when, upon closer inspection of Baldwin's work, particularly *Another Country*, Cleaver comes to the following conclusion: "There is in James Baldwin's work the most grueling, agonizing, total hatred of the blacks, particularly of himself, and the most shameful, fanatical, fawning, sycophantic love of the whites that one can find in the writings of any black American writer of note in our time" (99).

Leaving aside for the moment the incredibly facile reading of Baldwin that Cleaver offers here, at the heart of this statement is a common criticism of Baldwin lodged by African American readers and critics at the time. Many felt that Baldwin talked too eagerly and too exclusively to white America, and thus could be of no real use to *black* people (not Negroes or colored) in need of a revolution. Cleaver may have a good point about Baldwin's relevance, about his ability to speak truthfully about black experience to white people, about the usefulness of that project, about the effect of Baldwin's celebrity on his work. However, he leaves this argument aside, choosing instead to pursue the issue of self-hatred of black homosexuals:

> The white man has deprived him of his masculinity, castrated him in the center of his burning skull, and when he submits to this change and takes the white man for his lover as well as Big Daddy, he focuses on "whiteness" all the love in his pent up soul and turns the razor edge of hatred against "blackness"—upon himself, what he is, and all those who look like him, remind him of himself. He may even hate the darkness of night.... The racial death-wish is manifested as the driving force in James Baldwin. (103)

While Cleaver never actually identifies Baldwin as homosexual, the reader doesn't need much help making the connections Cleaver implies here. But just in case we need some help, Cleaver offers us the figure of Richard Wright to show us what a black male writer should be. He says of Wright, "Of all black American novelists, and indeed all American novelists of any hue, Richard Wright reigns supreme for his profound political, economic, and social reference" (108). As an added bonus, all the men in Wright's work are "strongly heterosexual" (106). The same cannot be said for Baldwin's characters, or, by implication, of Baldwin.

While Baldwin certainly didn't identify as "gay" or live his life "out" in the way we think of these terms post-Stonewall, neither did he hide his relationships with men. And while Cleaver doesn't exactly "out" Baldwin in this essay, his intent is clear.

The case of James Baldwin aside for the moment, it seems that many Negro homosexuals, acquiescing in this racial death-wish, are outraged and frustrated because in their sickness they are unable to have a baby by a white man. The cross they have to bear is that, already bending over and touching their toes for the white man, the fruit of their miscegenation is not the little half-white offspring of their dreams but an increase in the unwinding of their nerves— though they redouble their efforts and intake of the white man's sperm. (102)

Beneath the surface of this homophobic rant, Cleaver is accusing Baldwin of failing as a black artist because he fails as a black man (which, sad to say, Cleaver can only speak about in the most vulgar, patriarchal, heterosexist terms). Coming on the heels of Baldwin's transformation into a fiery black spokesman, Cleaver seems to be suggesting that Baldwin's anger is impotent, not only because of its late arrival in *The Fire Next Time*, but also because, according to Cleaver, it is born not of genuine frustration and exhaustion with the American racial predicament (as is presumably the case with black nationalism), or of a sincere desire for racial revolution, but rather of a kind of heartbreak. Cleaver portrays Baldwin as a jilted lover, rejected and acting out in pain. Couple this with the emphasis on embodiment during the Black Power and Black Arts movements (black male writers were supposed to *swagger* in person and in print) and we get a portrait of a decidedly counterrevolutionary Baldwin.

And it is revolution that Cleaver, and other nationalists, are interested in. For Cleaver, the future of black America is at stake. In order for black people to survive the American racial onslaught, they must experience a shift in their collective consciousness, a shift that will be facilitated by the work of revolutionary artists. As Cleaver states, "We are engaging in the deepest, the most fundamental revolution and reconstruction which men have ever been called upon to make in their lives, and which they absolutely cannot escape or avoid except at the peril of the very continued existence of human life on this planet" (*Soul on Ice*, 110). Baldwin's homosexuality, in his work and in his life, makes him unsuited, according to Cleaver, to prepare black people for this "reconstruction." Cleaver does not "think homosexuality is the latest advance over heterosexuality on the scale of human evolution. Homosexuality is a sickness, just as are baby-rape or wanting to become head of General Motors" (110).

Although Cleaver's essay sets the contours of the conversation (Baldwin is counterrevolutionary, Baldwin is only concerned with whites, Baldwin fails as a successor to Wright), other writers are more lucid and evenhanded in their criticism of Baldwin and their belief that his work is insufficient for the revolutionary cause. Larry Neal, a prominent writer and critic of the Black Arts movement and the editor, with Amiri Baraka, of the seminal anthology *Black Fire* (1968), begins his 1966 essay, "The

Black Writer's Role—James Baldwin," by acknowledging Baldwin's complexity. Rather than trying to place Baldwin somewhere on the protest continuum, though, Neal instead focuses on the "public character" of Baldwin's work: "It is as if the public were witnessing something on the order of a confession; and the only thing that finally saves it from being something so mundane is the excellence of the writing" (58). Despite this excellence, however, Baldwin fails to confront or reject mainstream white American ideals. He fails to replace those ideals with new ones derived from black America. Neal considers Baldwin the "conscience of a movement (civil rights) which has as its goal integration into a dying system" (60) and someone who cannot differentiate between the truth of the oppressed and the truth of the oppressor. Thus, Neal concludes, Baldwin fails not as a writer, but rather as a revolutionary. While willing to grant him intellectual and artistic complexity, Neal contends that Baldwin ultimately fails to aid black people in their quest for liberation.

J. Saunders Redding, a prominent African American literary critic in the 1960s and a frequent reviewer of Baldwin, assesses the African American literary landscape in 1966 in "Since Richard Wright." He laments that there are no "Negro writers" to take Wright's place because, while there were prominent black writers, "the best known of these were, in a most precise sense, eccentric and as creative writers—novelists—could scarcely be called Negro.... When they put on American spectacles to examine what they looked at, and when they reacted in the approved American way to what they saw—which was exactly and only what other Americans saw—they ceased being American *Negro* writers, and settled for being American writers" (21, original emphasis). Redding discusses in detail several black writers, and starts with Baldwin, perhaps because he is the most prominent at the time. While he grants that Baldwin displays "integrity" in his "honest and urgent" essays (23), he is disappointed in Baldwin as a novelist. Like Cleaver and Neal, Redding seems to look to black writers to reveal "the special truths that Negroes know better than anyone else" (22), believing that this revelation will have particular importance to black people fighting for liberation. Redding reads Baldwin as avoiding these truths, as accepting the "white man's view of reality" (22). Thus, no matter how superior he may be to Wright in craft, he cannot take Wright's place because he lacks the courage to reject the will of white America.

While all the critics discussed thus far have acknowledged Baldwin's exceptional artistic skill, their admiration of his gifts as a writer was not universally held. Robert A. Bone's *The Negro Novel in America* (1958) garnered much respect in African American literary critical circles. The 1965 revised edition features a blurb from a review in the *College Language Association Journal* (the College Language Association, the African American equivalent of the Modern Language Association):

"Bone has skillfully interwoven those varied themes into a highly sophisticated social and aesthetic critique. His technical facility as a critic, combined with a shrewd insight, a lively style and a flair for the well-turned phrase, combine to make *The Negro Novel in America* a remarkable piece of scholarship" (back cover). Another blurb, from *Interracial Review*, reads, "Mr. Bone is to be congratulated for the extent to which he illuminates the vicissitudes, aberrations, and achievements, of the Negro novelist in America. He brilliantly succeeds in bringing into a cohesive pattern the development of the Negro novel" (back cover). In the acknowledgements Bone thanks his "colored friends, who taught [him] what it is not possible to learn in libraries" (vii). Bone, not black himself, seems to be sincere in his project and seems to have the blessing of the African American literary establishment. The book remains one of the earliest serious, oft-cited extended treatments of African American fiction.

Bone's aim in this book is corrective. He contends that most criticism treats the "Negro novel ... primarily as social documents, and [they are] 'evaluated' according to the social bias of the critic" (7). Bone, instead, aims to offer "literary judgments" to "distinguish the peaks from the valleys, to determine which of these novels are worth remembering and which are best forgotten" (8). To do this he employs two concepts—"assimilationism and Negro nationalism"—because these concepts are "indispensable to understanding the cultural history of the American Negro" (7). Bone argues that recognizing that individual blacks as well as black culture and history travels between these two poles will better allow critical (rather than ideological) engagement of the "Negro novel."

Bone's project moves through the history of the Negro novel, beginning with late nineteenth-century works like *Clotel* and *The Garies and Their Friends*, establishing a tradition that runs between the poles of assimilationism and nationalism. Though there isn't space here to discuss all the specifics of Bone's argument, his discussion of Wright and *Native Son* is pertinent. Bone considers *Native Son* a part of the post-Harlem Renaissance period of the African American novel, and as part of the American tradition of the modern novel. He talks at great length about exactly where *Native Son* falls in these traditions. He has mostly words of praise for Wright and his most famous novel. He determines that of "the Negro novelists who wrote during the Great Depression, Richard Wright came closest to expressing the essential spirit of the decade" (151). He concludes that "Wright's contribution to the Negro novel was precisely his fusion of a pronounced racialism with a broader tradition of social protest" (152). For black writers interested in writing socially relevant novels that nonetheless maintained artistic integrity, Wright, according to Bone, served as an excellent template.

But, Bone contends, Wright was followed by pale imitators, a group he refers to as the Wright school:

> A novelist who wishes to transcend the limitations of naturalism must seek the meaning of events, must try to convey their impact on his characters. And this is precisely the difference between Richard Wright and his disciples: Wright sees the significance of Bigger Thomas, while his imitators seldom rise above mere sensationalism. For the Wright School, literature is an emotional catharsis—a means of dispelling the inner tensions of race. Their novels often amount to a prolonged cry of anguish and despair. Too close to their material, feeling it too tensely, these novelists lack a sense of form and of thematic line. With rare exceptions, their style consists of a brutal realism, devoid of any love, or even respect for words. (158)

What Wright does, and his disciples fail to do, is write novels of social protest (novels with racial conflict, according to Bone [166]) while maintaining the requisite psychological and emotional distance (echoing Howe's definition of good literature). It is exactly this lack of distance that Bone will criticize in Baldwin's novels.

The essay on Baldwin's novels is a postscript in the 1965 edition of *The Negro Novel in America*. The preceding chapter, on the "revolt against protest" in the 1940s, which features an extended reading of Ellison's *Invisible Man*, ends this way:

> In the end, Ellison succeeds brilliantly in rendering blackness visible. By far the best novel yet written by an American Negro, *Invisible Man* is quite possibly the best American novel since Word War II. In any event, Ellison has set a high standard for contemporary Negro fiction. There was a period in the history of the Negro novel when a simple literacy was to be marveled at. Now, a century after Brown's *Clotel*, historical relativity is no longer a valid attitude. With the appearance of such novels as *Cane*, *Native Son*, and *Invisible Man*, the reading public has a right to expect no less than the best from the serious Negro artist. (212)

Bone defines a set of expectations we can legitimately bring to the African American novel. We no longer have to excuse bad writing or forgive a too-political tone (as Howe suggests we do). We have arrived at a point, Bone implies, where the serious African American novel (and Baldwin would certainly be considered a serious black novelist) can be considered with the same "serious" critical tools we use to read other novels.

Bone considers Baldwin the "most important Negro writer to emerge during the last decade" (215). It is not clear, however, if he considers Baldwin important because of his success, popularity, influence, or talent. He does make clear, though, that we can't let Baldwin's popularity blind us to the unevenness of his work. As critics, we must put popularity aside, no matter how difficult.

> The author's popular acclaim, his current role as a political celebrity, and the Broadway production of his recent play have all tended to obscure the true state of affairs. But Baldwin must suspect that his hipster phase is coming to a close. He has already devoted two novels to his sexual rebellion. If he persists, he will surely be remembered as the greatest American novelist since Jack Kerouac. (239)

Hoping to save Baldwin from what Bone perceives as the sad fate of Kerouac (a writer he clearly holds in low esteem), Bone tries to get to the "true state of affairs" by dividing Baldwin's career in two parts, one controlled by the "emotion of shame," the other by the "emotion of rage."

> His first five books have been concerned with the emotion of shame. The flight from self, the quest for identity, and the sophisticated acceptance of one's "blackness" are the themes that flow from this emotion. His last three books [*The Fire Next Time, Another Country*, and *Blues for Mr. Charlie*] have been concerned with the emotion of rage. An apocalyptic vision and a new stridency of tone are brought to bear against the racial and the sexual oppressor. (218)

Baldwin can finally give himself over to this rage, argues Bone, because Wright has died. He no longer has to rebel against his father by avoiding protest. In turning from essays to novels and plays, Baldwin places himself firmly in Wright's literary shadow. And whereas Bone praises Baldwin's most prophetic, protesting essays, he places Baldwin's novels squarely in the Wright school of the Negro novel and judges Baldwin as a disciple who fails to live up to Wright's literary example.

Bone also seems to accuse Baldwin of dishonesty, a great insult indeed, considering the artistic goals Baldwin has set for himself. Rather than the "honest man and good writer" Baldwin strives to be, Bone instead sees that "good works and politics have been the recent bent of his career. Unable to grow as an artist, he has fallen back upon a tradition of protest which he formerly denounced" (217). Bone sees a career on the decline. The relative popular successes of *The Fire Next Time, Blues for Mister Charlie*, and *Another Country*, despite what Bone perceives as their artistic bankruptcy, are evidence of this.

Though Bone insists that we put aside Baldwin's popularity (presumably because only the words on the page matter), his own reading of Baldwin nonetheless depends on a particular understanding of Baldwin's biography. Bone argues that we can "account for the unevenness" in Baldwin's work through a "closer acquaintance with the author's life" (216). And when we look at that life we find that the "overwhelming fact of Baldwin's childhood was his victimization by the white power structure" (219). We might assume that Bone determines the "overwhelming fact" of Baldwin's life by studying closely the actual details of that life. However, the whole of Bone's essay suggests that his conclusions about Baldwin's life are based on an essentialist understanding of African American life.

The power of *Go Tell It on the Mountain*, the only one of Baldwin's novels Bone deems worthy of praise, seems to lie, for Bone, in its depiction of the black church and the role it plays in black life. For Bone, *Go Tell It on the Mountain* cuts through the walls of the storefront church to the "essence of Negro experience in America" (218), and that essence "is rejection, and its most destructive consequence is shame" (222). When Bone looks at the "Negro experience" he sees rejection, shame, and pain so deep that the black writer can hardly see around it. Bone is much like Howe in this respect. Both seem to believe that the black writer necessarily must grapple with the pain of his experience and the resulting anger. They disagree, however, about the consequences of this necessity. While Howe argues that the black writer becomes important (though probably not "good") when he embraces his anger, Bone sees this embrace as an aesthetic misstep. Rather than giving into the anger, the black writer must attempt to rise above it. Bone laments that Baldwin has been unable to do that.

Because Bone's project is an examination of African American fiction, he doesn't actually explore the anger of *The Fire Next Time* or *Blues for Mister Charlie*. Instead he devotes all of his critical attention to the three novels that had been published up to that point: *Go Tell It on the Mountain*, *Giovanni's Room*, and *Another Country*. Once he moves beyond the discussion of the "overwhelming facts" of Baldwin's life, Bone gets down to what seems to interest him most, namely, what happens when Baldwin stops narrating the experience of rejection, shame, and the American race drama. True, Baldwin is certainly not the first to do this. As Bone acknowledges in earlier parts of his book, writers like Frank Yerby, Ann Petry, and Chester Himes all set aside the Negro milieu to write "raceless" novels. But Bone dismisses them as pulp writers or as assimilationists or as of interest only in establishing a tradition.

But Baldwin, in 1965, is famous and popular, and the public pays attention to what he writes. He is not so easy to dismiss, yet it seems at several points that Bone *needs* to remind us that Baldwin is off his game. This is especially true in his intensely homophobic reading of *Another Country*. Here he describes the action of the novel:

> A Greenwich Village setting and a hipster idiom. A square thrown in for laughs. A good deal of boozing and an occasional stick of tea. Some male cheesecake. Five orgasms (two interracial and two homosexual) or approximately one per eighty pages, a significant increase over the Mailer rate. Distracted by this nonsense, how can one attend to the serious business of the novel? (230)

His tone suggests that we shouldn't take the novel seriously, nor, consequently, should we take its author seriously. Rather than living up to the promise we witness in the early essays and *Go Tell It on the Mountain*, we instead get a Baldwin in full sexual rebellion. Again, Bone goes back to the details of Baldwin's life to explain this rebellion. According to Bone, Baldwin's decline dates back to the moment his

> dawning sensuality collided with his youthful ministry. At first he rebelled against the store-front church, then Harlem, seeking to escape at any cost. Ultimately he came to reject the female sex [the only overt mention of Baldwin's homosexuality], the white world, and the Christian God. As rebellion grew, he discovered in his gift of language a means of liberation. Like hundreds of American writers, he fled from the provinces (in his case, Harlem) to Greenwich Village and the Left Bank. There he hoped to find a haven of sexual, racial, and intellectual freedom.
>   He quickly discovered, however, that he had not left the Avenue behind. In Greenwich Village or its French equivalent, he peered into the abyss, the demimonde of gay bars, street boys, and male prostitutes. This he recognized as Hell and recoiled in horror. But what alternative does he offer to promiscuity and fleeting physical encounter? He speaks in the rhetoric of commitment and responsibility, but what he has in mind is simply a homosexual version of romantic love. It is a familiar spiritual maneuver. Baldwin has built a palace on the ramparts of Hell and called it Heaven. Its proper name is Pandemonium. (237)

The seeming rampant immorality and sexuality in *Another Country* and the overt (angry) politics of *The Fire Next Time* and *Blues for Mister Charlie* all suggest to Bone that Baldwin's rebellion is in full swing and that this is hurting his work: "Evil has become Baldwin's good. The loss of meaning that ensues is both moral and semantic, and the writer who permits it betrays both self and craft" (239).

That Bone begins his essay on Baldwin dismissive of his popularity suggests that he, in part at least, blames that popularity for the decline of Baldwin's art. For Bone, Baldwin's fiction is uneven at best, artistically bankrupt at worst, and his skill and popularity as an essayist is blinding us to this fact.

Others critics share Bone's concern with Baldwin's popularity. In "Dark Angel: The Writings of James Baldwin" (1963), Colin MacInnes, like so many others during this period, acknowledges Baldwin's contemporary importance by attempting to define it. Comparing Baldwin to a blues singer, MacInnes writes that the "singer of the Blues must be a black man, but the paradox is that his audience must still be white. This is partly because there is no point in telling Negroes of the racial situation....

The next reason is that the Negro readership of 'serious' writing is still insufficient to sustain a major writer.... But the final reason why James Baldwin speaks to us of another race is that he still believes us worthy of a warning" (22–23). Sympathetic, liberal white Americans account for a large portion of Baldwin's reading audience during this period. And these readers seem to value Baldwin's willingness to dialogue and work with them. One can very well imagine how comforting this might be for his white readers as they watch the civil rights footage on their televisions and as they see the coming tide of black nationalism.

The Fire Next Time, then, may very well have been a discomfiting surprise to a reader like MacInnes. Here Baldwin preaches, through prophetic vision, damnation rather than love, and seems to fall into line with other black writers who focus on social protest. And the public rewards him for it. And while both Howe and Bone imply that social protest very often leads to bad art, and Cleaver argues that Baldwin's protest is, at best, ineffectual, MacInnes offers another criticism. According to MacInnes, Baldwin, civil rights spokesman and favored son of mainstream American media, really has nothing new to say: "Baldwin has told us, in the essays, how Richard Wright, his mentor, reached the point at which, on the 'colour question,' he had said his say but did not realise it. Might not now—though in an entirely different context—an identical danger threaten the hero of this essay? ... [O]ne must wonder what, as a writer, James Baldwin is going to tell us now? Could it not be the same tale told, even more profoundly, in an entirely different form?" (33). For MacInnes, Baldwin's sound and fury, so embraced by the American public, really signifies very little. But where he sees a failure on Baldwin's part (he certainly suggests that Baldwin could make different writerly choices and begin to matter again), others see inevitability.

Writing in *The Creative Present: Notes on Contemporary American Fiction* (1963) Harvey Breit gets right to the heart of what troubles him about Baldwin. "He has the talent, the sensibility, the psychology, the humanity to be a writer unqualified by race, color, nationality or class. But he is a Negro leader. It is a new eventuality" (7). Breit seems to grant (unlike other critics) that Baldwin's newfound popularity may not be all his own choosing. At a time when the very future of the nation seemed to hang in the balance, seemed to depend on how it addressed the "Negro problem," the public, of course, sought out those voices that helped make sense of it all. Baldwin's charm, wit, intelligence, and honesty helped him become a leading voice. Yet Breit is still troubled. He writes, "no matter how essential and necessary the essay, no matter how true it is that only Baldwin can force us to see and feel the fierce dilemma (the fiery furnace), one continues to feel anxious about his future as a creative writer" (17).

Breit feels anxious because he is a literary critic and wants, as Bone does, to treat Baldwin as a literary artist. Unlike Bone, however, Breit seems to recognize his inability to do so. Whereas Bone calls for critical objectivity just before offering an incredibly subjective reading of Baldwin's fiction, Breit laments his inability to be objective. Because Baldwin writes so publicly and so honestly about his experiences as an American black man and because he is called upon so often to speak on this topic (and seems so willing to), it seems a futile effort to consider his work in anything other than this context: "Even if one had the power to intervene, can one ask him not to be a Negro for the sake of his art, demand that he change his fine, living, thin skin, dissuade him from his confrontations and consequently his deflections, negate his eloquence, his eminence? Can one pull him out of the front lines?" (18).

Others, though, refuse to see Baldwin as the reluctant pawn of liberal white guilt. Some critics argue that Baldwin all too willingly and too easily sells himself and his art to a sycophantic public. Writing in *Partisan Review* in 1964, one of Baldwin's old stomping grounds, Robert Coles argues that Baldwin's message of love is cheap and that he writes from a place of vanity:

> He can't be satisfied simply with relating a critical time in his early manhood to the tragedies of our country. He is compelled to expand his feelings, make them into the feelings of all Negroes, make his struggle theirs, his conclusions their demands, his frustrations their accusations, his anger their treat. He is determined to offer a general truth out of the sphere of his own life, and has a grandiose remedy for our social ills. For Baldwin—a sharp critic of America's vulgar piety—it is love, love, love. (409)

The love that many of Baldwin's readers find so comforting and that later critics will identify as the most compelling aspect of his work gets dismissed here as "grandiose" and meaningless. Baldwin's burden, for Coles, lies in his inability to get outside his own head and the American press's willingness to entertain his delusions. Chief among these delusions is Baldwin's need to be accepted by a country that seems to be, paradoxically, beneath his contempt: "This dilemma—of demanding acceptance by a country simultaneously denounced as almost worthless—is more of Baldwin's fancy than fact, a result of romanticized notions which in themselves are part of the problem of racial unreason as it plagues the educated and the gifted" (414).

This notion that Baldwin, by 1963, is too much of the American mainstream media establishment to really be an "honest man and good writer" seems to drive much of the criticism of this period. Many critics respond to Baldwin's popularity as if a contract had been broken. Theodore Gross, in 1965, writes about Baldwin's honest man and good writer goal that "the two ideal states are inextricable; and the way of the prophet and literary priest, of the 'hero' who speaks apocalyptically for his race, is the ultimate way of dishonesty" (149). Baldwin can't be both a public witness and an honest man, according to Gross, because it "is not enough to have power of expression; the novelist has to decide upon what distance he will take to his audience, upon what role he wishes to assume" (139). Because Baldwin places no distance between himself and his reader (an ability that Gross actually praises in the essay: "he brings to a white person the Negro point of view with an intense honesty; and he implicates the reader by forcing him to share that point of view: it is terrible, an inexorable law, that one cannot deny the humanity of another without diminishing one's own: in the face of one's victim, one sees himself" [141]), he sacrifices the aesthetic power of his art, even if he increases its social power. And it is all the more upsetting for Gross, and for Bone and others, because Baldwin has so much artistic potential: "Talent of his order is so rare today in America that one fears he will make a martyr of his gifts—sell them to an audience more eager to hear bombast than disciplined reason" (149).

All of these critics seem to be in agreement with Bone—Baldwin has crossed a line, or is in serious danger of crossing it. He is no longer a compelling, provocative essayist urging white America, sympathetically, to look deep into its racial soul. He is now an angry black man making white America uncomfortable. And as Bone does in his essay on Baldwin's novels, rather than deal with this discomfort (whether it stems from the homosexual themes in the novels or the prophetic nature of the essays) these critics instead warn that the popularity Baldwin now enjoys will ultimately result in the demise of his craft, if it hasn't already. Baldwin can be an honest man and a good writer as long as he is not too honest.

While responding to Baldwin's increased popularity and determining his aesthetic worth in the face of that popularity is the primary critical project of this period, focusing only on that project causes us to overlook other insightful and important scholarship written during this period. In 1964 George Kent published "James Baldwin and the Problem of Being," in which he posits the major question driving Baldwin's work: "How can one achieve, amid the dislocations and disintegrations of the modern world, true, functional being?" (203). Like other critics of this period, Kent is concerned with taking stock of Baldwin's work to date. His conclusion is similar to that of other critics. He writes, "The conclusion, therefore, to which a full reading of Baldwin seems inescapably to lead, is that since his first novel he has not evolved the artistic form that will fully release and articulate his obviously complex awareness" (214). Where Kent differs from other critics, though, and what makes his essay so profound and fundamental in Baldwin scholarship, is his faith and interest in Baldwin's "obviously complex awareness" above all else. While the critics discussed in this chapter seem interested in Baldwin primarily for what he represents (the new black voice in literature, the assimilated token Negro, the writer as celebrity, the voice of his generation, the conscience of the nation), Kent's interest truly lies in the work Baldwin produces and the project undertaken in that work. Kent doesn't deride Baldwin's popularity. He doesn't attempt to stake ideological ground or position himself in the debate about "protest" in African American literature. He doesn't criticize or defend Baldwin's growing literary reputation. Instead, Kent does the work of the critic: he attempts to identify the writer's project, assesses how and how well the writer carries out that project, and identifies and participates in the larger conversation relevant to that project. "James Baldwin and the Problem of Being" stands out for its lucidity, but also because Kent manages to avoid many of the critical pitfalls we see in this period of Baldwin scholarship.

While Kent does seem to agree with others that *Giovanni's Room* and *Another Country* don't quite live up to the artistic promise of Baldwin exhibited in *Go Tell It on the Mountain*, he doesn't attribute this "failure" to Baldwin being too distracted by fame or succumbing to the trappings of protest. Instead Kent argues that Baldwin's literary project is profoundly difficult. "To define [the fluxions and fragmenting certainties of modern man] artistically would seem to demand extraordinary effort indeed, whether in traditional or experimental terms" (214). Kent argues that the form of the traditional novel is insufficient to Baldwin's project, suggesting that when, through experimentation, Baldwin finds his form, his fiction will be as powerful as his vision of "love that brings transcendence" (210).

I single Kent's essay out as an exemplary piece of Baldwin scholarship not because of Kent's clear praise of and faith in Baldwin's talent, but because, again, it stands out in this period. Very few critics during this period seem interested in Baldwin because of the work he produces. Rather, critics seem to come to him out of inevitable necessity—if you were a literary critic in the 1960s with any interest at all in African American literature or public intellectuals, you couldn't avoid writing about Baldwin. And, very often, you ended up using Baldwin to write about other literary, social, and political issues. Kent, on the other hand, seems interested in Baldwin first and foremost as a writer, seems to assume that Baldwin's aesthetic project can have profound consequences for understanding human thought and feeling, and implies that, while interesting perhaps, Baldwin's biography and political activities are in no way central to understanding that project.

Two other critics who add to the understanding of Baldwin during this period are Addison Gayle, a major African American literary critic and a prominent voice in the Black Arts movement, and Fred L. Stanley, an eventual prominent Baldwin scholar. In 1967 Gayle wrote two essays on Baldwin. The first, "The Dialectic of *The Fire Next Time*," defends *The Fire Next Time* against attacks from what Gayle terms "the

Negro intellectual." As with much of the criticism on Baldwin (and, often, literary criticism in general), we have to infer the conversation Gayle enters into here. First, the "Negro intellectual" Gayle addresses is not the black revolutionary embodied in someone like Eldridge Cleaver or Amiri Baraka, but instead someone who is committed to entering the American mainstream by working alongside that mainstream. Second, with the publication of *The Fire Next Time*, these intellectuals, according to Gayle, no longer claim Baldwin as one of their own. In response to these sentiments, Gayle begins by acknowledging Baldwin's intellectual complexity, a truth that goes almost completely unmarked in other criticism of this period.

Reminding us that *The Fire Next Time* is made up of two essays expressing disparate, if not unrelated, ideas, Gayle writes, "'My Dungeon Shook' could well have been written by Martin Luther King, and perhaps this is why the Negro intellectual is comfortable with it.... But Baldwin [also] wrote 'The Fire Next Time' and completely demolished the idyllic vision propounded in 'My Dungeon Shook'" (15). Here and throughout the rest of this essay, Gayle implies that the growing critical discomfort around Baldwin is not due to his popularity, but rather to the unforgiving scope of his vision. In "My Dungeon Shook," the first of the essays in *The Fire Next Time*, Baldwin gives some advice to his nephew:

> There is no reason for you to try to become like white people and there is no basis whatever for their impertinent assumption, that *they* must accept *you*. The really terrible thing, old buddy, is that *you* must accept *them*. And I mean that very seriously. You must accept them and accept them with love. For these innocent people have no other hope. (293–94, original emphasis)

This is the Baldwin that both whites and "Negro intellectuals" can embrace, the Baldwin who upholds his end of the social bargain, urging his nephew (and, by implication, all blacks) to accept (and, by implication, forgive) whites. It is the second, longer essay, "Down at the Cross," the one that expresses sympathy for Elijah Muhammad's Black Muslims and concludes by warning against the fire next time, that Gayle finds more compelling. That one mind can give rise, in the same volume, to both these essays, suggests to Gayle that Baldwin is more complicated and more insightful than he is given credit for by whites (who view him as a black redeemer), Negro intellectuals (who view him as a traitor to the cause of integration), or black nationalists (who see Baldwin as counterrevolutionary). Gayle concludes that too much honesty becomes Baldwin's undoing in the public eye. Baldwin is willing to face what others cannot. "As Baldwin suggests—perhaps most explicitly in *Blues for Mr. Charlie*, whites will not resurrect their society, and Negros cannot: therefore, the crushing realization that the society will not be resurrected" (16).

In a longer essay in 1967 Gayle explicitly takes on the task of defending Baldwin, primarily from the criticisms of Bone, Cleaver, and, to a lesser extent, Howe. His primary defense here is much the same as his defense of Baldwin in the last essay: "Critics, black and white, usually find it uncomfortable to confront the argument of many Negro novelists, and their reasons are similar; both would like to forget, to be able to nestle within the womb of their own illusions, clinging to that faith which has allowed them to live precariously in this society without, at present, attempting to exterminate each other en masse" ("A Defense of James Baldwin," 201). In other words, Baldwin makes it nearly impossible for people to live with their illusions.

What is most important in this essay is the attention Gayle devotes to the critical misreadings of Baldwin. In particular Gayle writes that, rather than judging Baldwin's work, Bone in fact defends the "'American Creed,' [and] Cleaver, with nothing but contempt for the 'Creed,' is intent on defending Negro manhood, and avenging Richard Wright" (204). The problem is that neither of these projects have anything to do with Baldwin's work, nor do they provide an adequate lens through which to view literature.

Gayle takes Bone to task especially for the assertion that Baldwin is in full sexual rebellion in *Another Country* and *Giovanni's Room*, and, thus, sacrificing aesthetic quality. Gayle counters, "Rebellion against sexual and social mores has been common in English Literature from Chaucer's *Canterbury Tales* to T. S. Eliot's 'Love Song of J. Alfred Prufrock,' and the critic who has not yet accepted such 'rebellion' as one of the chief motifs of the artist of the twentieth century, has ceased to dwell in the world of reality" (202). And, referencing Cleaver's baby rape and General Motors line from "Notes on a Native Son," Gayle responds, "Perhaps, but we must not forget that there is still truth in the old cliché, 'One man's sickness may be another man's cure,' and if we substitute 'sin' for 'sickness,' there are many people in this society who would suggest that the analogy between blackness and sin, woman-rape, baby-rape and crime is just as valid as that between homosexuality, sickness, and baby-rape" (206). Gayle displays in his criticism the same trait he seems to value most in Baldwin's work: unflinching, uncompromising honesty. The essays of Cleaver and Bone are both incredibly influential in understanding Baldwin's work, and so many other critics of this period are unwilling to grant that Baldwin is anything other than a liberal pawn riding an ego-driven wave of barely deserved popularity. Gayle steps into this conversation with a challenge. His bold defense of Baldwin is refreshing. Gayle is unafraid to assert that Baldwin has something important to say, even if we are afraid to listen:

> The race will only be saved, argued DuBois, by its "talented tenth," and Cleaver comes pretty close to arguing that it will be saved only

by its "masculine" Bigger Thomases. Only Baldwin adheres to the historian's formula of predicting the future in light of the past and present, and in so doing, arrives at the conclusion that salvation is impossible. This is a dangerous position to take, for Negroes are accustomed to having their doom prescribed in the old hell and damnation curses of the evangelist preacher, and few would consider the fact that it takes far more courage to do a jackknife off the Brooklyn Bridge than to utter futile, impotent curses from the cafes of Paris, or New York City. (208)

Fred L. Standley, another critic who often crops up in Baldwin criticism during this period and the next, also attempts to engage Baldwin's intellectual and artistic complexity. In "James Baldwin: The Crucial Situation" (1966), Standley, like Gayle, tries to define the problem many critics and readers have with Baldwin:

Many persons read Baldwin with what Silberman calls "the shock of discovery" and see only anger, hatred, violence, promiscuity, lust, obscenity and vulgarity in his works. To be sure, these elements are there. While such a response is a legitimate reaction for any reader, the inclination to see only those factors appears slightly absurd. For in his works the human personality in all of its baffling mystery, its enigmatic perplexity, its web of entangled desire, ambition, lust, frustration, and love is presented with intensity and poignancy. (380–81)

Standley implies that the contemporary problem with Baldwin's "anger" does not originate in Baldwin's work, but rather stems from readers' laziness. If readers push past their knee-jerk sense of "shock" they might see that Baldwin "attempts to go beneath the surface of human experience and to bring order into being out the fragmentary and chaotic conditions of disorder; and he exercises a personal and social responsibility for furnishing himself and his fellow men with a vision of themselves as they are," as all good writers do (374). Standley, in this essay, makes no distinction between Baldwin, Negro writer, and other writers. He simply attempts to illuminate the ways in which Baldwin excels at the project at which all writers find themselves at work: the illumination of the "crucial situation" of human existence. While this particular universalizing trend will become problematic (as I will explore in the next chapter), in this essay Standley, like Gayle, provides a refreshing respite from Baldwin as disappointing genius that defines so much criticism of this era.

That isn't to say that Standley avoids all discussion of Baldwin's politics. His 1970 essay "James Baldwin: The Artist as Incorrigible Disturber of the Peace" takes its title from Baldwin's definition of the artist. From this Standley infers that Baldwin understands that "the writer's peculiar nature as artist imposes on him a constant condition of 'warring' with his society" (21). Because Baldwin seems to freely accept a definition of artist that places him at odds with society, Standley further concludes that "Baldwin's concept of art and of himself as literary artist cannot readily be divorced from his concept of art as involving protest" (19). For Standley this reflects not a contradiction in Baldwin's philosophy, but rather a more complex understanding of Baldwin's work. Like Bone and others, Standley finds that the "art of [Baldwin's] novels frequently appears to be propagandistic, weakened by flaws of literary technique," yet his critique doesn't end there (28). Unlike Howe, who forgives flawed African American literature because of its importance, Standley concedes the flaws in Baldwin's novels while still finding in them *artistic* merit. He writes, "there are fundamental values informing it which give that art a maturity of insight not readily apparent to those who see in the novels merely hatred, violence, vulgarity, and promiscuity" (28).

By the end of this period (1973) the study of African American literature was influenced as much by theory of the black aesthetic as it was by the reaction against it. C. W. Bigsby's oft-cited 1969 collection, *The Black American Writer: Volume 1: Fiction*, begins with the "Critical Dilemma" facing scholars of African American literature. In his introduction he seeks to give an explanation of the "inferior quality of black writing until comparatively recent times" (5) and suggests that this inferiority is a "result of white influence on black creativity" and "can also be ascribed to the indecent eagerness with which the Negro writer has submitted himself to the dominating political and cultural philosophies of his day" (5–6). This seems to be an allusion to writers like Amiri Baraka who demand the politicization of African American art and a black aesthetic that make sense of this new political art. Those writers most often described as the best African American writers—Wright, Hughes, Baraka—all espouse a particular (ethnic) politics to which they are wed as writers; but their greatest artistic success, Bigsby asserts, "is built precisely on those works in which they fail to abide by their own strictures," suggesting "that these formulas fail to realize the full potential of the black writer" (6). The dilemma, then, for Bigsby, seems to be how to take the politics of these writers seriously if it is when they set these politics aside that they create great art. Should we read them as writers or as revolutionaries? Bigsby shares the same concerns as other critics in this period. Baldwin stands, in this introduction, as an example of a black writer struggling with and coming to the conclusion that this dilemma is untenable and that ultimately the writer must simply be a writer and not a spokesman. Two of the interviews in the book include Baldwin as a subject, two other essays are about him specifically, and several others include him in the general discussion of black writers. Baldwin becomes, then, a convenient foil for black aesthetic politics.

Others, however, view Baldwin's relationship to the black aesthetic differently. Stanley Macebuh's *James Baldwin: A Critical Study* (1973), the first full-length study of Baldwin's work, is heavily indebted to black aesthetic theory. The introduction of the book, despite being a full-length study of Baldwin, is a defense of this theory and, what is important, a criticism of some of its practitioners. Macebuh effectively describes the paradox of the black aesthetic:

> But what, ironically, a good many of the proponents of this concept do not seem to recognise is this, that if theirs is a "revolutionary" task, it is certainly less on account of their attempt to control the "verbal image," even less because of any observable seriousness in their elucidation of already existing literature, but primarily because, unlike what may generally be termed the conservative Western approach to aesthetics, theirs is, not an ex post facto exercise, but a prescriptive, a priori one. One need hardly labour the point that, in general, "Western" aesthetic theories, despite their occasional prescriptions, have been essentially analytic and descriptive, deriving their conclusions from the explication of already existing bodies of literature. The Black Aesthetic, on the other hand, is in essence a hypothetical one, a theory (or body of theories) dealing with a yet unborn, though sometimes nascent art. Rather than limit itself to the task of deducing principles from what already exists as art, it seeks boldly to invoke its own definition of art into being, the result being that we are confronted with an exciting, if somewhat unusual situation, one in which criticism virtually precedes art, its subject and reason for being. (21–22)

Macebuh grants that the works most closely connected to the black aesthetic are being created at the same time as the aesthetic is being articulated; yet he argues that it would be foolish to think that "black" literature has existed only as long as the black aesthetic has been an idea (about ten years). Macebuh's version of black aesthetic criticism of Baldwin proceeds "from three basic presuppositions: first, that he belongs, firmly and inseparably, to continuous tradition in Black Literature in America; secondly, that we assume a necessary link between 'politics' and 'literature' and that what follows is therefore much closer to 'cultural' than to 'practical' criticism; and finally, that the concept of the black aesthetic is an eminently useful one" (26).

The conclusions he draws about Baldwin and his work are not startling. He credits Baldwin's early formal control to the very personal stories he was telling and argues that Baldwin loses this control when he branches out in terms of content. Ultimately he finds that Baldwin begins as a writer with a private concern about "theological terror" and becomes one who writes out of "moral disgust and passionate fury" (185). Apart from what Macebuh specifically argues about Baldwin, though, *James*

Baldwin: A Critical Study is important for the critical trends it anticipates in the next period of Baldwin scholarship.

As we have seen in this chapter, Baldwin scholars during this period find it difficult to separate Baldwin the writer from Baldwin the activist and public figure. While this particular difficulty will persist in Baldwin criticism for some time, never again will that criticism be anchored by the work of specific critics or viewpoints. Perhaps only the advent of queer theory in the late 1980s and early 1990s (which I discuss in chapter 3) comes closest to providing the kind of boundaries that the work of Howe, Bone, and Cleaver provide for this period of Baldwin criticism. Despite the new insights queer theory will offer into Baldwin criticism, however, it will still be only one way of looking at Baldwin's body of work. Baldwin criticism after this point lacks a real critical center. What we find instead are critics searching for ways to keep Baldwin relevant as the nature of literary criticism, and the relationship of African American literature to that criticism and the academy, changes.

In the next chapter I will look at how much Baldwin criticism in particular, and African American literary criticism in general, from 1974 to Baldwin's death in 1987 is very much in reaction to the perceived excesses and limitations of black aesthetic theory. Ironically, the more established in the academy African American literature and black studies become the harder critics of African American literature rebel against the black aesthetic. And where this period sees Baldwin and his work getting caught up in debates about the role of the artist (can he be both popular and good? can he be both black and good? should he be a spokesman?), the next period finds his work tangled up in a movement to legitimate African American literature.

Notes

[1] Baldwin, *Collected Essays*, 9. All Baldwin citations are from the 1998 Library of America editions of *Early Novels and Stories* and *Collected Essays*.

[2] See also J. Saunders Redding, "Since Richard Wright"; Albert Murray, "Something Different, Something More"; Nathan Scott, "Judgment Marked by a Cellar: The American Negro Writer and the Dialectic of Despair"; Donald B. Gibson, "Wright's Invisible Native Son"; B. K. Mitra, "The Wright-Baldwin Controversy"; Morris Dickstein, "Wright, Baldwin, Cleaver"; and Jerry H. Bryant, "Wright, Ellison, Baldwin—Exorcising the Demon."

[3] This is, of course, the briefest of summaries of black power politics of the 1960s. For a fuller discussion of this period, see two works by Peniel Joseph, *Waiting 'Til the Midnight Hour: A Narrative History of Black Power in America*, and the edited collection, *The Black Power Movement: Rethinking the Civil Rights Black Power Era*.

[4] Cleaver's "Notes of a Native Son" first appeared in the journal *Ramparts* in June 1966.

2: Canonizing James Baldwin: 1974–87

BY 1974, THE FIFTY-YEAR-OLD BALDWIN had published four collections of essays, four novels, two plays, an unfilmed screenplay, two book-length dialogues, a collection of short stories, and numerous uncollected articles, reviews, and interviews. He had also purchased the estate at St. Paul-de-Vence, France, that would become his home. While he continued to travel between the United States and Europe (referring to himself as a transatlantic commuter), from 1971 on, his stays in the United States were shorter and less frequent. And though he continued to be an active writer and was in fact quite prolific until his death in 1987, he was no longer a prominent public face. His picture doesn't appear on the cover of magazines. Though he worked diligently alongside many civil rights leaders and was, for many, the movement's moral center, he is left out of civil rights histories.

In 1973 Henry Louis Gates, Jr., future director of the W. E. B. Dubois Institute for African and African American Research at Harvard, but then a Cambridge University graduate student and *Time* correspondent, planned an article on black expatriates. In August of that year he dined with Baldwin, Josephine Baker, and several others at Baldwin's French estate. While that evening would inspire Baldwin to write *The Welcome Table*, a play he completed just before his death, *Time* declined to publish Gates's interview, calling Baldwin "passé" (Leeming, 320). Baldwin had ceased to be America's brightest African American literary star.

This chapter considers the critical reception of Baldwin's work from 1974 to the year of his death, 1987. The collection that begins this period, Keneth Kinnamon's *James Baldwin: A Collection of Critical Essays*, the first to gather important criticism on Baldwin's work, includes the major players up to this point: Langston Hughes, Eldridge Cleaver, Irving Howe, Robert Bone, George E. Kent. Acknowledging that the final critical word had yet to be written, Kinnamon states, "Whatever the final assessment of his literary achievement, it is clear that his voice—simultaneously that of victim, witness, and prophet—has been among the most urgent of our time" (7). He also identifies trends in the "diverse critical opinions" surrounding Baldwin's work. These trends, already outlined in the previous chapter, stand as the very kind of criticism many critics of this period try to get away from.

I title this chapter "Canonizing Baldwin" because the critical impulse during this period seems driven by the need to salvage Baldwin's reputation and legitimate his work. There is some suggestion that Baldwin had been treated unfairly in previous criticism (judged on his celebrity and politics rather than his work) and that his reputation suffered because he didn't fit in easily with the Black Arts movement's definitions of blackness and masculinity. In addition, with the rise of black studies as an academic discipline, there is a move to legitimate all of African American literature (as well as history, art, music, etc.), and Baldwin, being one of the "big three" African American writers (with Richard Wright and Ralph Ellison), necessarily gets caught up in that critical project. As close readings are often taken to be fundamental to the study of literature, and "serious" literature identifies itself by its ability to stand up to the scrutiny of a close reading, this era of canonizing Baldwin features quite a number of close readings. This chapter also looks at the critics who revisit the Wright-Baldwin debate (in an attempt to have the final word on it), the critics who attempt to explicate Baldwin's notion of love, and, finally, the critics whose work holds critical sway but who don't fall easily within the other themes in this chapter.

If the Harlem Renaissance, to borrow a phrase from Toni Morrison, sought to turn a racist house into a nonracist home,[1] then Black Arts artists tried to burn that house down to the ground and erect in its place a monument testifying to all the glories of a beautiful black self. The architects of the Harlem Renaissance were willing to grant that American ideals, if not American practices, were a good idea.[2] Black Arts artists assumed no such thing and were as likely to condemn the United States in their art as symbolic of Western decadence and impotence as they were to praise the superiority of black diaspora culture.

In response to the February 1965 assassination of Malcolm X, Leroi Jones (Amiri Baraka) moved from Manhattan's Lower East Side to Harlem, thus giving spiritual birth to the Black Arts movement,[3] famously described by the critic Larry Neal as the "aesthetic and spiritual sister of the Black Power concept" (*Visions of a Liberated Future*, 62). Already a widely read, award-winning poet and critic, Jones's move made visible a larger political and ideological shift in African American culture. Despite the promise of the Civil Rights Act of 1964 and the Voting Rights Act of 1965, race riots in Harlem, Watts, Newark, Detroit, Cleveland, and other places marked the mid- and late 1960s. The assassination of Martin Luther King, Jr. in 1968 precipitated the political shift away from grassroots organizing and political protest toward an emphasis on independent political action and black cultural pride. Black writers like Jones wanted an art that reflected and facilitated the changes occurring in black culture.

The poet, critic, and Black Arts participant Kalamu ya Salaam describes the Black Arts movement as a "militant artistic movement" that advocated "artistic and political freedom 'by any means necessary'" (71). Indeed, Jones's seminal poem from this period reflects this characterization. In "Black Art" he calls for "'poems that kill'/Assassin poems. Poems that shoot/guns." The poem ends with a mission statement for a new generation of artists:

> We want a black poem. And a
> Black World.
> Let the world be a Black Poem
> And Let All Black People Speak This Poem
> Silently
> or Loud. (*Black Poets*, 181)

The movement lasted until the mid-1970s, which found many of its participants involved in other political endeavors, many of its institutions and ideas co-opted, and many of its ideas a mainstream success (black studies, for instance). Because of the harshness of its tone, the violence of its language, and its unrelenting commitment to nationalist politics, critics (until very recently)[4] dismissed the Black Arts movement as a movement defined by flamboyant polemical excess and given to the glorification of bad poetry.

Perhaps the most influential criticism in this vein comes from Henry Louis Gates, Jr. in the 1979 essay "Preface to Blackness: Text and Pretext." The essay appeared in *Afro-American Literature: The Reconstruction of Instruction*, itself the result of an MLA-sponsored, NEH-funded seminar that sought to "design courses in, and to refine critical approaches to, Afro-American literature yielding a 'literary' understanding of the literature" (vii). The seminar, in other words, was an attempt to define new rigorous rules of scholarship that would treat African American literature as works of art rather than as sociological artifacts. But where does this leave the literature of the Black Arts movement, literature that is unapologetically political, literature that rejects the idea that art can or should be separated from its social context?

Gates argues that the problem with Black Arts artists and critics is that they "concern themselves with futile attempts to make poetry preach, which poetry is not capable of doing so well" (58). Indeed, he agrees with Wittgenstein, who warns us, "Do not forget that a poem, even though it is composed in the language of information, is not used in the language of giving information" (60); and Gates goes on to state that "a poem is above all atemporal and must cohere at a symbolic level, if it coheres at all" (60). Gates spends the majority of the essay dismantling, through rigorous structuralist language, the critical assumptions of the Black Arts movement. He accuses Stephen Henderson, Addison Gayle, and Houston Baker, chief Black Arts-era critics, of shockingly bad scholarship. He asserts that only the study of language, the words on the page rather than the themes contained therein, will lead ultimately to the critical elevation of African American literature, which it sorely needs, according to Gates, after being plunged into the self-indulgent, tautological depths of the Black Arts movement. Near the end of the essay, Gates sums up the critical problem: "Afraid that our literature cannot sustain sophisticated verbal analysis, we view it from the surface merely and treat it as if it were a Chinese lantern with an elaborately wrought surface, parchment thin but full of hot air" (67–68). He thus dismisses the criticism and much of the art produced during the Black Arts era and in a few years would offer his own example of sophisticated verbal analysis, *The Signifying Monkey* (1989).

And so, clearly, Gates's goal, as well as the unstated goal of many of critics of this era of Baldwin scholarship, is to subject African American literature to sophisticated verbal analysis. This analysis comes mostly in the form of formalist criticism but also in the form of rigorous poststructuralist performance. The criticism is full of the kind of close attentive reading of Baldwin that the Black Arts movement seems to call for, but rejects the limiting, proscriptive aspects of the black aesthetic. Critics in this era are concerned with the words that Baldwin wrote (his "art") rather than the subjective details of his life, his participation in the civil rights movement, and his celebrity. These critical moves, however, elicit the following questions: What do we do with the autobiographical essays and novels if we ignore Baldwin's biography? How do we read African American literature if we reject the black aesthetic? How do we read Baldwin if the times he reflected so well have faded into history?

Ernest Champion's "James Baldwin and the Challenge of Ethnic Literature in the Eighties" (1981) is an interesting anomaly in this period. Champion makes no qualms about insisting that Baldwin's importance lies in what he reveals about the American racial drama. Lamenting that the "intensity" of the 1950s and 1960s has been lost in the present day, Champion contends that Baldwin never lost that intensity and continues to preach the message that "black people must fight the oppressor for equality and respect but that in so doing they will also help whites to a better way of life" (61). The paradox of Baldwin's career at this moment is that he is a major writer with, by the early 1980s, a minor presence. Champion's essay responds primarily to assertions that Baldwin is an irrelevant writer by making an argument for his continued relevancy. He contends that Baldwin's demand for the "Western world is a demand for a new morality and a new conscience without which neither the United States nor the Western world has any future" (62). This new morality and new conscience, according to Champion, is still very much needed: "Ethnic literature and writers such as Baldwin will and must play a very vital role in the education of this nation. Because in a very real sense, ethnic literature's role is the role of 'the other' or, according to Hawthorne, to cast Adam out of Eden, for Adam's own sake" (64).

Champion's essay stands out in this period because of its approach. Champion (and, by extension, other proponents of the relatively new discipline of ethnic and black studies) places Baldwin's importance squarely in Baldwin's politics as expressed through his writing. Baldwin is important not because his work transcends racial particularities. It is important precisely because he challenges us to see those particularities. This reading of Baldwin, however, would not become prevalent until after his death in 1987.

The first set of essays I discuss in this chapter reflect a corrective impulse in Baldwin scholarship. Many of them detail how past criticism has gotten Baldwin (or African American literature) wrong and offer their own corrective measures. For instance, Louis H. Pratt begins his 1976 essay "James Baldwin and 'The Literary Ghetto'" by discussing critics who have ghettoized African American literature, primarily by labeling it "protest literature." Protest, he argues, "is a designation reserved for literature written by black Americans, all of which is assumed to be a remonstration against the economic, social, and political condition of the black man in America. As a descriptive phrase, it becomes a literary innuendo which proclaims the inferiority and sterility of the Afro-American literary tradition" (265).

Pratt takes the term "literary ghetto" from John A. Williams, who argues that critics "limit severely the expansion of the talents of Negro writers and confine them to a literary ghetto from which only one Negro name at a time may emerge" (quoted in Pratt, "James Baldwin and 'The Literary Ghetto,'" 262). This, of course, is precisely what happens in the criticism of the previous chapter. "The one" had been Wright, and many critics (Cleaver, Howe) weren't ready to relinquish that spot to Baldwin. And during this period other writers—Amiri Baraka, Ishmael Reed, John Wideman, and black women writers like Toni Morrison, Toni Cade Bambara, and Alice Walker—are jockeying for position.

Pratt argues that this literary ghetto "tends to be representative of a subtly-masked form of racism which functions to stifle and suppress black talent and confirm the myth that blacks are limited in their capacity to produce serious literature" (263–64). Recalling the tenor of much of the criticism covered in my previous chapter, Pratt reminds us that many critics expect very little from the "limited capacity" of black writers, and work on the assumption that a preoccupation with race is the chief cause of that limitation. In Baldwin's case, with the publication of *Fire*, he gave up being a *serious* (universal) writer to be a *political* (black) writer. Pratt contends that critics come to this particular conclusion about Baldwin by focusing primarily on his essays, his most overtly political work. While critics of this period will try to remedy this misrepresentation of Baldwin's body of work by ignoring the essays altogether (focusing instead on Baldwin's fiction and drama), Pratt argues that this only masks the problem. The problem is not the essays themselves, but rather our reading of them.

To prove his point, Pratt offers a close reading of a passage from Baldwin's essay "Fifth Avenue, Uptown," collected in *Nobody Knows My Name*. Pratt argues that the repetitive subject-verb sentence constructions of the introduction form an "organic relationship" (268) with the essay's topic: the oppressive conditions of black life and the people who persevere despite those conditions. He also highlights the sense of urgency and outrage created by the repetitive and short sentences in Baldwin's "To Be Baptized," collected in *No Name in the Street*. Because the essay takes up the topic of justice or, rather, the lack thereof for people of color in America, the simmering rage suggested by Baldwin's style forces the reader into a "confrontation with reality" (269). In other words, Baldwin doesn't rely simply on a recitation of facts or a catalog of grievances to elicit a response from his readers. Instead, he carefully crafts an artful essay that in *form* and content communicates his thoughts on American racial politics.

In many ways Pratt's argument recalls George Kent's in "James Baldwin and the Problem of Being." As I discussed in the previous chapter, Kent posited that if Baldwin's work suffered from anything, it was that he had yet to find the form that could adequately contain his ideas. Pratt's reply seems to be that Baldwin had indeed found his form, particularly in his nonfiction, but that form had been inadequately studies by critics. Indeed, the critics in chapter 1 demonstrate nicely the "literary ghetto" Pratt discussed in the beginning of his essay. Because those critics substituted "social for artistic criticism," assuming that the "power of fact [was] the motivating force in [Baldwin's] essays," Pratt contends, they miss the artfulness and, therefore, much of the power of those essays (268).

He concludes his essay by issuing a challenge to other critics: "a brief and initial examination of the aesthetic basis of the essays such as this cannot be regarded as exhaustive. It is, nevertheless, an evaluation which critics thus far have not undertaken" (271). In short, a formalist reading, one that pays no heed to racialized or racist assumptions about African American literature, will get us to a better, more nuanced understanding of Baldwin's (and African American literature's) genius. Rigorous scholarship can correct the critical missteps of the past.

Pratt's own 1978 full-length study of Baldwin, *James Baldwin*, finds him turning his rigorous critical eye, as other critics in this chapter will, to Baldwin's fiction and drama. While notable for its critical impact, for our purposes it is most interesting for the critical missteps it challenges and those it perpetuates. Taking up his own challenge, seemingly, Pratt is concerned first and foremost with Baldwin's craft (rather than his biography or politics). Biographical detail may be interesting, but is largely irrelevant. "To the extent that a work of art presents vicarious experiences and viable alternatives, an artistic creation becomes an entity in itself, entirely separate from its creator. Therefore, it is legitimate to *interpret* autobiographical references within the work [i.e., you don't have to pretend to not see it], but one can never *impose* those personal elements which occur entirely outside of the context of the work of art and allow them to impinge upon the creation itself" (59, original emphasis). In the chapter on Baldwin's plays and screenplays, for instance, Pratt lays out a series of questions to consider:

> How do Baldwin's dramas, in fact, project beyond the world of protest and racism into the sanctuary of art? What are the dramatic techniques that he uses in his painstaking efforts to depict black life and culture and reveal the inherent universal values which emerge from the portraits he has drawn? What is there of human value in the ideas of these dramas? What illumination is shed on the "great wilderness of self" as man gropes amid the darkness in quest of self-identity and fulfillment? (83)

Here Pratt seeks to assess the formal qualities of the plays (the "dramatic techniques") as well as those qualities that move the plays beyond mere race commentary. In the "sanctuary of art" there is little concern with "protest and racism." Instead, we are concerned with the "great wilderness of self." This definition of art is very much like the one Howe and Bone were working with in the previous chapter, though Pratt differs from these two in that he is willing to extend the mantle of art to Baldwin's seemingly most propagandistic work.

Significantly, too, Pratt doesn't avoid the sexual content in Baldwin's work. He looks at the novels and Baldwin's use of issues of sexuality to explore the themes of identity construction and love and human connection. He concludes,

> In Baldwin's novels, love is extended, frequently denied, seldom fulfilled. As reflections of our contemporary, American society, the novels stand as forthright indictments of the intolerable conditions that we have accepted unquestioningly as a way of life.... Moments of love, Baldwin seems to say, are precious, rare occasions to be cherished, and we must create an atmosphere where they can survive and flourish. We must find the means of reestablishing the genuine concern for the fate of our brothers. We must discover that "other country" within the depths of ourselves so that love can again become a possibility in our lives" (80–81).

Here Pratt makes a move that many subsequent critics will echo—he places love at the center of Baldwin's ethos and identifies sexuality as the vehicle through which Baldwin explicates his vision of love. Pratt can't quite, however, move away from the discomfort with homosexuality displayed by earlier critics.

While acknowledging the possible homoeroticism of Elisha and John's relationship in *Go Tell It on the Mountain*, Pratt writes, "Yet it is also significant that he turns to Elisha after he finds himself totally unable to establish a single genuine relationship between himself and the other characters in the novel. Only Elisha is able to function as a father-surrogate for John because Elisha, unlike Gabriel, is attuned to the young boy's needs as John searches for his own identity" (57). This reading of John and Elisha is informed, in part, by Pratt's assertion that the details of Baldwin's life (particularly Baldwin's homosexuality) cannot be easily mapped on to Baldwin's work.

John T. Shawcross, in his essay "Joy and Sadness, James Baldwin, Novelist" (1983), agrees. He calls previous criticism of Baldwin "critical drivel" (100), objecting primarily to critics' habit of drawing a one-to-one correspondence between characters' beliefs and statements in the novels and Baldwin's own beliefs. He argues, "We cannot assume such statements in a novel, taken out of context, represent the author's beliefs or even the characters' essential beliefs, though they may help to epitomize the character, and the character may have representational value as a real-life person" (100).

Shawcross's corrective move is to offer readings of *Go Tell It on the Mountain* and *Giovanni's Room*, highlighting the ways he thinks previous critics got these books wrong:

> In all, Baldwin the novelist has achieved two fine novels with *Go Tell It on the Mountain* and *Giovanni's Room*, employing the materials of fictional art: narrative, structure and form, allusion and association, mythic substruct, contrast and comparison, onomastics, flashback and framing. The works deal with issues for Baldwin as a person, but these are issues for many others as well. Only with the eradication of critical prejudgment such as he has been subjected to in viewing these novels as fictionalized biography of the black and the homosexual will we recognize the achievement of James Baldwin, novelist. (109)

Note, here, the critical moves Shawcross makes, all of which are indicative of this period of Baldwin scholarship. He insists that Baldwin's work should stand alone from his biography and politics, for, while these may be interesting critical lenses, they are most often irrelevant and not very illuminating. In addition, his focus on the formal elements of the novel—"narrative, structure and form, allusion and association, mythic substruct, contrast and comparison, onomastics, flashback and framing"—shows Shawcross making the same explicit critical moves others will make, moving away from subjective criticism to a more objective discussion of form.

Craig Werner's 1979 essay, "The Economic Evolution of James Baldwin," also speaks directly to the lack of critical and emotional distance in previous criticism. He writes, "a number of factors have contributed to an atmosphere of confusion in the critical reaction to Baldwin's writing. Determining Baldwin's precise position at any time is no simple task, and as a result of the highly charged topical nature of his basic concerns, a great deal of analysis suffers from the intrusion of the critic's personal political prejudices" (12). Werner's essay displays the same corrective impulse as others from this period and his criticism of "personal political prejudices" coloring other criticism implies that he will avoid this in his own criticism.

Werner's purpose in this essay is to offer a Marxist reading of Baldwin's novels. Like others, he seeks to answer the question of what we will find in Baldwin's work if we put aside Baldwin's life and politics and critics' ideological soapboxes. For Werner, Baldwin's novels provide "a constantly refined critique of the American economic system and [a suggestion for] a general direction for future action" (31). Seeking to fill the gap left by a lack "of explicit analysis of the manner in which the novels reflect Baldwin's evolving public position [on economics] and even less recognition of the importance of economic pressures in shaping his characters' actions" (19), Werner proceeds to a close reading of the economic factors in each of Baldwin's novels.

For Werner, Baldwin's "economic evolution" is evident in his public pronouncements. Though Baldwin, according to Werner, remains committed to a "spiritual approach to problem solving" (16) throughout his career, his "militant" phase (after *The Fire Next Time*) saw him speak explicitly about the economic basis and consequences of oppression. Describing Baldwin's economic position in this phase as "socialist (though not Communist)" (16), Werner quotes Baldwin from his "rap" with Margaret Mead:

> One has been avoiding the word capitalism and one has been avoiding talking about matters on that level. But there is a very serious flaw in the profit system which is implicit in the phrase itself ... the Western economy is doomed. Certainly part of the crisis of the Western economy is due to the fact that in a way every dime I earn, the system which earns it for me ... is standing on the back of some black coal miner in South Africa, and he is going to stand up presently. (17)

This socialist politics, Werner argues, seeps into Baldwin's novels, so that by the time we get to *If Beale Street Could Talk*, Baldwin "establishes a spiritual economy which is created by very nearly inverting the material economic scale. Baldwin believes that the dispossessed must thoroughly and unambiguously reject the system which is oppressing them, and he approves solely of those characters who have dissociated themselves from the system's economic perception of value" (28–29). While Werner finds fault with this position, citing the difficulty of complete dissociation (he acknowledges that Baldwin recognizes this difficulty), he finds the position "sufficient in its fictional" (31) context.

There are two noteworthy things here. First, Werner's article seems to prove Pratt's point that a close formalist reading of Baldwin's work is rewarding and revealing. Not only does Werner's reading move Baldwin out of the "literary ghetto" by acknowledging the shortsightedness of critics who preceded him, but he also takes Baldwin seriously as a black writer capable of thinking seriously about something other than race. While essays like Werner's might look, thirty years later, like they are trying too hard to make Baldwin's work relevant outside of conversations about race, the corrective impulse at work here does move the critical conversation forward. Even as the number of essays and articles published on Baldwin during this period are fewer than the period that precedes it and the one that will follow, the diversity of ideas explored in them is greater precisely because critics seems to be trying hard to find new things to say about Baldwin's work.

Second, Werner's attention to the economic, rather than racial, philosophy in Baldwin reflects the times, as criticism often does. The 1960s saw race take center stage as the most pressing moral and legal issue of the day. To participate in public life, particularly on the national stage, one had to take some position on the "race question." As the civil rights movement died down and gave way to black nationalism, and as the Vietnam War moved to the top of the progressive hit list, raced ceased to be the most pressing issue of national politics. Thus, *Time* magazine can dismiss a story on Baldwin because he is a relic from an era in which people talked ceaselessly about race, and Werner can dismiss "the personal political prejudices" of critics who couldn't see past race and turn his critical attention to other progressive ideas in Baldwin's work.

While Werner's article seems to make the point that Baldwin remains politically relevant even though politics have changed, Mary Fair Burks's essay "James Baldwin's Protest Novel: *If Beale Street Could Talk*" (1976) takes issue with politically motivated criticism, particularly criticism coming from the Black Arts movement. While ostensibly a review of *If Beale Street Could Talk*, Burks really has a bone to pick with the "Black Revolution," which gave us "ethnocentrism" and "propagandists" rather than artists (83). Her initial description of *Beale Street* is telling.

> If one can judge by this single work alone, the trend [in Black writing] will be toward moderation and away from complete nihilism of the Black revolution. It will become more art and less an instrument of warfare. Politics and social protest will not disappear but

reality will replace pathological escapism, and ethnocentricity will be rooted not in empty rhetoric and mindless, irrational claims of the superiority and purity of Blackness but in the genuine conviction of self-worth and the belief that Afro-Americans possess a rich cultural heritage worthy of being shared, understood, and appreciated. (83–84)

Rather than introducing any of the novel's major characters or detailing any of the plot (that will come later), Burks instead points out all the flaws the novel *doesn't* have. These flaws—"irrational claims of superiority and purity," "pathological escapism"—are frequent criticisms of the Black Arts movement and the literature that stems from it. Baldwin, it seems, avoids these pitfalls and *Beale Street* could serve as a model of how to write about "post-revolution" black life.

But then Burks surprises the reader by offering an unequivocally bad review of the novel. She grants that Baldwin was never at his best as a novelist, "but if he chose to make his major post-revolution debut as a novelist, his readers had the right to expect new themes, new perspectives, deepened insights, greater comprehension of the subtleties and complexities of change" (84). *Beale Street* fails because Baldwin offers the reader nothing new; the "book is James Baldwin twenty years ago" (84). Burks charges that the story of the love affair between Tish Rivers and Fonny Hunt is marred by the inclusion of familiar Baldwin stereotypes—the white racist cop, white male sexual desire for black women, homosexuality, the black church, and the redemptive power of sexual love. While I might read the inclusion of these "stereotypes" (I might call them tropes), as placing *Beale Street* squarely within Baldwin's oeuvre, Burks reads it as "literary prostitution," as Baldwin's concession to the "protest" called for by the Black Arts movement. Burks's review of *Beale Street* is incredibly reductive and reveals more perhaps about her own stereotypes about blacks (she questions why the light-skinned Mrs. Hunt belongs to a "sanctified" storefront church rather than the "prestigious Abyssinia Baptist Church, Harlem's religious showplace" [86]) than Baldwin's; her essay, nonetheless, intrigues because of its conclusion.

Having just spent many paragraphs telling the reader that Baldwin had too many bad habits that he couldn't let go of, and maybe a few new ones he picked up from the Black Arts movement, Burks nevertheless concludes,

> Although Baldwin is unable to give up his own pre-conceived ideas and unable to accept the raucous nihilism of the revolutionaries, neither is he able to look at the post-revolution world with new eyes, new insight, new understanding. What remains, however, is an artist who has learned well the tools of his craft, and in spite of a predilection to create stereotypes born of his own psychic necessity, in spite

of his feeble effort to placate Black radicalism, he uses these tools adeptly, creating moments of moving, unforgettable beauty. Because of these moments, rare as they may be, *If Beale Street Could Talk* cannot be ignored and must be reckoned with by any serious scholar of Baldwiniana. (95)

Baldwin may not have been able to move African American literature as far forward as Burks would have liked, but he nevertheless remained a master of his craft. At the end of the day, despite the stereotypes and the old-fashioned notions, he could still create moments of "unforgettable beauty." For Burks, and for others, this is what ultimately separated Baldwin from the "propagandists" of the "black revolution," and why he continued to be a major American writer.

Burks is not the only critic who found this "post-revolution" moment useful. In *"Blues for Mister Charlie*: The Rhetorical Dimension" (1975), John L. Tedesco gives a reading of Baldwin's play *Blues for Mister Charlie* eleven years after its first production. Like other critics during this era, Tedesco shows very little interest in the life or politics of Baldwin the man. This doesn't mean, however, that he shies away from the very explicit politics of Baldwin's "Emmett Till play." In fact, he defends the play against charges of "disorderly plot development" by classifying it as "platform drama."

> This classification is suggestive for it points to a rhetorical dimension in the play which deserves close examination by the critic.... Therefore, to understand the play correctly, we must comprehend the rhetorical strategies which enable it to alter the attitudes, commitments, and behavior of its audience. Moreover, we must also understand the historical context for which it was intended. The assumption here is that like a rhetor, the writer of agi-prop drama employs strategies which meet the demands of a particular context by prompting some change in an audience's values and actions. (20)

He goes on to examine the dialectical structure of the play, focusing on three oppositions (black truth/white justice, Meridian/Parnell, Bible/gun) and the historical context of the play (the changing racial situation after 1964). This article offers exactly the kind of formalist close reading many critics seem to crave during this period (Tedesco here certainly seems interested in moving *Blues* out of the "literary ghetto"). What's more interesting, though, is that while Tedesco's reading itself is not particularly interesting (it is rather facile, actually), he chooses to do this kind of reading in 1975. This article was published a decade after the play's publication and production. It doesn't really have to engage the play's politics because, presumably, the country has moved on. We are, after all, in the "post-revolution" period. And in those places where it does engage the politics (i.e., address the racial turmoil explored in the play), Tedesco can do so safely under the cover of "historical context."

> Nowhere in this brief essay do I mean to imply that Baldwin's play is nothing more than a speech set in dialogue. Nevertheless, like the plays of Shaw, Brecht, Isben, Osborn, and Arden, it possesses an important rhetorical dimension—one which reflects the racial situation in America around 1964. To ignore this dimension and dwell only on plot development as do many who judge it harshly is to thwart proper understanding of the play. But attending to the rhetorical dimension does not suggest that *Blues for Mister Charlie* falls short of universality and therefore is not art. The universal and particular are always inextricably bound up with one another. Thus, in the process of teaching his audience a particular lesson about the state of race relations in America, he also captures something universal and true about the nature of man when he is caught in the turmoil of social change. (23)

Baldwin's "Emmett Till play" can be universal in part because Baldwin and the play's issues and questions had by 1975 left the political stage. There is enough critical distance to focus on the "rhetorical dimension of the play" and enough emotional distance to see the "universal" in the play despite its "particular" politics. Ultimately, I think the thrust of this argument is correct. The universal and the particular *are* always "inextricably bound up with one another." What's more interesting, though, is that implicit in Tedesco's reading of *Blues* is the problem many critics during this period face: How do you read Baldwin's work, most which is unapologetically engaged in the political conversations of its moment, when those politics, and politically engaged criticism, are out of fashion? Some, like Tedesco, foreground the historical context of Baldwin's work, while others look for the universal in the particulars.

Shirley S. Allen's essay "Religious Symbolism and Psychic Reality in Baldwin's *Go Tell It on the Mountain*" (1975) is a prime example of this critical move. Her essay is a critical reassessment of *Go Tell It on the Mountain*, a novel, she argues, that "deserves a higher place in critical esteem than it has generally been accorded." Despite its critical acclaim and its inclusion on syllabi, people "assume that the work is primarily important as an interpretation of the black experience" (173). She references Robert Bone's 1965 essay about Baldwin as a prime example of this kind of reading. Allen seeks to correct this reading by showing what is revealed if we think of the novel as something other than a story about a particularly black experience.

Rather than comparing *Go Tell It on the Mountain* to works like *Native Son* and *Invisible Man* (as is most often the case) or to Baldwin's essays, which would lead us to the black-white conflict, Allen argues that the major conflict in the novel is instead "the more universal problem of a youth achieving maturity, with literary parallels in *David Copperfield*, *Great Expectations*, *The Brothers Karamazov*, and Hawthorne's 'My Kinsman, Major Molineaux.' Its excellence as a 'Negro novel' has obscured its relevance to other human concerns, particularly the process [of] 'cutting the psychological umbilical cord'" (173). The central action is John's "initiation into manhood—a ritual symbolization of the psychological step from dependence to a sense of self; but most critics describe the conversion as the acceptance of his blackness" (174).

For Allen the key to understanding John's journey in this novel is understanding the symbolism Baldwin works with. Allen argues that Baldwin draws on the intimate, extensive knowledge of the Bible prevalent in the community he grew up in, and in the community he describes in the book, to narrate John's journey. Careful attention to this symbolism reveals how the story transcends its racial particularities:

> The effect of this religious symbolism is to keep the reader aware of the universal elements in John's struggle so that its significance will not be lost amid the specific details and particular persons complicating his conflict. The symbolism prevents us, for example, from mistaking John's peculiar problem as a black taking his place in a society dominated by whites for the more basic problem, common to all humanity, of a child taking his place in adult society. (179)

To prove her point, Allen offers an extensive formalist reading of the tensions between John and his parents/community and how that tension is resolved by his initiation/conversion: "In becoming a man he has rejected not only childish dependency on his mother and fear of his father, but also racial bondage.... Through religious symbolism Baldwin suggests that the conversion which frees John from sin is also his psychological initiation into maturity, which frees him from the umbilical cord and racial hatred" (198–99).

In her efforts to lift Baldwin out of the "literary ghetto," Allen convincingly argues for the significance of the religious symbolism in *Go Tell It on the Mountain*. Despite Baldwin's own religious ambivalence, Allen can still argue that his particular understanding of Christianity based on his personal experiences in Harlem (her essay very much depends on there being a particularly African American brand of Christianity) allows Baldwin to tell a universal story. What is important, though, is that *Go Tell It on the Mountain* can only be universal if it can transcend its racial particularities. Black people and racial bondage, then, become merely metaphors for the universal human condition.

Emmanuel S. Nelson, who will be at the forefront of "queering" Baldwin in the next chapter, here initiates a discussion of sexuality in Baldwin's work by arguing for its metaphorical nature, that is, the particular (homo)sexuality of Baldwin's characters can be read as metaphors for the universal human condition. In "James Baldwin's Vision of Otherness and Community" (1983), Nelson argues that Baldwin has translated his own struggle for self, as a black and homosexual man, into fiction. For Nelson, the search for self is the central theme in Baldwin's work and Baldwin shows how difficult that search can be. Often we are uncomfortable with what we find when we look too closely within:

> To Baldwin, personal as well as collective failures stem from the inability of individuals to confront the "darker" sides of their human nature. Out of this failure comes the mechanism of scapegoating: racial and sexual minorities become visible symbols of the "darker" side—the buried repressions, disturbing anxieties, and hidden pathologies—of the members of the Establishment majority. (27)

Baldwin's fiction is about these scapegoated racial and sexual minorities. Their suffering becomes instructive:

> Suffering, if endured creatively, leads to self-knowledge, which, in return, can offer the possibility of achieving a genuine sense of self. Hence, suffering has humanizing power, and redemptive potential. If many of the Black characters in Baldwin's fiction are presented as morally superior to most of the white characters ... it is *not* because those characters are Black, but because their blackness inflicts additional suffering on them, suffering that can be uplifting and humanizing. (27–28, original emphasis)

By implication, the same is true of Baldwin's homosexual characters: "Hence, blackness and homosexuality in Baldwin's fiction assume metaphorical functions: they are both sources of agony as well as means of redemption; they bring suffering, but, if dealt with courageously, they can lead to self-knowledge, self-acceptance, and the forging of a genuine self-identity" (28). Though Nelson will go on in later criticism to deal with homosexual characters as homosexual, here he seems to suggest that we understand Baldwin's fiction not as stories about black and gay identity, but rather as instructive of identity formation and that the particulars of his black and gay characters serve to highlight that process. While this move at times feels like an attempt to "save" Baldwin from blackness or nationalist politics by focusing in on the particular details of Baldwin's plots rather than simply generalities about race that can be gleaned from that work, Nelson opens the critical door to discuss topics other critics tended to avoid.

An example of a critic utilizing this newly opened space is Lorelei Cederstrom in "Love, Race, and Sex in the Novels of James Baldwin" (1984), a reading heavily influenced by second-wave feminism's redefinitions of gender and sexuality. Like Nelson, Cederstrom also attempts to tackle the issue of homosexuality in Baldwin's work. She acknowledges that though readers and critics generally love *Go Tell It on the Mountain*, as well as Baldwin's short stories and essays, his other novels are "regarded as artistically and intellectually inferior. Whites regard him as an artist with a special audience and irrelevant to their concerns; blacks chide Baldwin for his failure to come to terms with the real issues of their revolutionary movement" (175). Referencing both Bone and Cleaver, Cederstrom determines that the problem many have with Baldwin is his seeming "advocacy" of homosexuality. Countering the argument that Baldwin advocates homosexuality (or any particular sexual practice, for that matter), Cederstrom contends that Baldwin instead attempts to shed a light on basic human connection:

> The use of sex in his novels is not merely an objectification of the "emotional reflexes of his adolescence," as Bone would have it, but a keen, incisive view of the state of human relationships in contemporary America. Baldwin dissects, with precision, the quality of love and sex in a racist society and examines with acute political insight the sexual roles which are forced upon black and white alike as a result of their social conditioning. (176)

Cederstrom seems most interested in the way Baldwin's novels "reveal not only his interest in the relationship between racial and sexual politics, but also his vision of an alternative—a glimpse of love which is free of political patterns of dominance and subordinance" (176). This alternative vision is especially compelling for a feminist critic like Cederstrom (whose reading of Baldwin is heavily influenced by Kate Millet's *Sexual Politics* [1970]), as one of the driving concerns of second-wave feminism was the eradication of subordination and dominance in personal relationships. Like Nelson, Cederstrom reads Baldwin as interested in individuals' journeys of self-discovery, and she reads homosexual characters as metaphors of that journey.

Through readings of *Giovanni's Room, Another Country*, and *Go Tell It on the Mountain*, Cederstrom examines the romantic and sexual relationships presented there and Baldwin's commentary on them, all to conclude that Baldwin is, through looking at the particulars, giving us a model of love that has nothing to do with race or gender or sex and everything to do with universal humanity: "He has shown us that by giving up ideas of dominance, by eliminating the false assumptions of masculinity and femininity and of black and white with which we have been indoctrinated, we may achieve at last 'another country' where genuine love is possible" (187). While in some ways it can be frustrating to read Nelson's and Cederstrom's interpretation of homosexuality as metaphors for the universal human condition (rather than as homosexuality), it is nevertheless refreshing to have them discuss homosexuality as something other than an aberration or abomination. It is noteworthy that these critics attempt to deal with what is actually in Baldwin's work (in this case, a fair amount of sex and sexuality) rather than what they wished were in Baldwin's work.

Not all critics who argue for the primacy of the universal in Baldwin's fiction focus on sexuality, however. Sarah Beebe Fryer's "Retreat from Experience: Despair and Suicide in James Baldwin's Novels" (1986) looks at instances of suicide in Baldwin's fiction and argues that he draws on "experience of American racism to create a vehicle for the expression of his understanding of despair, the twentieth-century existential dilemma" (27). In a now-familiar legitimating move, Fryer argues for Baldwin's importance because of the universality of his work. "While James Baldwin's novels focus primarily on the experience of twentieth-century black Americans and are consequently often relegated to courses in 'black studies'—if they're included in academic curricula at all, Baldwin himself clearly grasps the universal political significance of the motifs of despair and suicide that pervade his works" (21). Fryer seems almost disdainful of "black studies" here, as if this new academic discipline were sullying Baldwin's reputation.

Indeed, while Fryer's essay is interesting for her study of the suicide motif in Baldwin's novels, it is more interesting for its implied criticism of black studies. While critics began this period attempting to rescue Baldwin from the Black Arts movement's racially essentialist excesses and others wanted to move Baldwin out of the "literary ghetto" of protest, Fryer's essay seems to argue that black studies (or, at the very least, a focus on race) will replicate these critical missteps. Furthermore, it will obscure the complexity of Baldwin's work. "Baldwin demonstrates that American society—with its preoccupation with superficial racial distinctions—undermines the common sense of humanity necessary for the emotional welfare of all its citizens, whites as well as blacks" (21). When we study Baldwin only, or primarily, in terms of his race or racial politics, according to Fryer, we miss the ways Baldwin speaks to us all.

Another corrective impulse involves the Wright-Baldwin "debate." Writers in this period seem to seek critical closure on this issue, which ceases really to be an issue in Baldwin scholarship after this period. Kichung Kim's essay "Wright, the Protest Novel, and Baldwin's Faith" (1974) offers a compelling account of how critical conversation about Wright and Baldwin (and, sometimes, Ellison) refuses to be confined to questions of craftsmanship. "It has continued to spill over into matters of social and racial consciousness and conscience, frequently becoming one of the critical issues over which people have been divided into opposing ideological camps" (387). His reading gives a good accounting of those camps.

Like Kim, Jerry Bryant in "Wright, Ellison, Baldwin—Exorcising the Demon" (1976) attributes much of the critical furor over the "debate" to ideological jockeying. He writes, "There was a good deal of abuse on both sides, and, probably, a good many bad judgments expressed. But all in all, the tendency toward using political and social criteria in judging black fiction was a healthy one" (174). He aims to "bring a balance to our view of these writers—to pass some literary judgments on their fiction without ignoring the political and social implications of their work and personalities" (174).

He treats all three writers fairly. His goal here doesn't seem to be to elevate one over the other two and he gives them all credit for creating artistic space for new writers. "The fight to break down the stereotypes to which Wright, Ellison, and Baldwin have devoted so much of their artistic energy is on the way to being won. On some fronts other stereotypes have simply been erected in the place of old—for example, heroic urban guerrillas, sensitive artists crushed by a racist America. But there are enough new voices claiming to be heard on their own grounds to assure us a new era of artistic independence and individuality that black writers have never enjoyed before" (188).

In "'... Farther and Farther Apart': Richard Wright and James Baldwin" (1982), Fred L. Standley, a major player in Baldwin scholarship and discussed in the previous chapter and in the next, offers an excellent overview of the actual words exchanged between Wright and Baldwin and of all the articles written about this "quarrel." Standley's essay appears in the collection *Critical Essays on Richard Wright*, and it is a testament to how influential and seminal Baldwin's "Everybody's Protest Novel" and "Many Thousands Gone" are that the conversation warrants an entire essay in this collection. For many people these essays remain the path through which they first encounter Baldwin. "Everybody's Protest Novel" is often used, in anthologies, as representative piece of Baldwin's criticism (despite the fact that his collections contain numerous critical essays on literature and film), making it possible for readers to know little about Baldwin other than that he once wrote a damning essay about *Native Son*. Despite this, however, critics of Baldwin's work lose interest in this "controversy" during this period.

During this period we also find critics tackling what is perhaps the most significant theme in Baldwin's work: love. While I think that critics still have yet to sufficiently define or explicate Baldwin's "love," critics during this period make several attempts.In "The Dilemma of Love in *Go Tell It on the Mountain* and *Giovanni's Room*" (1974), George E. Bell defines the issue as the paradox that only love can save you in a world where there is only a limited possibility of love. Yet Bell reads Baldwin as optimistic: "Love *is* an attainable goal. Love is possible if one is willing to live existentially, if one is willing to abandon the puritan mythology of man's corruption, of the body's evil, of the necessity of sin and guilt, and to live freely, unashamedly, and unselfishly as a trusting and committed person" (397, original emphasis). He argues that Esther, Richard,

Elizabeth, John, and Elisha in *Go Tell It on the Mountain* and Giovanni in *Giovanni's Room* provide answers to the dilemma of love.

His close readings are notable, in part, because he matter-of-factly acknowledges the homoerotic tension between Elisha and John (this will not become a widespread reading of these characters until the next critical period in Baldwin scholarship) and doesn't fret about the lack of black characters in *Giovanni's Room* (he is one of the few critics who doesn't think this lack notable). He contrasts the characters mentioned above, characters who can give and receive love, with those who cannot, primarily Gabriel in *Go Tell It on the Mountain* and David in *Giovanni's Room*. He concludes that both novels have a primarily pessimistic thrust: "Both novels hold that the path to love is full of theological and psychological pitfalls. Only by successfully overcoming a puritanical sense of evil and guilt can a man gain the release needed to attain a mature, committed, loving, and hence meaningful relationship with another person" (406). Despite these pessimistic stories, though, Bell ultimately positions Baldwin as hopeful writer, one who holds out for the possibility of love, of true human connection, despite the impossible-seeming odds.

Peter Bruck, on the other hand, isn't as optimistic. In "Dungeon and Salvation: Biblical Rhetoric in James Baldwin's *Just Above My Head*" (1984), he argues that Baldwin's enthusiastic reception in the 1960s made him a "pampered child of the white liberal establishment" (130) and that the "morally oriented nature of his writings, his commitment to a philosophy of inter-racial love seemed to be outdated in a time which witnessed the formation of the Black Power and Black Panther movements and increased interest in the teachings of ethnic separatism" (131).

Rather than having something to teach us still, as Champion argues, or continuing to believe in the power of love, as Bell states, Bruck argues that in Baldwin's characterization of Arthur in *Just Above My Head*, the "pessimism here apparent reveals the deep resignation of an author who had once set out to proclaim the idea of brotherly love" (140). Bruck sees in this novel a Baldwin who has been broken and who has, perhaps, betrayed his own progressive politics.

> More than any other work, *Just Above My Head* demonstrates that the author, who had set out "to shake up whites and wake up blacks," has now lost his political and linguistic orientation. This novel shows none of his former desire to enlighten, but rather declares that salvation is now only possible as an individual process and not as a political vision of the future. (142)

Bell's and Bruck's articles quite nicely demonstrate the primary contours of this corner of Baldwin scholarship. Critics continue to try to determine if Baldwin offers us love as hopeful and redemptive or if he reflects back to us a world in which love ultimately fails.

As with chapter 1, focusing only on the major critical trends doesn't allow an opportunity to discuss important work that falls outside of those trends. For instance, during this period Fred L. Standley and Nancy Standley published *James Baldwin: A Reference Guide* (1980), an excellent reference for Baldwin's published work and criticism up to that point. The criticism is annotated, making it particularly useful for Baldwin scholars. Standley acknowledges in his introduction that proper criticism of Baldwin doesn't begin until the 1960s; most commentary on his work previous to this had been in reviews.

We also see the emergence of Trudier Harris as an important Baldwin scholar. Her two essays on Baldwin during this period—"The Eye as Weapon in *If Beale Street Could Talk*" (1978) and "The South as Woman: Chimeric Images of Emasculation in *Just Above My Head*" (1984)—not only treat works rarely ever discussed by other critics but also, without fanfare, contain the kind of close reading called for by other critics during this period. Harris's readings of Baldwin are notable because they are provocative. Her argument about *Just Above My Head* is: "If the South is painted in Baldwin's fiction as a female image which emasculates black men, and yet it is the males in that environment who most frequently carry out that gruesome emasculation, then the logical extension of the argument is that Southern white men are 'faggots.' Those who are without sexuality use the racial power they do have to acquire symbolically the manhood they have somehow lost" (108). And she avoids the trap of nostalgia when reading Baldwin's later work. Of *Beale Street* she writes,

> Baldwin has denuded his plot of the encumbrances that created problems for his characters in his earlier works. The major characters in *Beale Street* are not fanatically committed to organized religion and church affiliation. They are not subject to the torment of interracial sex/love relationships. They are not immobilized by involvement in homosexual affairs. They are just folks who love each other and who are committed to the human; however, it is the intensity of their concern for each other and the intense way in which Tish presents the story that makes it special. By allowing Tish, with her central involvement in the story, to relate in her own creative, though unsophisticated way, Baldwin has made graceful simplicity the force or art. He has thereby moved his own creativity to a new level. (66)

The prominent literary and cultural critic Harold Bloom edited a volume on Baldwin for his Modern Critical Views series in 1986. A volume edited by Bloom carries a certain cultural cache because of his Harvard faculty position and his reputation as a prominent literary critic outside the academy. It is important to note that Bloom advocates a formalist aesthetic, as do other critics discussed in this chapter. Editing a volume on Baldwin, then, implies that Baldwin is important and well-known enough, and no longer so controversial that Bloom can dedicate an entire book to him. It also implies, I would argue, that Baldwin's body of work can stand up to the scrutiny and rigor of formalist criticism that Bloom advocates. This collection, eleven essays on Baldwin's nonfiction and fiction, is a bit of a paradox, however.

Bloom, in an "Editor's Note," assures us that the collection "gathers together what its editor considers the most useful criticism yet devoted to the writings of James Baldwin" (vii). The essays range from 1962 to 1985 and cover Baldwin's most popular works: the essays, *Blues for Mister Charlie*, *Go Tell It on the Mountain*, *Another Country*, and *The Fire Next Time*. In the introduction, however, Bloom makes clear which Baldwin he finds worthy of praise. He writes that whatever "the ultimate canonical judgment upon James Baldwin's fiction may prove to be, his nonfictional work clearly has permanent status in American literature" (1). Note that the Baldwin that Bloom attempts to canonize here is Baldwin the essay writer. Bloom's introduction then proceeds through a very compelling close reading that traces Baldwin's prophetic vision through his major essays. The esteem in which Bloom holds Baldwin's talent as an essayist is evident in the essayists he compares Baldwin with: Orwell, Emerson, Carlyle, Nietzsche. Bloom's reading leaves the reader with a sense that Baldwin is not only an important writer but also a great writer whose grasp of the human soul is matched by few others. Bloom's introduction, however, is followed by essays that all argue the same basic point: Baldwin is a talented writer whose early promise was never fulfilled.

While the specific arguments made in these essays echo those we have already seen in this and the previous chapter, it is worth noting that Bloom sees fit to collect not that criticism that gives credence to his reading of Baldwin, or at least criticism that looks primarily at Baldwin's essays. Instead we get criticism that finds Baldwin's attachment to blackness aesthetically troubling and ultimately ironic, and finds his prophetic vision ultimately overcome by ambivalence. Ambivalence, indeed, is the word to describe this collection's attitude toward Baldwin. Coming, as it did, shortly before his death in 1987, and representing a fairly mainstream critical view of Baldwin's work, this collection stands as a seeming bellwether of how critics will read Baldwin after his death.

In the introduction to *Black Women in the Fiction of James Baldwin* (1985), Trudier Harris gives a good assessment of Baldwin scholarship near the end of his life. In response to the relative lack of knowledge about Baldwin, even among those who claimed to have read his work, Harries concludes,

> Baldwin seems to be read at times for the sensationalism readers anticipate in his work, but his treatment in scholarly circles is not commensurate to that claim to sensationalism or to his more solidly

justified literary reputation. It was discouraging, therefore, to think that one of American's best-known writers, and certainly one of its best-known black writers, has not attained a more substantial place in the scholarship on Afro-American writers. (4–5)

Though Harris doesn't speculate on the reason for the dearth of good Baldwin criticism, the absence seems related to the assertions and conclusions in Peter Bruck's "Protest, Universality, Blackness: Patterns of Argumentation in the Criticism of the Contemporary Afro-American Novel" (1982). In this piece Bruck contends that together "with the idea of universality and the concept of mainstream literature, the ideal of assimilation constitutes the semantic field used by critics up to the mid-1960s to discuss and evaluate both the Afro-American novel and the role of the writer" (8). The mid-1960s response to this, the call for a criticism rooted in a black aesthetic, according to Bruck, results in a "prescriptive canon" (23), a canon that dismisses Baldwin as assimilationist and counterrevolutionary and therefore not worthy of study. In response to these two strains of criticism, there is a call among other critics (Henry Louis Gates, Jr. chief among them) to treat African American literature as an "evolutionary system" (26). Bruck endorses this move, stating that such criticism would break "with the established canon of the critical community which is still preoccupied with the writings of Wright, Ellison, and Baldwin. *Native Son*, *Invisible Man*, or *Go Tell It on the Mountain*, for all their thematic richness, are not the yardstick by which to measure other Afro-American novels, nor can they stand as tokens for them" (26). The contents of Bruck's collection, *The Afro-American Novel since 1960* (1982), bears out this sentiment in that it includes not a single essay on Wright, Ellison, or Baldwin. Baldwin, who, unlike Wright or Ellison, continued to publish extensively during this period, becomes a casualty of well-meaning attempts to broaden the African American literary tradition.

Critics of this period try to demonstrate Baldwin's continuing relevance to a world and discipline seemingly no longer interested in the answering the question, What does the Negro want? Yet Baldwin ends this critical period much the same way he began it: passé. Other African American writers, some of whom, like Toni Morrison, cite Baldwin as a major influence, become critical and popular darlings during this time. However, renewed interest in his work and life after his death and the advent of cultural studies will breathe new life into Baldwin studies in the next period.

Notes

[1] See the collection *The House That Race Built: Original Essays by Toni Morrison, Angela Y. Davis, Cornel West, and Others on Black Americans and Politics in America Today*, edited by Wahneema Lubiano.

² Alain Locke wrote in his famous "New Negro" essay, "The Negro mind reaches out as yet to nothing but American wants, American ideas. But this forced attempt to build Americanism on race values is a unique social experiment, and its ultimate success is impossible except through the fullest sharing of American culture and institutions.... The racialism of the Negro is no limitation or reservation with respect to American life; it is only a constructive effort to build the obstructions in the stream of his progress into an efficient dam of social energy and power. Democracy itself is obstructed and stagnated to the extent that any of its channels are closed. So the choice is not between one way for the Negro and another way for the rest, but between American institutions frustrated on the one hand and American ideals progressively fulfilled and realized on the other" (12).

³ For detailed discussion of the history and philosophy of the Black Arts movement, see the *Oxford Companion to African American Literature*, edited by William Andrews, et. al.; *American Literary Criticism since the 1930s*, edited by Vincent R. Leitch; and *The Black Arts Movement* by James Smethurst.

⁴ See especially James Smethurst *The Black Arts Movement* (2005); and Lisa Gail Collins and Margo Natalie Crawford, *New Thoughts on the Black Arts Movement* (2006).

3: Retheorizing James Baldwin: 1988–2000

BY THE TIME OF BALDWIN'S DEATH from stomach cancer in 1987, there were several assumptions about James Baldwin and his work on which most Baldwin scholarship was built. There was general agreement that he was an important African American writer, though his relevance was primarily historical (that is, he wrote several seminal essays that were important at a particular point in time). Critics generally agreed that his career peaked in the mid-1960s, and that while he excelled in the essay, with the exception of *Go Tell It on the Mountain* he fell short in other genres. (Notably, there will be no critical evaluation of his poetry until the end of this period.) And finally, critics generally worked with the assumption that Baldwin spoke most passionately about race, downplayed his sexual orientation, and denounced Christianity.

These assumptions are reflected in *Critical Essays on James Baldwin*, a 1988 anthology edited by Fred L. Standley and Nancy V. Burt. After giving a quick overview of the critical reception of Baldwin's work (derived mostly from reviews), Standley and Burt offer their rationale for the collection: "This book has been designed to exemplify the evolution of scholarship during approximately the last decade and a half.... While it is true that some of James Baldwin's books have not received the same critical attention as in previously published collections of essays, it is equally the case that his total achievements have received here a more balanced examination and objective evaluation than previously available" (28). The essays are reprints of reviews and critical articles (many of them discussed elsewhere in this book), in addition to new pieces commissioned expressly for the anthology. The collection is notable for reviews of stage productions of *Blues for Mister Charlie* and *Amen Corner* and of the PBS production of *Go Tell It on the Mountain*. What strikes me most about this collection, though, is that all entries generally praise Baldwin's artistry, moral steadfastness, and political astuteness. There is very little that is "critical," in all senses of the word, in this book. *Critical Essays on James Baldwin* is as much a homage to Baldwin as it is a collection of recent criticism. The critical assumptions around Baldwin's work seem so set in stone that there is nothing left to do but pay tribute to Baldwin during this period.

And there certainly were a great many tributes to Baldwin. The University of Massachusetts Press published the proceedings of a 1988 conference reconfigured as a tribute to Baldwin after his death. The collected proceedings, *Black Writers Redefine the Struggle: A Tribute to James Baldwin* (1989), edited by Jules Chametzky, feature writers engaged in conversation about Baldwin's influence on African American literature. A similar volume, *James Baldwin: The Legacy* (1989), edited by Quincy Troupe, features individual writers offering their remembrances of Baldwin, though they studiously avoid the political, artistic, and ideological divisions that plagued Baldwin throughout his career. Included are Henry Louis Gates's famous interview with Baldwin and Josephine Baker; Richard Goldstein's interview, which provides much fodder for those critics in this era trying to pin down Baldwin on homosexuality and gay identity (discussed later in this chapter); and the last interview Baldwin gave, conducted by Troupe. Among the writers eulogizing Baldwin are Mary McCarthy, who confesses she read none of Baldwin's books after *The Fire Next Time* because she was "shaken a little by it" and did not want to change the idea she had of him (49); Maya Angelou, who writes of "my friend and brother" rather than the artist and prophet everyone else knew (41); Amiri Baraka, who speaks of "Jimmy, this glorious, elegant griot of our oppressed African-American nation" (127); and Toni Morrison, who wrote of Baldwin's gift of giving "us ourselves to think about" (75).

Maria Diedrich, in "James A. Baldwin—Obituaries for a Black Ishmael" (1991), surveys all these obituaries, eulogies, and remembrances and writes that while during Baldwin's life his writing "provoked a variety of reactions that comprised the whole gamut from enthusiastic appraisal and lionization to denunciation and violent rejection," after his death something changed:

> It became clear that our dreary, materialistic, and disenchanted world is still a world of magic: for the death of this multifaced, rebellious and controversial writer caused his miraculous metamorphosis into the universally acknowledged forefather of contemporary black American literature, into the accepted spokesman of black rage, black pride, and black love, into everybody's best friend. Respect and reverence for the dead, and perhaps, the feeling that no justice had been done to the live writer tempted those who felt inspired to write his parting praise to deprive this knotty, strong trunk of its edges and to polish an attractively rough surface until the true beauty and strength of the original vanished. James Baldwin was domesticated and reincarnated as everybody's Jimmy. (130–31)

Baldwin clearly meant a great deal to other writers, particularly writers younger than he, like Morrison and Angelou, who had personal and professional connections to him. No doubt the recollections offered reflect a sincere outpouring of grief and affection from those who knew him. At the same time, though, there is something a little disingenuous about the transformation of Baldwin into "everybody's Jimmy." His death came in the wake of poor reviews of his final full-length works, the novel *Just Above My Head* and the book-length essay *Evidence of Things Not Seen*. A retrospective collection spanning his entire career, published almost simultaneously with *Evidence*, garnered reviews that longed for the days of a politically relevant, artistically competent Baldwin. I don't mean to suggest that those eulogizing Baldwin needed to enter the critical minefield of Baldwin scholarship. It is telling, though, that Baldwin's importance at the end of his life seems to be historical and inspirational rather than artistic. This embrace of Baldwin the man rather than artist (Mary McCarthy's affection for him even though she couldn't bring herself to read his work) leaves his position in American and African American letters as a major critical question.

This chapter looks at the ways in which Baldwin scholarship after his death, from 1988 to 2000, challenges common assumptions and silences surrounding Baldwin's work. Critics during this period, having the benefit of being able to survey the entirety of Baldwin's career and use feminist, postmodern, cultural studies, and queer theories, attempt to challenge us to rethink what we know and understand about Baldwin's work. This is done primarily by recontextualizing and queering Baldwin's work. Though other critical conversations are taking place (notably those about Henry James's influence on Baldwin,[1] Baldwin's expatriation and his critical reception abroad,[2] and the fortieth anniversary of *Go Tell It on the Mountain*[3]), they don't lead to the same kind of broader reshaping of the critical terrain as the ones I'll discuss. Baldwin's death in 1987 coincided with significant shifts in critical theory. Though the history of those shifts and definitions of specific terms can be found in a number of places,[4] a brief summary of the pertinent details is necessary here. Feminist theory, queer theory, cultural studies, and postmodernism, all key critical lenses in this period of Baldwin scholarship, bring to the table a new set of questions for literary scholarship. These questions largely center on issues of evaluation and inclusion: What do we consider "good" literature and why? How are our evaluative lenses shaped by the power dynamics and politics of our particular cultural moment? How do literary texts function as a mechanism by which a culture constructs what it means to be black, or gay, or female, etc.? All of these questions are undergirded by the poststructuralist notion that power is created and mobilized by representation. At the same time, these approaches, which are often employed in pop culture criticism, also often deliberately shelve the question of literary value, with the assumption that by this point everyone recognizes that value is a relative scale shaped by power dynamics, the historical moment, etc. That is, while questions of evaluation and inclusion are always lurking, in practice many of these critics just go ahead and write about what they want to write about without feeling that they have to prove that it is worthy.

Critics' willingness to discuss Baldwin's sexuality and the sex and sexuality in his books is also a part of a larger conversation about black men and sexuality happening at this time. The 1980s saw what some people term a "black gay male renaissance." Marlon Riggs's controversial and seminal documentary *Tongues Untied* (1989) offered a frank and powerful portrayal of black gay life and Isaac Julien's film *Looking for Langston* (1989) encouraged audiences to reconsider what they knew of the famous poet and of the literary period he is most associated with, the Harlem Renaissance. Essex Hemphill's *Brother to Brother: New Writings by Black Gay Men* (1991) and Joseph Beam's *In the Life: A Black Gay Anthology* (1986) offered us a new array of black male voices. Marcellus Blount and George P. Cunningham's *Representing Black Men* set the stage for critical discussions of these issues. And images of black male bodies dominated popular culture because of, among other things, the work of Robert Mapplethorpe, the music videos of Madonna, and the popularity of drag queen RuPaul.[5]

The critical and cultural landscapes are primed for a discussion of black gay identity and issues and the queering of James Baldwin, then, becomes the most significant and provocative critical move during this period of Baldwin scholarship. William J. Spurlin, in an article tracing the queer reception history of Baldwin, explains the critical space opened up by queer theory.

> I must acknowledge that contemporary work in American lesbian and gay studies, academic queer theory, and post-Stonewall activism has enabled a space for me to (re)read the cultural lenses that helped interpret Baldwin and his work and constitute his reception in the early 1960s, and that my readings and critique of the claims made about homosexuality in the period under discussion make rhetorical use of queercentric interpretations of gay identity by these disciplines and social practices in the present. ("Transgressing Boundaries," 47)

In other words, Spurlin can revisit Baldwin scholarship from earlier periods and address explicitly the homophobia informing that scholarship. Indeed, Eldridge Cleaver's and Robert Bone's critiques of Baldwin continue to resonate in part because they make such excellent fodder for queer theory.

One of the results of queer theory's influence on Baldwin scholarship is that it sheds new light on a popular Baldwin work, *Go Tell It on the Mountain*, and it brings oft-maligned work, like *Giovanni's Room*, to the center. In "Critical Deviance: Homophobia and the Reception of James Baldwin's Fiction" (1991), for instance, Emmanuel S. Nelson (whom we saw in the previous chapter discussing sexuality in Baldwin's work, and who will go on to publish frequently on gay and lesbian authors) calls *Giovanni's Room* "a classic work in modern gay fiction" (92) and describes *Go Tell It on the Mountain* as a "complex text" that "offers one of the most poignant portrayals of developing adolescent homosexual consciousness in American fiction" (94–95).

His readings of both novels stem from his desire to not limit Baldwin to being simply a gay or black writer. "We have to explore the combined cultural, political and artistic consequences of both ... racial awareness and his homosexual consciousness on his literary imagination" (91). The problem he sees in Baldwin scholarship has been an inability on the part of critics to deal adequately with the complexity of Baldwin's identity. "Many white critics are uncomfortable responding to a writer who is doubly different; many Black critics, though often enthusiastic about Baldwin's handling of racial themes, seem embarrassed and angered by his explicit treatment of homosexuality" (92). As a result, then, Nelson asserts that a major aspect of Baldwin's work, his exploration of homosexuality and the influence of sexual identity on human society, gets lost in the critical shuffle.

As if responding to a challenge, or merely playing in the critical space that had been opened up by queer theory, other critics begin to attend to the overt homosexual themes, characters, and stories in Baldwin's work. They begin to fill this critical void. Almost all of these critics focus their attention on Baldwin's second novel, *Giovanni's Room*. In "Dividing the Mind: Contradictory Portraits of Homoerotic Love in *Giovanni's Room*" (1992), Yasmin Y. DeGout argues that the novel is ultimately about our inability to believe one another because of failed social systems. And she argues that Baldwin does not offer homoerotic love as an answer to the problem. This is in sharp contrast to earlier critics who often read Baldwin as offering homosexuality as a superior alternative to heterosexuality, and, just as often, judged him harshly for this.

For DeGout, Baldwin's depiction of homosexuality is ambivalent at best:

> Baldwin depicts homoerotic love as the natural and wholesome interaction of innocent characters whose love transcends the degeneracy of the gay Parisian underground and is capable of healing and reformation. But he also depicts homoerotic love as deviant behavior that proceeds from both psychological and socioeconomic depravity within the microcosmic home environment and within the larger society. (426)

This contradiction makes the novel a "literary Rorschach test for the reader's sexual consciousness," allowing "readers to approach the work in a way that suits their own psychological needs or social value systems" (434–35). It also allows DeGout to suggest that the ambiguity in the novel stems from Baldwin's own ambivalence about homosexuality, an assertion based on Baldwin's public statements about homosexuality and gay identity.

Unlike critics in the previous chapter who were loath to consider Baldwin's biography in their readings of his work, critics from this period return to that biography with a vengeance. This move is helped, in part, by the appearance of two biographies during this period, *Talking at the Gates: A Life of James Baldwin* (1991) by James Campbell, and *James Baldwin: A Biography* (1995) by David Leeming. These biographies, as well as the advent of "identity politics" during this period, give tacit permission to scholars to once again consider the effect Baldwin's life experiences had on his work. In addition, the growth of cultural studies and, with it, critics' willingness to work intertextually, or to abandon the text altogether, means that the critical anxiety around Baldwin's biography (is it critically relevant? is it critically off limits? does it reveal anything at all about his work?) is all but gone during this period.

The problem with looking into Baldwin's own life to provide insight into the homosexual themes in his work is that he spoke very little about his own homosexuality, and when did he speak it was to express his discomfort with a "gay" identity and to assert that ultimately sexual preference is a private matter. Outside of the essays "The Male Prison" (1961) and "Freaks and the American Ideal of Manhood" (1985), Baldwin wrote very little autobiographically about homosexuality. In 1984, Richard Goldstein, a senior editor at *The Village Voice*, interviewed Baldwin with the expressed purpose of asking about his sexuality. In the interview Baldwin stated that he felt a "responsibility ... to be a kind of witness" to "that phenomenon we call gay" (175), though he doesn't necessarily identify as gay.

> GOLDSTEIN: Do you feel like a stranger in gay America?
>
> BALDWIN: Well, first of all I feel like a stranger in America from almost every conceivable angle except, oddly enough, as a black person. The word "gay" has always rubbed me the wrong way. I never understood exactly what is meant by it. I don't want to sound distant or patronizing because I don't really feel that. I simply feel it's a world that has very little to do with me, with where I did my growing up. I was never at home in it. Even in my early years in the Village, what I saw of that world absolutely frightened me, bewildered me. I didn't understand the necessity of all the role playing. And in a way I still don't. (174)

Yet in novels like *Giovanni's Room*, which sees a critical resurgence during this period, Baldwin displays a very intimate and convincing understanding of gay life. Criticism during this period sought to reconcile the homosexuality in Baldwin's fiction with Baldwin's seeming resistance to identify as gay.

Raymond-Jean Frontain's 1995 article, "James Baldwin's *Giovanni's Room* and the Biblical Myth of David" is provocative in that it reads

Giovanni's Room as a retelling of the biblical story of David and Jonathan.[6] While he argues convincingly for this reading, citing the wealth of Christian imagery in Baldwin's work and Baldwin's own extensive knowledge of the Bible as evidence, it is important to note that Giovanni is not, in fact, the Italian equivalent of Jonathan. Giovanni translates as John, and this calls into question Frontain's assertion that "Baldwin signals to the reader his intention to offer in *Giovanni's Room* a meditation on the conditions of a modern love 'passing the love of women' (41)." That said, the secondary argument in this essay remains compelling. Because Frontain considers Baldwin "one of the great poets of human redemption" (54), he is surprised and disappointed at the lack of redemption for any of the characters in *Giovanni's Room*.

This can be explained, according to Frontain, by looking at Baldwin's own life. Frontain can only speculate here (and he owns up to that) because details about Baldwin's lovers and love affairs, even his long relationship with Lucien Happersberger, are scarce. Frontain maintains, however, that *Giovanni's Room* can help us fill in some of the blanks.

> Baldwin polarized heterosexual and homosexual relations so dramatically, presenting the former as socially licit but suffocating in their mediocrity and the latter as enlivening and redemptive but socially suffocating. The reader can only accept this as part of the novel's worldview. And I suspect that in addition to its neglecting the racial themes that his readers had come to expect—and to the homosexual content that many mainstream American readers in the 1990s still find as difficult to accept as did Baldwin's original readers in 1956—one of the reasons *Giovanni's Room* remains possibly the least discussed of Baldwin's novels is its inability to imagine a successful love relationship of any kind. (53–54)

Perhaps, Frontain implies, Baldwin fails to portray redemptive love in his novel because he had been unable to find it in his own life. He finds it especially significant that Baldwin only "dares explicitly describe a male sex scene of mutual enjoyment" in his last novel, *Just Above My Head*. Either Baldwin only dared present a successful homosexual relationship at the end of his career or he found love only at the end of his life. Like many critics of this period, Frontain reads Baldwin as a man of his time: though he seemed to have accepted his own homosexuality, he nevertheless remained ambivalent about it, and his work reflects that.

Critics like Kendall Thomas, on the other hand, assert that the ambivalence Frontain notes is almost completely beside the point. What is more interesting to Thomas is how Baldwin's sexual identity has informed the critical treatment, particularly African American critical treatment, of his work. His essay "'Ain't Nothin' Like the Real Thing': Black Masculinity, Gay Sexuality, and the Jargon of Authenticity" (1996), a seeming response to postmodernism's dismantling of identity, uses Baldwin the author as a site from which to retheorize identity as something rooted in corporeality rather than in ideological authenticity.

Thomas begins his essay by citing Michael Thelwell's review of James Campbell's 1991 biography of Baldwin. A virtue of the biography, according to Thelwell, is Campbell's assertion that Baldwin was "essentially androgynous rather than homosexual" and that his androgyny allowed him to teach a "generation of us how to be black men in this country," despite his open homosexuality (quoted in Thomas, 57). Thomas objects to this not only because it is an oversimplification of Baldwin's sexual identity, but also because of what it implies about black liberation politics. "Stated bluntly, Thelwell's vision of a 'neutered' Baldwin betrays a deep and disturbing ideological investment regarding the connections among masculinity, sexuality, and 'authentic' black identity" (57).

The article was published as the US neo-black nationalist movement was waning. Rap groups like Public Enemy, whose 1990 hit "Fight the Power" provided the anthem for this movement, presented a strong, aggressive, hypermasculine, and politically progressive version of black masculinity for the public. Other so-called gangsta rap acts like Dr. Dre, Ice Cube (former members of the group NWA—Niggaz with Attitude), Snoop Dogg, and Ice T offered a version of black masculinity that was often physically threatening and (hetero)sexually promiscuous. And the 1995 Million Man March, convened by the Nation of Islam leader Louis Farrakhan, called on black men to step up to their responsibilities as husbands and fathers. It is against this backdrop that Thomas, again reflecting the influence of pop culture and cultural studies criticism on this generation of critics, refers to the "heteronormative logic that conditions the ascription of 'authentic' black identity on the repudiation of gay or lesbian identity. The jargon of racial authenticity insists, as the gangsta-rapper Ice Cube put it, that 'true niggers ain't gay' (59)."

This is a problem for Thomas not just because of the inherent homophobia of this position, but also because of the internal divisions it creates: "My hypothesis, in brief, is that the homophobia and virulent masculinism that underwrite the politics of racial authenticity in the current conjuncture are best understood as the displaced expression of internalized racism, which is in turn a symptom of a sexual alienation among black Americans of epidemic proportions" (61). Thomas offers, in the place of ideological authenticity, corporeality as means of bringing people together. Working with Cornel West's assertion that identities are things that people die and kill for, and thus are not simply postmodern linguistic constructions, Thomas argues that this "reworking of the terms of the identity debate from questions of ideology and consciousness to material matters of bodies, life, and death is an important one because it clears the ground for fuller consideration of issues that have been submerged by both the jargon of racial authenticity and its antiessentialist critique" (63). In other words, Thomas encourages us to consider questions of identity not as postmodern constructs but rather as real questions about actual physical survival.

Thomas's ultimate concern seems to be how best to pursue antiracist and antihomophobic change without forcing black gays and lesbians to "choose sides." In this way Thomas's work shows the influences of not only queer theory but also the black feminist theory developing during this period. Kimberele Crenshaw coined the term "intersectionality" to describe the experience (of black women, according to her argument) that is "greater than the sum of racism and sexism" (40). Baldwin, then, serves as an excellent theoretical site for Thomas because Baldwin's work gives evidence that he shared these political goals, and his reception in black intellectual and liberation circles demonstrates the limits of choosing sides. If we recognize that Baldwin's black body, regardless of whom that body chooses to love, belongs to "us," to the black community, then it becomes more difficult to dismiss him or portions of his work because he is gay. Thomas concludes, "To understand that antiracist and antihomophobic politics are informed by a common corporeal interest in survival is to create the possibility of coalition across difference" (65).

The kind of opening up of critical space around Baldwin and sexuality in the essays we have seen so far allows critics not only to reexamine critically marginalized works, but also allows us to rethink all the critical conversations Baldwin participated in. Up until this point, critics primarily discussed Baldwin as a voice within the critical conversations about African American protest literature, the role of the writer, the effects of racism on black and white Americans, and, occasionally, the consequences of expatriation. But with the emergence of queer theory and the new questions and critical tools they offer, we can begin to think of Baldwin as participating in other conversations.

For example, two 1993 articles place Baldwin in conversation with Audre Lorde. Lorde's death in 1992 almost certainly suggests that critics were undertaking with her the same kind of project that is happening concurrently with Baldwin—an assessment of her entire body of work and her legacy. Both Shelton Waldrep in "'Being Bridges': Cleaver/Baldwin/Lorde and African-American Sexism and Sexuality" and Donald H. Mengay in "The Failed Copy: *Giovanni's Room* and the (Re)Contextualization of Difference" argue that Lorde's legacy is challenging reified notions of identity and difference and that Baldwin's work is a stepping stone to that ideological point.

Waldrep's essay begins with a long reading of Cleaver that points out the homophobic irrationality outlined in the first chapter of this book. However, I find his discussion of Baldwin and Lorde, and his implication that these three writers exist on the same intellectual continuum, more compelling. He reads Baldwin as far more complicated a writer, particularly in matters of form, than critics usually give him credit for. "First, Baldwin was an individualist. He did not follow a strict methodology, but rather wrote criticism that was an eclectic blend of textual analysis, biography, history, and pure speculation" (176). He highlights how central a theme sexuality is in Baldwin's work and stresses the interconnectedness of race and sex in the essays and novels. He then relates all of this to Baldwin's prescription of love. (Note how Waldrep's understanding of Baldwin's work builds on the formalist criticism discussed in chapter 2.) He praises Baldwin's ability to see that race doesn't trump sexual identity and that sexual preference doesn't preclude the capacity or desire for love. Yet he finds that Baldwin doesn't go far enough, or at least not as far as Lorde will take us: "Any claim to universality or common humanity, such as he has made, would appear to her naïve. She feels that she must write poetry that attempts via self-reflexiveness to come to terms with basic questions about sexuality by isolating the experience of African-American women in order that it might be analyzed" (177). Whereas Baldwin wanted us to see that all men were the same, despite their perceived differences, Lorde encouraged us to look head-on at those differences to recognize that not all people are men: "[Baldwin] was unafraid to look at what Cleaver would only consider the other, the enemy. Yet Lorde's comments show that Baldwin ignores much complexity within gender debate by his positing of brotherly love as a panacea for society's ills" (179). Waldrep doesn't dismiss Baldwin or downplay his importance, but he does highlight significant aspects of Baldwin's work that we might otherwise miss if we assume him to be only a writer about race. He also demonstrates that it is possible to challenge and question the ideas found in Baldwin's work without dismissing him as a writer preoccupied with race or discounting his artistry.

The same is true of Mengay's article. He reads *Giovanni's Room* as challenging sexual hierarchies at a time when other writers and novels didn't even acknowledge that these hierarchies existed: "What separates *Giovanni's Room* from other novels written before it is Baldwin's unrelenting crossing of so many elements of subjectivity, including class, nationality, regional identification, and religion, but particularly gender, race, and sexuality" (59). Like Waldrep, who argues about Baldwin's "brotherly love," Mengay argues that "the heroes of *Giovanni's Room* seek to (re)contextualize difference, in its many identificatory modes, in such a way that it is rendered neutral both personally and politically" (59). And like Waldrep, Mengay finds the gender politics of this move troubling:

> Baldwin alludes to the difficulties women face in his portrayal of the David-Giovanni and Hella-David relationships, in Hella's exasperation with David's chauvinism, but he doesn't go so far as actually to

> reconfigure or even reenvision the gender hierarchy in the text. The
> main contribution of *Giovanni's Room* appears to be its critique of
> racism within a gay context and the way race is inextricably bound to
> other modes of difference. (69)

Lorde, however, provides the critical tools to "reconfigure or even reenvision the gender hierarchy," and emphasizes difference. Lorde, then, moves us further along a path first chartered by Baldwin, though she takes that path in a new direction.

Mengay asserts that Giovanni is coded as black in the novel. That is, if we understand blackness to be a social construction (rather than a biological fact), specifically a linguistic construction, then what we see in *Giovanni's Room* is that language applied to Giovanni. Mengay writes, "One finds the identificatory nexus of gender/race/sexuality in both David and Giovanni, but it is the latter who represents the black/gay/male position—that is, Baldwin's own. Giovanni's race dimension is historical mostly, evoking the rhetoric of American slavery, the repoliticized African-American identity of the 1950s, and an African genealogy" (60). A number of other critics, like Mengay, will argue not that Giovanni is actually "black" (of African descent), but rather that his circumstances and relationships with and to other characters in the novel place him in the typically socially, economically, and politically marginalized position of the black.

The most anthologized contemporary essay on Baldwin's work makes a similar argument. In "Tearing the Goat's Flesh: Homosexuality, Abjection, and the Production of a Late Twentieth-Century Black Masculinity" (1996),[7] Robert Reid-Pharr argues that the "question of Blackness, precisely because of its very apparent absence, screams out at the turn of every page.... I will suggest that Baldwin's explication of Giovanni's ghost-like non-presence, his non-subjectivity, parallels the absence of the Black from Western notions of rationality and humanity while at the same time pointing to the possibility of escape from this same Black-exclusive system of logic" (387). Giovanni's blackness is important to Reid-Pharr's argument because he wants to explore the homosexual as both a scapegoat (in a move that echoes Emmanuel Nelson's 1983 essay on Baldwin) and as a source of possibility within the black community.

Because, according to Reid-Pharr, "the Black as been conceptualized in modern (slave) culture as an inchoate, irrational non-subject, as the chaos that both defines and threatens the borders of logic, individuality, and basic subjectivity" (373), the black community watches vigilantly at the borders of blackness in order to keep the chaos out. "The scapegoat, then, would be the figure who reproduces this undifferentiation, this chaos, this boundarylessness. The violence directed against the goat would mitigate against prior violence, the erosion of borders that has beset the entire community" (373). Homosexuals function as these "scapegoats" in the black community. Homophobic attacks, then, both physical and those in literary criticism, function as attempts to secure the borders of blackness. Like many other critics discussing Baldwin and sexuality, Reid-Pharr returns to Cleaver's "Notes on a Native Son." "To date no one has examined closely Cleaver's tragicomic struggle to construct a Black heterosexuality, to finally rid the Black consciousness of the dual specters of effeminacy and interracial homoeroticism. One might argue, in fact, that Cleaver's woman-hating and fag-bashing were, for all his bravado, failed attempts to assert himself and the Black community as 'straight' (375)." Reid-Pharr is critical of Cleaver's efforts to present the black community as straight because this is exclusive and unjust and dangerous to members of the black community who are not straight. Because it is so often reprinted, it comes to stand in as the quintessential queer reading of Baldwin's work, and because it is reprinted more often than any other contemporary treatment of Baldwin, it also suggests that a queer reading is the most appropriate reading of Baldwin.

By the mid-1990s the queer theorists' love affair with Baldwin had begun to wane, but the effect of their scholarship could still be felt. While queer theory certainly opened up space to talk about those aspects of Baldwin's work that had been silenced in the past, it also allowed critics in general to ask different questions about Baldwin. Whereas chapter 1 saw critics almost blinded by their inability to see around questions of race and race politics, and chapter 2 saw critics almost paralyzed in their efforts to avoid questions of race, queer theory (as well as the influence of feminist theory, cultural studies, and postmodernism in literary criticism) allowed critics to acknowledge that Baldwin wrote about race, but also wrote about a variety of other topics. One of those other topics is religion.

Two 1997 essays, "'Come-to-Jesus Stuff' in James Baldwin's *Go Tell It on the Mountain* and *The Amen Corner*" by Barbara K. Olson, and "*Just Above My Head*: James Baldwin's Quest for Belief" by Michael F. Lynch, offer reconsiderations of Baldwin's use of religion and religious imagery. While other critics have taken note of the religious aspects of Baldwin's work, most often tying religion to Baldwin's notion of love, none have, as Lynch does in his essay, posited a Baldwinian theology.

For Lynch the "most pervasive problem with Baldwin criticism is the projection of a dichotomized scheme onto an artist whose method is fundamentally dialectical" (285). Here Lynch echoes Waldrep's assessment that Baldwin is a far more complicated writer than he is given credit for being, but also echoes Addison Gayle's 1967 essay on *The Fire Next Time*, which urges us to recognize the dialectical nature of Baldwin's work. Like Gayle, Lynch recognizes that the critical tide turned against Baldwin after the publication of *The Fire Next Time*, when critics seemed to have decided that Baldwin had become too angry and too polemical:

> But the inaccurate charge that he polemicizes his writing from that point on is rooted in critics' positing the political against the individual and/or spiritual, which opposition Baldwin attempts to reconcile. In my view, his middle and later work achieves more complex works of art than the prevailing assessment contends largely because he does not become a polemicist and because as a dialectical thinker he continues to respect and maintain the necessary vital tension between political reality and spiritual vision. (285)

Out of this dialectical thinking comes a theology that Lynch argues Baldwin "develops more as a corrective to than a repudiation of Christian theology as understood and practiced, and might be called 'radical' in the sense of being faithful to the spirit of the early church" (292). Baldwin's theology, he argues, "considers three complementary aspects of, or avenues toward salvation: saving oneself through developing the ability to survive and to love, saving another through preferential or erotic love, and saving others through selfless action based on accepting responsibility for all people" (293). Lynch then roots commonly discussed themes in Baldwin's work—eroticism and love—firmly in Baldwin's Christian faith. I find this reading particularly compelling not only because of the assumption of complexity in Baldwin's work (indeed, the notion of a Baldwinian theology developed in his novels demands further consideration), but also because Lynch refuses to throw out one Baldwin in order to privilege another. By assuming a complicated, dialectical Baldwin, Lynch creates a critical space where both Baldwinian eroticism and spirituality can live.

Barbara Olson is not as optimistic. Olson's essay begins with a quote from Baldwin describing the origins of his play *The Amen Corner*. Coming to the conclusion after *Go Tell It on the Mountain* that he was "a writer, a Negro writer, ... expected to write diminishing versions of *Go Tell It on the Mountain* forever" (295), he set about the task of writing something that would free him from his first success. *The Amen Corner* (finished in 1954, but not published until 1968), is the result of this "writing exercise" (295). As if anticipating Lynch's criticism that Baldwin's "implicit, deep faith in (some) God and in Christian ideals has gone all but unrecognized and certainly unexplored" (284), Olson performs close readings that attempt to make clear the details of Baldwin's faith. For Olson the most significant aspect of Baldwin's faith is his ambivalence, though her article implies that Baldwin himself was unaware of this ambivalence. *The Amen Corner* "was the young Baldwin's attempt to make *Mountain*'s ambiguous criticism of the faith he had abandoned more explicit, more pointed. Ironically, however, this second attempt is only slightly more successful than the first, in large part because Baldwin's return to the church idiom riddled his message more than redeemed it" (297). Whatever kind of criticism Baldwin attempts to lodge at the Christianity of his youth is always undermined, Olson argues, because the language he uses to launch that criticism is steeped in that very tradition. Even the alternative Baldwin offers in the place of religion, brotherly love, is, Olson argues, "love in the Christian tradition. The sicknesses he bewails find their diagnoses and their cures within the Christian tradition itself" (300).[8] While Olson comes to a different conclusion about Baldwin and religion than does Lynch, her argument is nonetheless compelling because of the assumption of complexity we find in Baldwin. Like queer theory that asks new questions or approaches old questions with new eyes, thus allowing us to come to new and different conclusions about sex and sexuality in Baldwin, Olson and Lynch reject old formulations of religion in Baldwin. And they do so without simply re-creating old arguments.

The desire to avoid old arguments and chart new critical territory appears to be the driving force behind two groundbreaking anthologies, *James Baldwin Now*, edited by Dwight A. McBride (1999) and *Re-Viewing James Baldwin: Things Not Seen*, edited by D. Quentin Miller (2000), that close out this period. McBride's introduction to *James Baldwin Now* asserts that this anthology offers "new ways of thinking about the life and work of James Baldwin, one of the most prolific and influential African American writers ever to live, but also open[s] up new ways in which his work helps us understand many of our contemporary societal problems" (1). What marks this anthology as different, the introduction goes on to state, is not simply what will be said about Baldwin, but also the who and how of the saying.

> Written as they are by students and scholars who are still in the early stages of their careers, and who either were trained or are being trained in the academy during a time when interdisciplinary work and cultural studies are at what seems their nadir, these essays offer perspectives which are unique, in that they are not shackled by the traditional modes of conducting scholarship but rather are informed by a host of approaches that provide fresh, innovative analyses, distinguishing themselves from much of the earlier work on Baldwin. (1)

Important here is the assertion of Baldwin's importance (particularly for a generation of scholars who know him primarily as an "important black writer" rather than those who remember him as an important political figure), his significance to a variety of different disciplines and identity groups (not all the critics are literary scholars, not all of them are black or gay or male), and the assertion that the scholarship that had come before was insufficient to the task of treating well Baldwin's complexity. Referring to previous critical treatment, McBride writes, "The fascination is with Baldwin's life, his presence, his political thought, as well as his work. This is evidenced by the paucity of real critical treatment of

Baldwin's work in favor of the more biographical portraitures of the man. This book of essays represents a Baldwin revival of sorts" (8). And, finally, McBride asserts that we have only now arrived at the critical moment that can treat Baldwin in all his complexity: "With the advent of cultural studies, it is finally possible to understand Baldwin's vision of and for humanity in its complexity, locating him not as exclusively gay, black, expatriate, activist, or the like but as an intricately negotiated amalgam of all those things, which had to be constantly tailored to fit the circumstances in which he was compelled to articulate himself" (2).

There are five sections in the book: "Baldwin and Race," "Baldwin and Sexuality," "Baldwin and the Transatlantic," "Baldwin and Intertextuality," and "Baldwin and the Literary." Each of the essays is notable for its theoretical rigor and its connecting of Baldwin's work to contemporary political issues. The entire collection, in fact, brings Baldwin scholarship full circle, treating Baldwin as a politically engaged writer and using him as a means to navigate complex political issues.

For example, Marlon Ross's "White Fantasies of Desire: Baldwin and the Racial Identities of Sexuality" compares Baldwin's work to that of Langston Hughes. He also examines the speculation and rumors around each man's sexuality, particularly the closely guarded "secret" of Hughes's homosexuality. Rather than looking to Baldwin's statements in interviews to get a sense of Baldwin's positions on homosexuality, Ross instead looks at the homosexual characters in Baldwin's work.

> Baldwin's contribution to African American culture lies in his ability to imbalance the cultural conception of normalcy and in his linking of normalcy to racist ideology. The concept of normalcy, according to Baldwin, is the legacy of a European American system of racism. White supremacist culture needs a norm in order to trust its own illusion of black inferiority and white supremacy. More precisely, it needs a sexual norm in order to perpetuate the myth of whiteness as a racial norm. If African Americans are to think clearly about the behavior of racism, we must be able to disentangle the image of sexual desire projected onto us by white society from our own dread of sexual desire fostered by this projection. If we search our own communities, articulate our desires, so that we have nothing to hide and nothing to purge (insofar as this is possible), we shall be better able to dismiss and disregard the white obsession with policing our sexualities—a policing that we ourselves have unfortunately, on occasion, internalized as a self-project, in effect attempting to do their dirty work for them. (44–45)

In other words, if the sexualization of black culture by the dominant culture, and the resulting homophobia and/or sexual violence within the black community, is a political concern, and Ross assumes that it is, then

Baldwin's work offers us a solution to that problem. Baldwin's work provides a model of abnormality, a rejection and suspicion of conformity and the status quo (*Giovanni's Room* is particularly provocative in this regard) that allows is to investigate the ways in which "normalcy" reinscribes white heteronormative patriarchy. Ross doesn't lament Baldwin's own ambivalence about gay identity (and, in fact, his argument implies that Baldwin's ambivalence may be a rejection of another kind of conformity) nor does he try to parse out Baldwin's own sexual politics. In fact, Baldwin's specific political agenda or beliefs are not as important as the opportunity Baldwin provides to rethink our own politics.

Another notable essay in *James Baldwin Now* examines Baldwin the listener. Josh Kun's "Life According to the Beat: James Baldwin, Bessie Smith, and the Perilous Sounds of Love" reminds us that "Baldwin said that music was his salvation; that he wanted to write the way jazz and blues musicians sound; that he wished he could be as free as Billie Holiday and Bessie Smith and as triumphant as Aretha Franklin; that music, not American literature, was his true language; and that it was only through music that the Negro in America has been able to tell his story" (309). Kun's reading of Baldwin the listener is influenced by his understanding of the blues as a tradition that "explicitly links musical performance to the articulation of love, the enunciation of desire, and particularly, in the case of 'classic blues' singers of the 1920s, the play of sexuality" (321). He begins by delineating the importance and primacy of Bessie Smith in Baldwin's life. For instance, after his "nervous breakdown" in Paris, he retreats to a village in Switzerland with then lover Lucien Happersberger, taking only his typewriter, a phonograph, and his Bessie Smith records. Kun claims that "Baldwin's identification with both the persona and the voice of Bessie Smith reveals as much about his approach to race as it does about his belief in the possibilities of gay male desire" (309). Note here the biographical detail at play. Rather than trying to pin down Baldwin on this or that political point, or trying to find the real world event that finds life as a fictional account in one of the novels, Kun instead mines Baldwin's biography for evidence of his artistic heritage. And because cultural studies allows, even encourages, us to place "high" art alongside "low," Kun can see Bessie Smith's influence on Baldwin whereas others, particularly in early Baldwin scholarship, saw only Richard Wright's.

Kun's is not only a fascinating reading of the presence of Bessie Smith throughout Baldwin's life and work, particularly in *Another Country*, it is also a repositioning of the blues as a repository and articulation of black gay desire. Kun argues for the importance of Bessie Smith in this regard. Smith was famous for her "fierceness, her toughness, her celebration of her body, her open bisexuality, her pain, her triumph over poverty, and ultimately, her freedom—her ability to escape the world's definitions and be that rare, unattainable thing: herself" (317). This reading not only challenges what Kun considers the "oppressive hush" (314) around Baldwin's sexuality and the nature of his identification with Bessie Smith, but also challenges silences around other aspects of African American culture that explore the "various possibilities of sexual existence" (Hazel Carby, quoted in Kun, 323).

The final chapter of *James Baldwin Now* is a selected bibliography compiled by Jeffrey W. Hole. He focuses his attention on criticism after 1985 and assesses Baldwin's place in criticism up to that point. He cites Baldwin's inclusion in disparate anthologies such as *Growing Up Gay/ Growing Up Lesbian: A Literary Anthology* (1994), *Altogether Elsewhere: Writers on Exile* (1994), and *Blacks and Jews: Alliances and Arguments* (1994) as evidence that "Baldwin is representative of not just one of these categories; rather, his is a voice that contributes to all these diverse conversations, a fact that hence further problematizes the essentialist positions these categories can sometimes elicit" (394–95). He also reiterates the premise of the entire anthology, that the "inroads that cultural studies has made are better able to complicate the notions of race, sexuality, gender, and class" (395), and that Baldwin and his work are provocative sites for this complication. The bibliography includes essays and books on Baldwin since 1985, as well as dissertations that look at Baldwin's work. He also includes a bibliography of the juvenile works on the life and works of James Baldwin, which includes Randall Kenan's biography of Baldwin for the Lives of Notable Gay Men and Lesbians series. The bibliography as a whole demonstrates the continued, and varied, critical interest in James Baldwin and his work and, by beginning in 1985, reiterates the anthology's aim to begin new conversations about Baldwin's work.

The anthology that ends this century, *Re-Viewing James Baldwin: Things Not Seen*, takes on a different, though equally groundbreaking, critical task. Miller notes in his introduction that writers are often known only for a small portion of their entire body of work and that this happens for a number of reasons. A work may be a prize-winning novel, or appear repeatedly on "top" and "best" lists. A particular work may be the favorite, for reasons unknown, of whimsical critics. Or a work may be chosen as "representative" of an author's career, and anthologized for use in courses, so that students encounter that same work over and over again. In the case of Baldwin, Miller contends, he falls out of favor in 1963 (after the publication of *The Fire Next Time*, as discussed in chapter 1), resulting in a frozen image of a writer who expresses anger, frustration, and pain without making his (white, middle-class) reading audience too uncomfortable. Consequently, "what has been lost is his trait of tremendously rich intellectual inquiry that illustrates the direction of African American thought and culture in the late twentieth century. Also lost has been a widely varied oeuvre of an experimental writer who never was content with retelling the same story using the same voice, or speaking to the same audience. Lost, too, is the legacy of Baldwin's considerable influence" (2–3). This anthology, then, seeks to "examine works by Baldwin that have not received much critical attention in the past, approach some of his more canonical works from fresh critical perspectives, or both" (8).

Although the collection doesn't quite succeed in its ten chapters in covering all of Baldwin's neglected works, it does succeed in reminding us that Baldwin was much more than the author of *The Fire Next Time*. Two of Baldwin's least discussed, or even acknowledged, books—*Nothing Personal*, a collaboration with high-school friend Richard Avedon, and *Jimmy's Blues*, a collection of poetry—have their own entries in this collection. Joshua L. Miller's "'A Striking Addiction to Reality': *Nothing Personal* and the Legacy of the Photo-Text Genre" considers the text, a collection of photographs by Avedon complemented by text from Baldwin, as meeting at the crossroads of documentary-based social activist literature and an African American tradition of photo-text narratives. Miller speculates that the critical and scholarly neglect of *Nothing Personal* may stem from the difficulty in categorizing the book's form. Though bringing words and pictures together is as old as photography itself, "the photo-text genre runs parallel to and often calls into question other literary forms such as realism and reportage. The works in this form rarely depend on an uncritical mutuality between image and text" (155–56). The importance of *Nothing Personal*, then, may "lie in its rejection of the terms of its predecessors, opening the doors to daring experimentation that combines photographic iconography and text" (155). Miller echoes critics like Lynch and Olson and Ross, who demand with their criticism that we recognize the complexity of the ideas found in Baldwin. Doing so allows us to see how Baldwin pushes against the restrictive ideological boundaries around race, sex, desire, difference, etc. Miller asserts that the forms Baldwin chose to write in exhibit this same complexity. Rather than dismiss *Nothing Personal* as the self-indulgent vanity project of two high-school friends, as some reviewers did (and as I will discuss in chapter 5), instead we should investigate what the photo-text form offered to a writer like Baldwin, who was in a constant search for a form that matched his artistic vision and goals.

D. Quentin Miller provides the anthology's reading of Baldwin's only book of poetry, *Jimmy's Blues*. Miller spends the first part of the essay detailing the numerous ways in which this text has been neglected by critics. None of Baldwin's poems have ever been anthologized. The collection is regularly left out of lists of his publications and is mentioned in none of the major American and African American anthologies in which Baldwin is published. Miller speculates that critics have spent so much time debating whether Baldwin is a better essayist or novelist that his skill as a poet never comes into question. Miller's purpose in this essay, then, is "to inquire about the reasons for its neglect, and finally to analyze it not as some anomalous afterthought to the rest of his career but as an important work that contains the essence of his vision" (234).

Miller identifies the metaphor of blindness and Baldwin's theme of love as central to understanding *Jimmy's Blues*:

> By understanding the clear-eyes message of the poems in *Jimmy's Blues*, we are closer to understanding two related themes that evolve in Baldwin's work throughout his career: learning to love and America's failed attempts at national unity through the fulfillment of the promise of equality. His frequent use of blindness as a metaphor for these failures reifies the connection between Baldwin's work and the majority of African American literature following World War II. Although Baldwin's contributions were unique, this metaphor of blindness in *Jimmy's Blues* demonstrates his alliance with the theme of invisibility that dominates African American literature from Ellison on. (240–41).

While Miller's critical move feels similar to those made by critics discussed in chapter 2, demonstrating the ways in which Baldwin falls in line with the African American literary tradition rather than standing outside it, Miller is, I think, actually offering something more substantial. In offering Baldwin's poetry collection as one that fits easily and well with the African American literary tradition as we understand it, he implicitly challenges us to rethink that understanding. It is a call to reconsider the authors and work that make up that tradition, as well as a call to reconsider the work we leave out. Although Miller doesn't take up canon reformation as a cause in this essay, his reading of Baldwin's poetry further illustrates how Baldwin and his work often provide the first step to grappling with larger critical issues and problems.

Both *James Baldwin Now* and *Re-Viewing James Baldwin* set the stage for critics in the twenty-first century to look at Baldwin anew. Armed with critical tools from postmodernism, queer theory, and cultural studies, but also with a solid foundation in formalist criticism, contemporary critics seem eager to mine Baldwin's rich body of work for ever-new insights and provocations. We also find an incredible diversity of approach and interest in contemporary Baldwin scholarship. In current criticism Baldwin assumes the role of a major African American writer who is also a major gay writer, a prominent expatriate writer, a chronicler of American religion, and window into midcentury politics and letters, among many other roles. Baldwin's work resonates with critics interested in African American literature, gay literature, feminist criticism, religious studies, urban studies, expatriates, civil rights, politics, film criticism, and the role of the artist, to name only a few of the critical topics in Baldwin criticism. Ultimately, there is no critical center in contemporary Baldwin scholarship, but this seems more than fitting for a writer who spent his entire career resisting easy answers and intellectual stagnation.

Notes

[1] See, especially, Horace A. Porter, *Stealing Fire: The Art and Protest of James Baldwin* (1989), a work that attempts a "reinterpretation of James Baldwin's genesis as a writer" (xii) by examining the influence of Richard Wright, Harriet Beecher Stowe, and Henry James on Baldwin's early work.

[2] See *James Baldwin: His Place in American Literary History and His Reception in Europe*, ed. Jakob Köllhofer (1991); and *The Critical Reception of James Baldwin in France* by Rosa Bobia (1997).

[3] See *New Essays on "Go Tell It on the Mountain,"* ed. Trudier Harris (1996).

[4] See especially Terry Eagleton, *Literary Theory: An Introduction*; M. H. Abram, *A Glossary of Literary Terms*; Judith Butler, *Bodies That Matter*; Eve Kosofsky Sedgwick, ed., *Novel Gazing: Queer Readings in Fiction*; and Iain Morland et al., eds., *Queer Theory*.

[5] The hyper-heterosexual black male body is also on display in this period, in rap videos and hip hop culture and sports. While I argue that these representations are not a part of this mid-1980s to early 1990s black queer male conversation, many contemporary cultural critics do argue that this hyper-hetero masculinity is incredibly homoerotic. See Michael Eric Dyson, *Know What I Mean?: Reflections on Hip Hop* (2007) and Byron Hurt's 2007 documentary *Beyond Beats and Rhymes*.

[6] The biblical story of David and Jonathan, two friends who delight in each other but whose friendship is ultimately threatened by Jonathan's father, King Saul, who is jealous of David's popularity with people (he killed Goliath, after all), is considered by some to be a biblical sanction of homosexuality. Though the Bible makes no explicit reference to sex between the two men, and the more common reading of their relationship is one of platonic love, many nevertheless read this story as a positive portrayal of homosexuality.

[7] Originally published in *Studies in the Novel* (1996), Reid-Pharr's essay has also appeared in *African American Literary Theory: A Reader*, ed. Winston Napier (New York: New York University Press, 2000), and Sedgwick, *Novel Gazing: Queer Readings in Fiction* (1997).

[8] See also Hardy, *James Baldwin's God*, for a discussion of Baldwin and religion.

Part II

4: The Critical Reception of "Sonny's Blues"

THE CHAPTERS IN PART 1 have considered the critical reception of James Baldwin's entire body of work. In truth, though, taking a broad view of Baldwin's critical reception allows us to consider only a handful of the full-length works he published. As I will discuss in chapter 5, scholars have established a hierarchy of Baldwin's works and, consequently, our understanding of Baldwin as a writer rests on the merits of a few essays and a couple of novels. If we step outside of this "canon" we find another work, Baldwin's 1957 short story "Sonny's Blues," receiving considerable attention. Yet that particular conversation proves to be an anomaly in Baldwin scholarship.

I've separated the criticism on "Sonny's Blues" from the criticism on Baldwin's other work because, in large part, the critical life of "Sonny's Blues" is separate from the critical life of Baldwin's other work. By far Baldwin's most anthologized work, "Sonny's Blues" is a well-crafted, highly readable, and accessible story. And because it lacks the possibly polemical and alienating quality of the essays or other short stories like "Going to Meet the Man," it is a natural fit for introductory college literature courses. In addition to being included in the *Norton Anthology of African American Literature* and *Call and Response: A Riverside Anthology of the African American Literary Tradition*, it is also included in, among other anthologies, *Fiction 100* and *The Short Story and Its Writer*, two popular and widely used fiction anthologies, and in *Literature: An Introduction to Fiction, Poetry, Drama, and Writing*, as an illustration of point of view. When the story is included as simply one story among ninety-nine other stories, anthology editors tend to focus on the universal themes and appeals of "Sonny's Blues." In the autobiographical note on Baldwin in *Fiction 100*, the editor cites a "recent critic" who states that the "final and most persuasive assumption found in Baldwin's art is that all mankind is united by virtue of their humanity" (1457). Consequently many readers' first (and often only) exposure to Baldwin is "Sonny's Blues." And just as the story is often experienced as separate from Baldwin's other work, the critical reception of the story is separate as well. Rather than participating in critical conversations about the role of the artist, the relationship between art and politics, Baldwin's skill as a fiction writer, or his merit as an activist, the scholarship on

"Sonny's Blues" is almost always self-contained. This chapter considers the most influential voices in this conversation and is arranged chronologically rather than thematically, as most of the articles build on those that came before it. Note, though, that whereas the critical conversation around "Sonny's Blues" is mostly self-enclosed and rarely references any of the critics or issues we have seen in previous chapters, critics like Pancho Savery and Jacqueline Jones nevertheless gesture toward larger Baldwin conversations.

The plot of "Sonny's Blues" follows the unnamed narrator, an algebra teacher in Harlem, as he reconciles with his estranged brother, the heroin addict and musician Sonny. While the story features a number of wonderfully moving and evocative scenes, including a flashback that details the death of their uncle, and the scene in which the narrator and Sonny both listen to a group of gospel singers performing on the street, two particular scenes capture the attention of critics. The first is the first real conversation Sonny and the narrator have after Sonny comes home from jail. The narrator tries to understand something about Sonny's pain and music and addiction. Sonny tries to explain:

> "It's terrible sometimes inside," [Sonny] said, "that's what's the trouble. You walk these streets, black and funky and cold, and there's not really a living ass to talk to, and there's nothing shaking, and there's no way of getting it out—that storm inside. You can't talk it and you can't make love with it, and when you finally try to get with it and play it, you realize *nobody's* listening. So *you've* got to listen. You got to find a way to listen." (857)

The second scene comes at the end of the story when Sonny and the narrator go to a nightclub and Sonny joins his old bandmates for a jam session. They play, among other things, "Am I Blue?," which the narrator calls "sardonic" (862), and which Sonny seems to come alive playing:

> Then Creole stepped forward to remind them that what they were playing was the blues. He hit something in all of them, he hit something in me, myself, and the music tightened and deepened, apprehension began to beat the air. Creole began to tell us what the blues were all about. They were not about anything very new. He and his boys up there were keeping it new, at the risk of ruin, destruction, madness, and death, in order to find new ways to make us listen. For while the tale of how we suffer, and how we are delighted, and how we triumph is never new, it always must be heard. There isn't any other story to tell, it's the only light we've got in all this darkness. (862)

After his revelation the narrator orders drinks for the whole band, specifically a "Scotch and milk" for his brother. The story ends with an image of the drink atop Sonny's piano, where it "glowed and shook above [Sonny's] head like the very cup of trembling" (864). These two scenes are most compelling for critics because, first, they carry the emotional weight of the story. It is in these scenes that Sonny and his brother make true, if largely unspoken, connections. Second, critics of this story understand "Sonny's Blues" to be first and foremost a story about music (or art, generally), and these are the two scenes that most vividly portray the power and function of music in the lives of the characters. And, finally, critics focus their attention on these scenes in large part because other critics focus their attention on these scenes. "Sonny's Blues" criticism is incredibly insular; critics refer repeatedly to one another's readings of the story rather than to other Baldwin or African American literary scholarship. These two scenes become central in the critical conversation precisely because the critical conversation has deemed them important.

John M. Reilly's 1970 essay, "'Sonny's Blues': James Baldwin's Image of Black Community," in *Negro American Literature Forum* (later *African American Review*), is treated as the earliest definitive assessment of "Sonny's Blues." His primary concern in this essay is Baldwin's use of the blues and the function of the blues within the black community. He reads "Sonny's Blues" as a blues story and Baldwin as a blues writer who offers us a blues aesthetic:

> The implicit statement of the esthetics of the Blues in this story throws light upon much of Baldwin's writing. The first proposition of the esthetics that we can infer from 'Sonny's Blues' is that suffering is the prior necessity. The second implicit proposition of the Blues esthetics is that while the form is what it's all about, the form is transitory.... This will not justify weaknesses in an artist's work, but insofar as Baldwin identifies his writing with the art of the singers of the Blues it suggests why he is devoted to representation, in whatever genre, of successive moments of expressive feeling and comparatively less concerned with achieving a consistent overall structure. The final proposition of the esthetics in the story of 'Sonny's Blues' is that the Blues functions as an art of communion. (59)

Several key assumptions that ever after shape the conversation around "Sonny's Blues" come from this essay. The first is that Baldwin is a blues writer, by which Reilly seems to mean a writer who is dedicated to the black community first and to aesthetic form second, as the blues exists as a vehicle of African American expression first and an aesthetic form second. (This begs the question, of course, of how we read "Sonny's Blues" when it is removed from an African American context, such as when the story is included in short fiction anthologies or introductory composition texts. Critics never really address this question.) Second, Reilly collapses the actual music in the story (bebop) into the music of the title (the blues), a move critics will repeat until Pancho Savery's article on "Sonny's Blues" and bebop (1992). Third, Reilly defines a blues aesthetic, and though other critics will take this task on more explicitly (see especially Houston A. Baker, *Blues, Ideology, and Afro-American Literature: A Vernacular Theory* (1987), it is Reilly's definition of this aesthetic that holds sway in this conversation. By extension, his fourth assumption is that a blues aesthetic is the most useful tool with which to read African American literature. This is placing "Sonny's Blues" squarely in an African American literary tradition in a way that closes off, almost completely, readings of other sorts. (Although critics will not always read "Sonny's Blues" within an explicitly African American context, none of them talk explicitly about what it means to remove it from that context.) And, finally, the assumption from which all the others follow: Reilly assumes that this story is about music and its function within the black community.

Other critics tend to agree that the story is ultimately about music or, at least, speaks its message through music. Jay Bruce Jacoby, "The Music Is the Message: Teaching Baldwin's 'Sonny's Blues'" (1978), traces the author's efforts to engage students in this story by using music. The pedagogical focus of this essay reflects the story's most frequent literary home—the classroom. Jacoby talks about the difficulty of getting his students, presumably white, to discuss this story because of their reluctance to discuss race. "Sometimes Baldwin's story is the only work that represents modern Black writers in [short story] anthologies. In teaching 'Sonny's Blues,' I have found that an initial discussion of Baldwin, the Black experience in America, or the question of Black identity is often the quickest way to turn off students" (2). In order to move students past their discomfort, Jacoby first asks them to consider the "character of the narrator," his pain and grief over the death of his daughter and his estrangement from his brother. Jacoby does what many teachers write of doing: using the narrator as an entry point for students. Once students have identified the conflict of the story (as narrated through the brother's point of view), which results from "how each brother chooses to cope with his racial background" (3), Jacoby then asks students to consider the music in the story, arguing that the music "serves a twofold, interrelated function" (3). First, music "has some kind of regenerative, curative power. It eases pain by permitting such pain to be expressed" (3). Second, music "serves to establish a necessary sense of communal identity that is especially linked to the Black heritage" (4).

The pedagogical nature of this essay reflects a constant thematic strain in "Sonny's Blues" criticism. Even though Jacoby offers a critical reading of this story, one that echoes Reilly's, he is more concerned with reading his students. Ultimately Jacoby wants his students to see that "Sonny's Blues" is about the way music, particularly the blues, functions in the black community to ease pain and smooth conflicts. Jacoby's use of this story and his students' reactions to it provide an excellent snapshot of the way many readers, perhaps the majority, come to Baldwin. Rather than learning about him as a politically engaged major black author of autobiographical essays that challenge our ideas about race and history and sexuality, readers often first encounter Baldwin as simply a black writer who provides a brief realistic glimpse into African American life. This view of Baldwin allows students to come to the kind of uncomplicated revelation one of Jacoby's students offers: "Music, for the Black American, has been the means by which an entire people has expressed its pain and degradation; yet the very fact that a people retains this capacity for expression represents triumph, however meager, over the environment that seeks to grind them under" (4). This particular view of African America, peopled with oppressed souls who overcome by singing the blues, is a prevalent one and probably provides very little challenge to the view of black people that Jacoby's students bring into his classroom. And while I do not mean that as a criticism of Jacoby or his classroom technique, I do question the way "Sonny's Blues" is used in the classroom and the conclusions students come to as a result. The pedagogical essays that treat "Sonny's Blues" tell us a great deal about Baldwin in the popular, as opposed to critical, imagination. For his popular audiences, the ones looking to the reviews discussed in chapter 5, the ones likely to have encountered Baldwin for the first time in "Sonny's Blues" in a classroom, Baldwin's importance and power lie in his ability to translate and make beautiful the black experience, despite his own suspicions about the sentimentalism of such a sentiment.

Edward Lobb's 1979 essay, "James Baldwin's Blues and the Function of Art," turns the critical conversation back to Reilly's essay and his argument about music in "Sonny's Blues." In particular, he takes issue with Reilly's definition of the blues as a metaphor of the black community: "But the meaning of the blues is, as I hope to show, rather wider than Reilly seems to think, and is part of a larger theme which is conveyed almost wholly through the story's images. 'Sonny's Blues' is Baldwin's most concise and suggestive statement about the nature of and function of art, and is doubly artful in making this statement through life situations" (143). Lobb goes on to examine the darkness/light and sound/silence imagery in the story (many critics pay particular attention to these images), arguing for the dialectical nature of these seemingly oppositional terms. Referring to Sonny's assertion that "you've got to listen" even when "listening" may kill you, Lobb writes: "The dialectic of the story so far is uncompromisingly bleak. The only thing worse than the pain of existence is full consciousness of that pain; knowledge is presumably desirable but unquestionably dangerous, and there seems to be no way of acquiring it without being annihilated, mentally or physically, by its blinding white light" (144–45). And moving to the final scene, he argues,

"In this scene, as Reilly rightly points out, the narrator comes to understand his brother and his own place in the community. The community he acknowledges, however, it is not the black community alone but the whole human community of suffering" (145).

For Lobb, an examination of the story's paradoxical, dialectical symbolism, rather than the story's content (contradicting Reilly in this regard), reveals that "Sonny's Blues" is about art and human suffering rather than about the black experience. Lobb's argument speaks to what perhaps makes this story so popular. Despite the setting, 1950s Harlem, and the black cast of characters, readers are nonetheless able, because of the symbolism and the metaphorical quality of the music, to read this story as about something other than race or addiction, or even black music. In Lobb's reading, "Sonny's Blues," even in its "most casual details," becomes a story about the dialectical triumph and pain of art:

> Art is distinguished from fantasy by contrast with heroin and the cheap satisfactions of film and television; it is associated with light, sound, and form, and stands against darkness, silence, and "fear and trembling." But if it is to be good art and provide a true picture of experience, it must include the elements it fights against—hence the paradoxical nature of Baldwin's emblems of art: the union of darkness and light, of form and the trembling which shakes things apart, of the roar from the void and the order of music. (148)

Lobb's argument is not wholly unconvincing. His attention to the light and dark imagery does bring into sharp focus Baldwin's remarkable skill as a writer and the magic that happens when that skill is wed to the complexity of Baldwin's ideas. But it is those ideas that Lobb seems far too willing to push aside in his final analysis. While Baldwin seeks to highlight the "contrast" between the brothers in this story, he certainly also asks us to consider how the particular racialized experience of the brothers (they live in Harlem, their uncle comes to a horribly violent, racist end, the music we see and hear in the story is "black" music) produces that contrast.

Lobb's argument demonstrates how well "Sonny's Blues" holds up to the kind of new-critical close reading that often gets taught in introductory literature classrooms (and sometimes practiced in academic journals), but it is not the kind of close reading that will prevail in the critical conversation about this story. Keith Byerman's 1982 essay, "Words and Music: Narrative Ambiguity in 'Sonny's Blues,'" also considers dichotomies in the story and will go on to become, like Reilly's, another touchstone essay in "Sonny's Blues" scholarship.

Byerman focuses primarily on the last scene and the narrator's gift of Scotch and milk to Sonny. He reads the drink as "an emblem of simultaneous destruction and nurture to the system; it cannot be reduced to one or the other. Sonny's acceptance of it indicates that his life will continue on the edge between the poison of his addiction and the nourishment of his music" (371). Byerman disagrees with previous critics who contend that the story resolves itself (indeed, a common reading of the conclusion is that the brothers are reconciled in the nightclub). Instead, Byerman writes, "If resolution is not assumed but taken as problematical, then new thematic and structural possibilities are revealed. The story becomes a study of the nature and relationship of art and language" (367). If we assume that the story's conclusion is, at best, problematic, then, Byerman argues, we see that "Sonny's Blues" is actually about the narrator's "misreadings" (367).

Reading the nightclub scene as a reconciliatory moment depends on believing that the narrator-brother has a revelation as he listens to Sonny and his friends play, as many critics do. Byerman, however, contends that this is a faulty assumption. "Little preparation has been made for such a reaction to the music. The act of the musician seems a creative response to the impinging chaos described in the opening subway scene. But this perception springs full-bodied from the brow of a man who had repeatedly indicated his antagonism to such music" (370). This can be explained, for Byerman, by the fact that language is very often insufficient to express human thought and human feeling. "'Sonny's Blues,' then, is a story of a narrator caught in the 'prison-house' of language.... In the very act of telling his story, the narrator falsifies (as do all storytellers) because he must use words to express what is beyond words" (371). Thus the Scotch and milk, along with the entire story, is ambiguous rather than redemptive. Because the narrator has to "lie" about his experience of hearing Sonny play, the tensions in the story cannot be resolved. All that we are left with, all that we can be left with, is the ambiguity and limits of language.

Richard N. Albert, in "The Jazz-Blues Motif in James Baldwin's 'Sonny's Blues'" (1984), also reads the story's conclusion as ambiguous. Rather than focusing on the Scotch and milk, though, Albert instead reads the bandleader Creole and the song "Am I Blue?" as not "black" in the same way the blues are "black," and, thus, we cannot assume that black music reconciles the black brothers in the end. Perhaps this ambiguity is purposeful, though, contends Albert, as Baldwin encourages us all toward change and connection to the entire human family rather than a specific racial community.

Albert reminds us that "Sonny's Blues" is a "popular selection among editors of anthologies used in introductory college literature courses" (178) and argues that the story endures because it is "less polemical than many of his later efforts and because it offers several common literary themes: individualism, alienation, and 'Am I my brother's keeper?'" (178). Albert's essay seems an attempt to parse out some of these themes. He acknowledges the previous criticism that focused on the blues as metaphor. However, he writes, "none of the criticism bothers to look more closely at the significance of the jazz and blues images and allusions in relation to the commonly agreed-upon basic themes of individualism and alienation" (178). He grants that the story "seems to emphasize the importance of the strictly black experience and tradition," as the narrator's revelation comes as a result of a black musical form. However, he still finds the last scene ambiguous, particularly because of its use of Creole and the song "Am I Blue?" He provides a long explanation of why Creole (whose name connotes a particular interracial experience in French Louisiana) and the song (a synthetic, commercially popular blues song written by two white men) don't really fit into the black experience, indicating, for Albert, that this final scene is not about blackness at all. So why use these two elements in the final pivotal scene? "Is it possible that in 'Sonny's Blues' [Baldwin] is indicating that tradition is very important, but that change is also important (and probably inevitable) and that it builds on tradition, which is never fully erased but continues to be an integral part of the whole?" (184). Albert reads Baldwin as implying that

> we are an amalgam of many ingredients that have become fused over the centuries. We cannot separate ourselves, *all* people, from one another. Having Sonny, inspired by Creole, playing "Am I Blue?" for what we assume must be a racially mixed audience in a Greenwich Village club gives credence to these ideas and helps to explain what might otherwise appear to be some inexplicable incongruities. (184)

Albert's earlier assertions of the prevalence of "Sonny's Blues" in anthologies and on college introductory literature syllabi are instructive when considering his conclusions. His goal seems to be not only an analysis of this story but also an explanation of its continued popularity and resonance with students and teachers. For Albert, the power of "Sonny's Blues" goes far beyond its racial dimension because "blackness" is too limited an experience for all of us to share. But if Baldwin is indeed, with Creole and "Am I Blue?," encouraging us to step outside our own limited individual experiences to connect with other humans and our humanity, the story then becomes available to all of us.

Two mid-1980s essays continue in this vein and reflect well the critical preoccupations in "Sonny's Blues" scholarship at the time. In addition to arguing increasingly for the transcendent humanity of the story's characters, critics also pay a great deal of attention to the dark and light imagery and the notion that "Sonny's Blues" presents music and art as a respite from the brutal reality of human existence.

Michael Clark's 1985 essay in the *College Language Association Journal* takes aim at Reilly's assertion that Baldwin's blues aesthetic is "alien from a conception of fixed ideals and forms" and concerned more with "successive moments of expressive feeling" than with "achieving a consistent overall structure" (59). Clark insists that the task Baldwin sets for himself in this story, nothing short of illuminating various facets of human existence, could not be achieved without a great deal of craftsmanship. And since Clark reads "Sonny's Blues" as "a tour de force, a penetrating study of American culture" (197), his task as a critic is to highlight that craftsmanship. Typical of critics who seek to show how "Sonny's Blues" is a great work of art, Clark focuses on the images of light and dark. Where he departs from other critics is his assertion that these images are in support of the story's primary metaphor, childhood.

His basic argument is that light in the story is associated with childhood and with possibility, while darkness is associated with adulthood and the pain of human existence. In Sonny's seemingly irresistible urge to play music, to connect with his own childhood and the communal past of black people, he strives to bring a little light in to the darkness. The Scotch and milk at the end of the story glows and indicates, according to Clark, Sonny's success and his "reconciliation with reality" (205). I have summarized Clark's argument not because it is central in "Sonny's Blues" scholarship, but because it is representative. "Sonny's Blues" lends itself very well to this kind of new-critical close reading, in which the tensions and conflicts in a work are resolved neatly in the end. These readings abound in the scholarship, alongside others that seek to complicate the "neatness" of the story. This is one of the reasons criticism of this story exists alongside but apart from criticism of Baldwin's other work.

The other reason, of course, is the popularity of this story among anthology editors and teachers. Another mid-1980s article reminds us of this. Susan Robbins's "Anguish and Anger" is as much about her students as it is about "Sonny's Blues." "Anguish and anger are the fires that burn away innocence in … James Baldwin's 'Sonny's Blues'" and are "the same fires that smolder in our students" (58). In this short essay she offers "Sonny's Blues" (and James Joyce's "Araby") as an opportunity for students to reflect on their own "anger and anguish" and their relationships with authority figures. She finds the brother's narrative arc particularly instructive: "As he changes from the man who reads about his brother's addiction and arrest in the newspaper to the man who goes to the bar to hear his brother playing the blues, the students trace his change in their notes and discussion and become more tolerant of teacherly types and authority figures" (60). Pedagogical arguments like these have little interest in the craft of "Sonny's Blues" or in its place in the African American literary tradition (or any other tradition for that matter). They are primarily interested in the pedagogical work this story performs in the classroom, and, as this story is used quite often in the classroom, this is a significant thread in "Sonny's Blues" scholarship.

Patricia K. Robertson's "Baldwin's 'Sonny's Blues': The Scapegoat Metaphor" (1991), returns us, however, to the critical fascination with the story's final scene. In this essay Robertson offers a reading that she explicitly states does not "compete with interpretations by others that involve social criticism, philosophical changes, prophetic voice, or Baldwin's place in Black literary history" (196, footnote 1). She is instead more interested in the biblical allusion of the "cup of trembling."

> The Old Testament allusion to the "cup of trembling" leads directly to the scapegoat metaphor and the idea of pain and suffering of a people. The New Testament story of hope is carried in Sonny's name which suggests Christ symbolism and leads to the New Testament message of the "cup of trembling" as the cup of Gethsemane which Christ drank, symbolizing the removal of sins for all who believe and hope for eternal life through belief in him. Sonny's name echoes this special relationship. Sonny, the scapegoat, is the hope of his particular world. (189)

She offers a standard definition of the scapegoat, who, "through his own personal suffering or by his metaphorical sharing of his own sorrow, may allow us to see into life and into ourselves and thus vicariously transfer our guilt and pain through him and his suffering" (190). Sonny, then, plays this role in the story and says as much when he tries to explain to his brother how the heroin helps him deal with what he hears when he "listens." Robertson disagrees with Byerman, who argues that the drink of Scotch and milk means Sonny will continue to walk a fine line between addiction and nourishment. She writes, "But Sonny *has* drunk the cup of pain before; now the brother joins in, empathizes, understands. Sonny drinks the Scotch and milk and continues to suffer, but part of his suffering is removed by his brother's understanding. For the brother, the action itself suggests increased understanding and a sharing of Sonny's pain" (195). While agreeing with Byerman and Albert that the final scene holds the key to unlocking the meaning of the story, she disagrees that this meaning is ambiguous. Robertson's reading, like Lobb's and Clark's, demonstrates the ability of "Sonny's Blues" to stand up to rigorous close reading. More important, though, Robertson's very self-conscious removal of her argument from other critical conversations about "Sonny's Blues" specifically or Baldwin generally (she doesn't wish to "compete" with other criticism) demonstrates how useful this story is for critics who write about Baldwin but who wish to stand apart from Baldwin criticism. The same features that make this story so useful in the classroom—relatively easy to read, evocative use of literary language, expert use of metaphor and symbol, open to multiple interpretations—also allow Robertson to remove "Sonny's Blues" from its (black) cultural context and still have her interpretation make critical "sense." It is the cultural context, though, and the music that grows out of that context that will continue to engage critics.

Pancho Savery's 1992 essay, "Baldwin, Bebop, and 'Sonny's Blues,'" moves the critical conversation in a different direction by, ironically, returning it to its roots: the music in "Sonny's Blues." He prefaces his argument with the argument of those who doubt Baldwin's place in the African American literary tradition. Quoting Amiri Baraka, who in 1966 calls Baldwin the "Joan of Arc of the cocktail party," and Larry Neal, who laments Baldwin's "uncertainty over his identity and his failure to utilize, to its fullest extent, traditional aspects of Afro-American culture" (quoted in Savery, 165), Savery extends the critical conversation about "Sonny's Blues" beyond its insular confines. To prove his point that Baldwin is in fact a formidable fiction writer and that his fiction deserves a prominent place in the African American literary tradition, Savery focuses on the music in the story. And rather than reading the music metaphorically or symbolically as previous critics have done, Savery attempts a reading of the music actually played in the story—bebop. In doing so, he complicates the story by adding a political dimension not rooted in Baldwin's own politics.

Savery's first critical move is to place the story in time. He convincingly determines through textual cues that, despite being published in 1957, the story takes place in 1952. Consequently, the music most important to the story, the music Sonny would almost certainly have been playing (considering, especially, that his musical hero is Charlie Parker), is bebop. Why does this matter? "What I am arguing in general is that music is the cornerstone of African American culture; and that, further, Bebop was an absolute key moment.... Musically, Bebop was to a large extent a revolt against swing and the way African American music had been taken over, and diluted, by whites" (169). Savery goes on to connect bebop to the radicalizing of black politics in the 1950s, which results in a new reading of the brother-narrator: "In light of this historical context, Sonny's brother's never having heard of Bird is not only a rejection of the music of Bebop; it is also a rejection of the new political direction Bebop was representative of in the African American community" (172–73). Like other critics during this period (1988–2000), Savery here broadens the intellectual traditions Baldwin participates in. Though it is not his stated project (unlike those critics in chapter 3 who explicitly attempt to broaden the critical conversation in Baldwin scholarship), Savery nevertheless rejects the conventional wisdom about this story (that it is about the blues) and about Baldwin (that he is a blues writer) and, consequently, opens up new critical terrain.

Interestingly, despite the fact that Savery's reading of "Sonny's Blues" stands mostly outside of the kind of queering and retheorizing of Baldwin we see in chapter 3, his foregrounding of radical black politics in the 1950s in an article published at a time when African American politics was undergoing a reradicalization[1] connects his project to the critics in the previous chapter. Savery further complicates the relationship between Sonny and his brother by foregrounding the political implications of Sonny's music and indicting the brother for his seeming lack of sympathy with these politics. By foregrounding radical politics in Baldwin's fiction, Savery also makes an implicit argument for the continuing intellectual relevance of Baldwin at the end of the twentieth century. Rather than adhering to conventional wisdom that Baldwin mostly falls short in his fiction and that he owes his literary reputation primarily to guilty white audiences, Savery makes an argument for re-viewing Baldwin. Instead of reading Baldwin as making ineffectual, at best, use of African American culture (as Neal does), he reads Baldwin as better than most at capturing the vanguard nature of African American music. Calling our attention to Baldwin's use of the word "sardonic" to describe the standard "Am I Blue?" played by Sonny, Creole, and the band at the end of the story, Savery highlights the chief characteristics of bebop. As Baraka writes, bebop musicians "openly talked of the square, hopeless, corny, rubbish put forth by the bourgeoisie" (quoted in Savery, 173). The sardonic rendition of "Am I Blue?," then, is "exactly the type of song that by itself wouldn't do much for anyone, but which could become rich and meaningful after being heated in the crucible of Bebop" (173). And Baldwin's fiction, similarly "heated" in the "crucible" of renewed critical attention, would also reveal new, even radical, reworkings of "traditional aspects of Afro-American culture."

Jacqueline C. Jones's 1999 essay, "Finding a Way to Listen: The Emergence of the Hero as an Artist in James Baldwin's 'Sonny's Blues,'" on the other hand, studiously avoids the political dimensions of Baldwin's work, a move that aligns Jones's article with the criticism of chapter 2. Jones explores the artist-hero figure in "Sonny's Blues" and argues that the recurrence of artist characters in all of Baldwin's work "illustrates Baldwin's primary identity, that of an artist" (462), not, notably, an activist or witness or public personality. For Jones, it is important to articulate Baldwin's theory of art and the artist because this forces us to push to the critical margins theories of race and sexuality that cloud our critical vision. She argues that Baldwin defines "the primary function of the artist as the role of truth seeker and witness" and that the character of Sonny "explicitly critiques the price an artist pays to pursue his interests" (465). The rest of her argument is as much about the pain and suffering the artist undergoes as it is about how not gay this story is. Of Sonny, she writes that Baldwin implies that through suffering and the courage to listen to his own pain and the pain of others, the artist can come to "an acceptance of self that transcends racial, sexual, and social stereotypes" (470), and that Sonny's "gut-wrenching rebirth" is "pristine, untouched, and unclouded" because "sex and sexuality do not complicate the plot of the story (467). Though her essay never comes right out and says this, Jones is clearly making an argument about this story's superiority over Baldwin's other fiction. The loaded language she uses to describe the story—"pristine, untouched, and unclouded"—suggests that the "sexual conflicts" we see in other Baldwin works like *Giovanni's Room*, *Another Country*, or even *Go Tell It on the Mountain*, are dirty and murky. Considering that this article appears after a decade of queer theorizing of Baldwin and of foregrounding his most controversial and explicitly (homo)sexual works, Jones's argument seems a very pointed backlash against Baldwin criticism of the 1990s. Unlike Savery, Jones never states explicitly that her critical goal is to challenge the conventional wisdom surrounding Baldwin or this story. Yet her essay clearly has in mind what had become, by 1999, a fairly standard reading of Baldwin's work in general, namely, that his work, particularly his fiction, is as much about questions of sexuality and sexual identity as it is about anything else. In going back to the kinds of critical moves we saw in chapter 2—focusing on the ways Baldwin's fiction transcends particular politics, highlighting Baldwin the artist rather than Baldwin the prophet and witness, arguing for the universal qualities of the story—Jones attempts, at least implicitly, to push queer readings of Baldwin back to the margins.

Tracey Sherard's 1998 essay, "Sonny's Bebop: Baldwin's 'Blues Text' as Intracultural Critique," looks to move the critical conversation surrounding "Sonny's Blues" in yet another new direction. Rather than continuing the argument that the story offers the blues, or black music generally, as a vehicle with which the black community navigates pain and suffering (which, by 1998, had become the standard reading of the story, even if there is disagreement about the particulars of the pain and suffering, and the ability of the blues to work through it), Sherard argues, instead, that "Sonny's Blues" is in fact a critique of this very notion:

> "Sonny's Blues" deals not only thematically with the crossroads between the blues and jazz, but addresses the need for a new form of cultural narrative as a repository for the experiences of African Americans. When the narrator comes to understand his brother Sonny through the latter's apparent struggle to strike out into the deep, unexplored waters of jazz improvisation, the metanarrative quality of jazz is foregrounded; the "blues" Sonny plays are a commentary on the historical context and the function of the blues Baldwin suggests are inadequate to convey the "sad stories" of urban Harlem. (691)

Rather than arguing that the story offers a positive or negative vision of the blues, or debating the nature of the music in the story, as other critics have done, Sherard instead attempts to engage the complexity of black music as it functions in the black community. If, as other critics in this chapter have argued, black music is the most important cultural expression in the black community, it stands to reason that it would be used not only as an emotional release or forum from which to speak but also as means to critique and challenge particular aspects of that same community. Sherard's article is important because of its critical dissonance. She doesn't read "Sonny's Blues" as a celebration of all things black or the blues as redemptive. Instead, she reads this story as a critique of the very notion of embracing something simply because it is black. The blues are a failure in Sherard's reading.

While "Sonny's Blues" continues to be a popular choice of fiction anthology editors, increasingly other works of Baldwin's are being included in American and African American literature anthologies. Perennial favorites like the essays "Notes of a Native Son," "Everybody's Protest Novel," and "Stranger in a Village" continue to be selected. But editors are also choosing, at an increasing rate, "Going to Meet the Man" (which, on occasion, replaces "Sonny's Blues" as a representative Baldwin short story) and the play *Blues for Mister Charlie* to represent Baldwin's work. I attribute this to the success of the critics in chapter 3. In retheorizing Baldwin, in placing him in new and different critical contexts and intellectual traditions, they have forced the literary establishment to recognize the artistic and intellectual diversity of Baldwin's entire body of work. So while anthology editors have long recognized Baldwin's importance, and thus have repeatedly included "Sonny's Blues" in their texts, they are now forced to reconsider which works really best represent Baldwin in all his complexity.

Yet it is still likely that students' first, and only, exposure to Baldwin will be "Sonny's Blues." And this fact highlights once again the paradoxical nature of Baldwin's place in American and African American literary history. "Sonny's Blues" is a fine introduction to Baldwin's work. Baldwin is in complete control of his craft in this story—the language is concrete and evocative; the themes of brotherhood and the artist's burden are effectively developed and well paced; his concern for the condition of black Americans in particular, but also his interest in the human "problem of being" (to go back to George Kent's phrase), are also on display. In most ways, this is the Baldwin piece that makes the most sense for inclusion in an anthology because it is so self-contained as a text and as an example of Baldwin's work. Indeed, many of us who love and teach Baldwin would offer this story to the student just discovering Baldwin. The problem, of course, is that "Sonny's Blues" is only a small snapshot of Baldwin's career (as any single short story is for most writers, but even more so with Baldwin because of his long and prolific career). Not only that, but offering "Sonny's Blues" as the best example of Baldwin's work is akin, perhaps, to taking the path of least resistance. Teaching "Sonny's

Blues" in an African American literature course, a short story course, or an introduction to fiction course to the exclusion of all of Baldwin's other work allows one to sidestep the sticky questions of politics, sexuality, and artistry (or lack thereof) that are unavoidable in his other work, especially the novels. "Sonny's Blues" allows us—teachers, editors, critics—to acknowledge the importance of Baldwin without actually having to address or investigate what makes him important.

In a similar vein, inclusion of "Sonny's Blues" (rather than some other short story, or essay, or novel excerpt) in so many non-African American literature anthologies suggests that Baldwin is an easier fit in the African American literary canon than is actually true. In these contexts, his story often comes to stand in for a certain kind of midcentury, blues-influenced African American meditation on the burden of blackness, when, in fact, the story, and Baldwin's place in African American literary history, are more complicated than that.

Notes

[1] For a further discussion of this period of African American history and culture, see Nelson George, *Post-Soul Nation: The Explosive, Contradictory, Triumphant, and Tragic 1980s as Experienced by African Americans (Previously Known as Blacks and Before That Negroes)* (2004), and Greg Tate, *Flyboy in the Buttermilk* (1992).

5: James Baldwin and the Popular Reviews

OVER THE COURSE OF his long and prolific career, James Baldwin published twenty-two full-length works (in addition to numerous essays, short stories, and interviews). With only a couple of exceptions, all the works were reviewed widely in mainstream, high-circulation magazines, newspapers, and journals, though they were not all well received. Though this study has considered the critical reception of Baldwin's work, and thus has focused on critical reviews and articles in academic and scholarly publications, no such study would be complete without a consideration of popular press reviews. The reasons are twofold.

First, many critical articles, especially at the height of Baldwin's popularity (1963–73), are in conversation, either directly or indirectly, with popular press reviews and Baldwin's popular reputation. Whether critics are debating the merits of a best-selling novel (*Another Country*), or a poorly reviewed play (*Blues for Mister Charlie*), or resuscitating neglected aspects of a work (the homoeroticism of *Go Tell It on the Mountain*, for instance), or simply responding to what has been said (Addison Gayle responding to the critics of *The Fire Next Time*), popular reviews shape much of the critical response to Baldwin's work.

More important, however, confining ourselves to academic criticism means that we confine ourselves to Baldwin's "canon," namely, the five works most often discussed in criticism: *Notes of a Native Son*, *Go Tell it on the Mountain*, *Giovanni's Room*, *Another Country*, and *The Fire Next Time*. This seems to me a disservice to Baldwin's body of work, since the last work in the "canon," *The Fire Next Time*, was published in 1963, while his last full-length book was published in 1985. In those intervening years Baldwin published sixteen other full-length works, including several novels, two plays, a collection of poetry, a screenplay, and a children's book. Our best and often only sense of how these works were received comes from reading the reviews in the popular press.

Not surprisingly, we see in these reviews a reception trajectory similar to that in the critical articles—a period of adoration followed by periods of varying levels of disappointment and frustration. And much like the critical articles, Baldwin's reception in these reviews often seems to have little to do with him or his work. On the other hand, however, the reviews differ from critical articles in that they offer a finite, immediate response to each of Baldwin's full-length works. Unlike the criticism of *The Fire Next Time*, which now spans more than forty years and reflects changing views of Baldwin, as well as shifting critical tastes and methods, *reviews* of *The Fire Next Time* (and the other works) provide a snapshot of a particular literary historical moment and help us better understand some of the conversations happening in the criticism.

This chapter is organized by form rather than chronologically, as in the previous chapters, for readability and functionality. As in the previous chapters, I have chosen representative reviews for discussion rather than attempt an exhaustive survey. I will begin with what I am calling Baldwin's canon, the five works critics and reviewers consistently identify as his best and most important: *Go Tell It on the Mountain, Giovanni's Room, Another Country, The Fire Next Time,* and *Notes of a Native Son*. I then move to sections on the remaining essay collections, the remaining novels, plays and screenplays, the short stories, poetry, and children's literature, and end, finally, with dialogues and collaborations. While chronological organization would offer a glimpse into the ebb and flow of Baldwin's popularity and demonstrate which works were well received and when, the discrete nature of the popular reviews prevent any sort of compelling narrative from taking shape. While both *No Name in the Street* and *One Day When I Was Lost* (Baldwin's Malcolm X screenplay) were published in 1972, for instance, reviews of either work rarely acknowledge the other. A chronological survey of the popular reviews is rather like looking at a stranger's photo album with no guidance—the scenes may look vaguely familiar but the pictures have very little meaning.

On the other hand, reading reviews of *No Name in the Street* alongside reviews of other essay collections, or reading reviews of *One Day When I Was Lost* with reviews of other neglected works, proves more useful. As popular reviews often concern themselves more with whether or not a given work fulfills the expectations of a genre or form rather than how that work fits in with a writer's entire body of work, and because Baldwin scholarship often divides along genre lines, grouping these reviews by form may prove useful for future scholarship.

Baldwin's Canon

The academic conversation discussed in chapter 1 is, in part, a response to the views and attitudes expressed in these reviews. This is primarily because, prior to 1963, most of the conversation about Baldwin happened in popular reviews and review essays. Criticism from 1963 to 1973 concerns itself in large part with the trajectory discussed below—namely, Baldwin moving from being a lauded, nonthreatening translator of black life for white audiences to being someone whose growing celebrity and frustration with and sympathy for black nationalism makes him suspect to that same audience.

The first work in Baldwin's canon is the novel *Go Tell It on the Mountain* (1953), the story of the Grimes family framed by the religious conversion of fourteen-year-old John. Praise for this novel usually comes in a form that implies Baldwin succeeds where other African American authors have failed. Writing about African American literature of the "protest school" as much as about Baldwin's first novel, many reviewers agreed with Robert R. Brunn, who writes that when the Negro problem "emerges [in *Go Tell It on the Mountain*] there is a sharp and vivid realization of the problem's place in the Negro life as a haunting presence— but rarely the dominant, all pervasive substance or experience" ("About People," 13). Baldwin, in other words, maintains a proper perspective. He acknowledges American racism's existence, but doesn't place it at the center of African American experience. J. Saunders Redding, an important African American literary critic who will go on to review most of Baldwin's work, praises the "surprising" maturity of such a young writer (Baldwin is twenty-nine) and argues that the "fact of [John Grimes's] being a Negro has little significance other than as a description.... John could have been any susceptible fifteen-year-old, illegitimate boy, hated by his stepfather, estranged by younger children from his mother, and forced to live within himself.... What James Baldwin seems to be saying is that the human being's need for identification with others is one of the major drives in life" ("Sensitive," 5).

For reviewers the universality of the novel rests in its religious themes and the character of Gabriel Grimes, John's stepfather. (Most are unmoved or uninterested in the novel's frame story, the conversion of John Grimes, a marked difference from critical treatments of the novel.) Richard K. Barksdale in *Phylon* asserts that the "conflicts which sear the soul of each character are conflicts which are concerned with ethical values and patterns of conduct, and these are preeminently the concern of religion, whatever the color a man's skin" (326). Ironically, the universality so praised by reviewers depends wholly on those reviewers foregrounding the Negro-ness of both Baldwin and his characters. Reviews of *Go Tell It on the Mountain* are, invariably, also implicit discussions of African American literature. They are either criticisms of protest literature (in the form of praise of Baldwin for moving away from "Negro" themes) or attempts at salvaging African American literature (in the form of praise of Baldwin for treating Negro themes in a new manner).

On occasion the discussions become explicit, as in the review by Harvey Curtis Webster in *Saturday Review Magazine*. Webster writes that the Negro novels of the early twentieth century "were usually cries of anger without measure or pleas for condescension," but with the publication of Richard Wright's *The Outsider*, Ralph Ellison's *Invisible Man*, and *Go Tell It on the Mountain*, "the Negro novel has finally come of age. Sensibly, the protagonist is a Negro in all of these books, but he is a Negro enmeshed in the human dilemma, not just a victim of underprivilege, segregation, and unreasoning violence" (14). He goes on to say that although "Mr. Baldwin does not have either Wright's or Ellison's capacity to take all modern problems as his province, he never descends into the provincialism that has made so many Negro novels read like footnotes to Myrdal's *An American Dilemma*" (14). *The Nation*, too, compares him to Ellison, stating that "Mr. Baldwin has placed himself, along with Ralph Ellison, in the advanced path of Negro writing today; he is determined to break out of the 'cage' of his material, which might also be viewed, however, as the source and spring of his art" (488). Ironically, while Baldwin is praised here in the reviews for his perceived attempts at universality, he will be judged in the criticism at the height of his career by how well he reveals truths about black people and race in America.

The longest review in this vein, indeed the longest review of *Go Tell It on the Mountain* in general, occurs in the pages of *Commentary*. Significantly, *Commentary* published Baldwin's first proper essay, "The Harlem Ghetto" (which will later be published in *Notes of a Native Son*), and his first professional short story, "Previous Condition," as well as several of his book reviews. The journal clearly has an interest in Baldwin specifically and in the Negro question in general. Steven Marcus's review considers, as was often the practice of reviewers at the time, the novels of Ellison, Wright, and Baldwin. Though Marcus rests his argument on a rather spurious assertion (that "African culture, with its essential stasis, its meager history, and the narrow possibilities its rituals afford, could hold little interest for the novelist, who is concerned above all with the fate of the complex personality against a complex social background" [456]), he does write convincingly of American writers' (white and black) inability to fashion a complex Negro identity in fiction. After an extended discussion of *The Outsider*, in which he asserts that Wright "leaves American Negro life as undiscovered and inarticulate as if he had never actually participated in it" (458), and *Invisible Man*, which he praises as the "first novel by a Negro to break away from the old, constrictive [racial] ideology" (459), Marcus moves on to Baldwin and *Go Tell It on the Mountain*, "the most important novel yet written about the American Negro" (459).

Why is this the most important novel? Because, Marcus writes, "Mr. Baldwin's concern with Negro culture is not so much to deny or discover it, but to present it in its pitifully tragic contradictions. His portrayal of Negro life demonstrates how the myth of African savagery is perpetuated among Negroes themselves both by the condition of the Negro community in America and by the institution that affords their principal refuge from that savagery, religion" (459). The review goes on to explicate the novel, lavishing similar praise as other reviews. He comes to the conclusion that Baldwin "has written a novel which is the strongest protest that can be made, because it intelligently faces the complex dilemma of its characters" (461). Marcus's review stands out because it is emblematic of the positive reviews of this novel. In *Go Tell It on the Mountain* Baldwin seems to have achieved what discerning readers had been waiting for: a "Negro" novel that sought to transcend its blackness.

Other reviews, however, while positive, offered, at best, backhanded praise. *Time*, referring to Baldwin's desire to write about Negroes as people as a "silly statement," states that "People they certainly are, but so movingly and intensely Negro that any reader listening to them with the compassion Baldwin evokes will overlook this cliché" ("Lord, Hold My Hand," 128). In a similar vein John Henry Raleigh in *New Republic* writes that Baldwin "is eminently successful, yet, paradoxically, he at the same time manages to convey more of the essential story of the American Negro than do most avowedly historical or hortatory books on the subject" (21). These reviews, and others like it, remind us that neither the novel nor the novelist can escape blackness, no matter how much he or she may wish to transcend it.

While praise of the novel centered on its compelling characters and transcendent racial narrative, criticism almost always centered on craft. Marcus, in fact, accuses Baldwin of littering the novel with clichés and of keeping an "affected distance from his material" (463) because he is unsure of what he wants to say. And the *The New Yorker* compares *Go Tell It on the Mountain* unfavorably with *Invisible Man*, stating that "Ellison's novel was emotionally disturbing and extremely serious, but it was also rich in comic invention." ("Sorry Lives," 93). The review states that *Go Tell It on the Mountain*'s "perfections are wooden and it is without vitality in its realism" (93). These kinds of criticisms haunt Baldwin throughout his career, particularly when it comes to his fiction. The very traits reviewers will find so compelling in his essays—his ability to distance himself from the subject at hand, his ability to present time-worn themes in fresh language, the technical proficiency of his prose—will grate in his novels.

The reviews of Baldwin's next full-length work, *Notes of a Native Son* (1955), now widely considered to be Baldwin at his best, offer no consensus on the relative merits or demerits of this collection. Grounds for the work's primacy in the Baldwin canon can be seen in some of the superlative remarks in the reviews. *Library Journal* opens its review by describing Baldwin as "the most gifted young American with a black skin," and praises Baldwin for his "breadth of vision" and "an objectivity that is piercing." *Library Journal*'s assessment that Baldwin "looks at the Negro from the point of view neither of attack nor of defense" (Byam, 2602) was by 1955 a fairly standard assessment of Baldwin the writer, an assessment that contributed greatly to his rising popularity. For many, Baldwin offered a respite from the angry, accusatory literature of other African American writers, particularly as the American civil rights movement gained momentum in the wake of the 1954 *Brown v. Board of Education* decision.

The superlatives continue in the *Phylon* review, which asserts that "one cannot help being moved and disturbed" by "one of the most important works yet written on the Negro in America and abroad" (T.D.J., 87). Dachine Rainer in *Commonweal* waxes almost philosophic about the unprecedented insight evidenced in Baldwin's style and content:

> Mr. Baldwin has been enraged into a style; the harshness of his lot, his racial sensitivity, and the sense of alienation and displacement that is frequently the fate of intellectuals in this country has moved him to portray in lyrical, passionate, sometimes violent prose the complex, oblique endless outrages by which a man, particularly a black man, can be made to feel outside the established social order. (385)

Reviewers are particularly impressed by the essays that will go on to become among the most anthologized of Baldwin's work: "Notes of a Native Son," "Stranger in a Village," and "Everybody's Protest Novel." Reviews generally agree that these essays provide the most vivid displays of Baldwin's strength as a writer, namely, his ability to take biographical minutia and build it into commentary about the larger issues of race, class, history, politics, and religion. Interestingly, much of the praise of this collection stems from the impression of reviewers that Baldwin is not laying the blame for the "Negro problem" completely at the feet of white America. This impression, and the adoration it engenders, informs, in part, Eldridge Cleaver's and other black nationalists' reading of Baldwin.

The *United States Quarterly Book Review* praises Baldwin's recognition of the universal plight of the American Negro: "Although his observations of the marginal Negroes' emotional attitudes are sharp-edged and cutting, he recognizes the facts that hatred is self-destructive, and that in the larger perspective, human, not exclusively American, nature is to be considered" (Review of *Notes of a Native Son*, 36). The *Christian Science Monitor*'s reviewer agrees, stating, "Perhaps the most encouraging thing about Mr. Baldwin's book is to see an evident swing away from an early harshness and uncompromising anger and frustration toward a willingness to recognize that it is not the American character that caused the 'Negro problem,' but rather human nature" (Brunn, "In a Negro's Shoes," 13). And in what will become a typical tone where Baldwin is concerned, *Time* asserts that "unlike Fellow Novelist Wright and other self-exiled American Negroes, Author Baldwin does not pretend to have found the good, free life in Europe" ("In the Castle of My Skin," 114). For these reviewers, Baldwin provides a much needed breath of fresh air and respite from a literature that had become, in their estimation, bogged down in blame and hatred. For these reviewers, Baldwin brings a new insight that reveals the "Negro problem" to be something other than the result of a morally bankrupt and corrupt American system. His seeming lack of "anger and frustration" relieves them of their discomfort and, what is important, their culpability in the plight of the Negro.

African American reviewers have a somewhat different reaction to *Notes of a Native Son*. His most famous reviewer, Langston Hughes, believes that Baldwin shows promise. Writing in *The New York Times Book Review*, Hughes states that Baldwin is like "many another writer who deals in picture captions and journalese in the hope of capturing and retaining a wide public." He continues, "When the young man who wrote this book comes to a point where he can look at life purely as himself, and for himself, the color of his skin mattering not at all ... America and the world might well have a major contemporary commentator" (26). J. Saunders Redding is more biting in his criticism. Arguing that, like *Go Tell It on the Mountain*, *Notes of a Native Son* is burdened by the question of identity, Saunders writes, "Now there is nothing wrong with this question as an apparatus for exercising the powers of abstract thought, but it becomes rather silly when, in the elucidation of it, one begins to argue, as Baldwin does, that the Negro American is by the nature of his being and his experience disqualified to find and unlicensed to seek his identity in the very environment which he helped create. On the abstract level, this is more nonsense. On the personal level, it is sheer madness—or leads to it" ("James Baldwin Miscellany," 4). Redding concludes by arguing that when Baldwin settles this question of identity, he may become "one of the best writers of his generation" (4).

Hughes and Redding zero in on the same qualities in Baldwin's work that so strike other reviewers—the lucidity of his nonfiction and the use of his personal identity quest to speak to something larger. But, unlike other reviewers, they identify these traits as shortcomings. Though neither man, certainly, urges Baldwin to "protest" or to other sociopolitical pronouncements, they do seem to lament his lack of urgency and seeming obsession with the self. They want to see him turn that keen eye, reserved in *Notes of a Native Son* primarily for reflection on his own life, outward. This opinion is shared by the reviewer in *Commentary*, who writes that *Notes of a Native Son* is "the work of a born novelist whose political and social opinions, however just, are uniquely private and, from a purely political standpoint, frustratingly circular" (Flint, 495). Interestingly, this reviewer, like Hughes and Redding, reads *Notes of a Native Son* as an interesting side note to what (they believe) will be a brilliant career in the novel. None of them could have anticipated that Baldwin's next novel would be *Giovanni's Room*.

In 1954 Baldwin wrote to a friend that he was working on a new novel in which he "wanted to convey something of the intensity of a particularly American insecurity and loneliness, and for that he had to use 'the good, white, Protestant'" (J. Campbell, 88). That novel would turn out to be *Giovanni's Room* (1956). Set almost entirely in the homosexual "milieu" of Paris and featuring no black characters, this story of the love affair between the American David and the Italian Giovanni is a seeming departure for Baldwin. Indeed, the reviews of *Giovanni's Room* seem to acknowledge this departure by rarely referring to Baldwin as a "Negro" writer, as happened, almost without fail, in reviews of *Go Tell It on the Mountain* and *Notes of a Native Son*. To be sure, we are reminded of who Baldwin is and of his race by the mention of his previous works, but the focus in these reviews is more often his Americanness or his bravery in writing so forthrightly about a homosexual relationship.

The reviewer in *New Republic* praises Baldwin, stating that he "successfully avoids the cliché literary attitudes: overemphasis on the grotesque, and the use of homosexuality as a facile symbol for the estrangement which makes possible otherwise unavailable insights into the workings of 'normal' society and 'normal' people; in short, the Homosexual as Artist" (Esty, 26). (Note that many critics, as discussed in chapter 2, come to the opposite conclusion, namely, that Baldwin uses homosexual characters quite skillfully to offer insights in to the human condition.) Though not satisfied with the ending (this reviewer calls it "lame"), he is nevertheless impressed with Baldwin's unwillingness to forgo the "complexity of things" simply because he is dealing with homosexual themes.

The review in *Saturday Review* follows along these lines, praising Baldwin for the "great artistry and restraint" with which he treats homosexuality. The review goes on to state that Baldwin "manages to retain a very delicate sense of good taste so that his characters never really offend us even when they appear most loathsome, most detestable" (Karp, 34). Many reviewers had apparently come to expect only the worst from novels dealing with homosexuality and are simply grateful that Baldwin resists sinking to the level of the prurient. What Baldwin actually has to say in *Giovanni's Room* seems to be quite beside the point to these reviewers.

Other reviewers, however, expect more from Baldwin. The reviewer in *The New Yorker* does not take David's homosexuality seriously at all. He expresses great frustration with David's "flirtations" and with Baldwin's betrayal of the literary promise evidenced in *Notes of a Native Son* and *Go Tell It on the Mountain*. This review quotes the Baldwin blurb from the dust jacket of *Giovanni's Room*: "David's dilemma is the dilemma of many men of his generation; by which I do not so much mean sexual ambivalence as a crucial lack of sexual authority" (West, 220). The reviewer responds by suggesting that the real dilemma is David's and Baldwin's outsider status—they are both "inevitably cut off by a barrier of language and experience from the texture of life as its being lived around him" (222). The review ends with the hope that Baldwin would "soon return to the American subjects he dealt with so promisingly and with so much real understanding" in his previous works (222). Charles Rolo in *Atlantic Monthly* also references the book jacket blurb and pronounces it "pretentious nonsense" (98), though he acknowledges that Baldwin still possesses the talent that so impressed him in *Go Tell It on the Mountain*. He describes Baldwin as a writer "endowed with exceptional narrative skill, poetic intensity of feeling, and a sensitive command of language. This endorsement is made despite the fact that Mr. Baldwin's subject is one of which I have had my fill" (98). These reviewers seem to want to return to discussions of American and race and leave the topic of homosexuality behind.

At least one reviewer, though, Granville Hicks in *The New York Times Book Review*, seems to immediately see in *Giovanni's Room* what many will come to take as the major theme in Baldwin's entire body of work. He sees no sensationalism in Baldwin's treatment of homosexuality, nor does Hicks feel that Baldwin has chosen to write about subjects unworthy of his talent. Instead he recognizes in David's relationships with Hella and Giovanni, in his search for some kind of peace in the world and within himself, Baldwin's desire to talk about the difficulty of finding and accepting love. "This is Mr. Baldwin's subject," Hicks writes, "the rareness and difficulty of love, and, in his rather startling way, he does a great deal with it" (5).

Surprisingly, reviewers speak much more openly and deliberately about the homosexuality in *Giovanni's Room* at the time of its publication than critics will until the advent of queer theory. In fact, as we saw in chapter 3, it isn't until queer theory takes firm root in the academy that *Giovanni's Room* moves back to the center of Baldwin scholarship. Reviewers, though, in having to describe the novel's content in order to assess it, are forced to acknowledge David's homosexuality.

Another Country (1962) also forces reviewers to grapple with homosexuality. Baldwin's third and perhaps most ambitious novel, about the suicide of Rufus Scott and its effect on his family and friends, sells quite well. It is the second best-selling book of 1963, after William Golding's *Lord of the Flies*, and secures Baldwin's fame and wealth. It is ironic, then, that *Another Country* receives, at best, a lukewarm reception in the popular press. What saves the book from a being a complete critical disaster is reviewers' tendency to forgive Baldwin, a reputedly gifted writer, for writing a "bad" book, a trend that continues from this point until the end of Baldwin's career.

The New Yorker review of *Another Country* is titled "Wrong Pulpit" and details the novel's many failings (unsympathetic characters, unbelievable situations, improbable sex), but concludes by asserting that "Baldwin the polemicist-moralist-essayist" keeps us reading because he "never forgets the power he can achieve with words or the exhilarating vision he has so often raised with those words. And neither do we"

(Malcolm, 69–70). Saul Maloff of *The Nation* echoes the sentiment when he writes that *Another Country* is nothing "but a tale in which ciphers are moved about for the wholly willed purpose of illustrating a tortured thesis; a group of singularly uninteresting people moving from one odd bed to another with the most astonishing alacrity and versatility" (15). In other words, *Another Country* is not a very convincing book. Yet Maloff comes to the same conclusion as *The New Yorker* review, that despite the failure of this novel, Baldwin is "an authentic, and in many ways superbly gifted, writer" (16).

The best example of this line of thought is James Finn's review in *Commonweal*. Finn details what is good or promising in each of Baldwin's preceding books before he gets to what fails in *Another Country*. It is as if he needs to give us evidence so that we will believe him when he asserts that Baldwin is "a fine and imaginative writer" despite *Another Country* offering evidence to the contrary (113). Finn, though, doesn't simply, grudgingly, forgive Baldwin for this literary misstep. He offers hope that the best is yet to come from Baldwin and that *Another Country* is simply evidence of a true master failing to find a proper outlet for his genius. "What seems to be the case," he argues, "is that Baldwin has yet to find the artistic form that will reveal the mystery, that will uncover the truth he knows is there" (116). It is not, then, Baldwin who has failed in writing this novel, but rather the novel that has failed Baldwin. (George E. Kent in "James Baldwin and the Problem of Being" comes to a similar conclusion, as discussed in chapter 1.)

Other reviewers are much more specific in their disappointment. While the reviewers mentioned above are disappointed because Baldwin seemingly fails to live up to the literary talent he displayed elsewhere, some reviewers take issue with Baldwin's failure to use *Another Country* to further the racial themes explored in his essays. Many people came to *Another Country* expecting a novel rooted in the civil rights sensibility Baldwin displayed in his essays. Needless to say, a novel about a multiracial group of disaffected Greenwich Village types engaged in interracial and homosexual liaisons to no real end did not quite satisfy people looking to Baldwin for answers to the perpetual "Negro problem."

William Hogan in the *San Francisco Chronicle* finds that *Another Country* tries to tell us something about American black-white relations, but fails "because of its preoccupation with totally destructive sex.... Baldwin, it seems to me, has tried too hard to make a believable comment on this American sub-culture and the American Negro-white relationship. Instead of establishing new dimensions in fiction, his book is merely irritating and shrill, and a disappointment" (35). It seems not to occur to Hogan that Baldwin's project may be something altogether different. Roderick Nordell in *Christian Science Monitor* too feels that Baldwin has more to say on the subject of black-white relations than is present in *Another Country*. He argues that there is "more hate than love" in the novel that makes "the reader re-examine himself for the earmarks of prejudice." He wishes though that "Baldwin would turn his talent now to those healing gestures across barriers of race that are surely, in all conscience, more frequent in actual life than the examples touchingly present in the brutal context of this book" (11). Baldwin's essays and public appearances offered hope to many and it seemed a cruel joke that *Another Country* was devoid of that hope.

For other reviewers, the explicit sex scenes and overt homosexuality were no joking matter. *Library Journal* warned that "careful book selectors will want to know that this is another 'problem' book—all the Miller vocabulary, race, and the gamut of sex from near-rape to homosexual, they are all here, everything the cautious will want to avoid" (Moon, 2154). The reviewer in *The New Statesman* objected to the "sloppy sentiment" among "queers" (Taubman, 53) and Augusta Strong in *Freedomways* blames the "dreary, sordid stretches" of the book on Baldwin's "intimately personal preoccupations and uncertainties" (503).

As with *Giovanni's Room*, reviewers are unable to avoid discussing the depiction of homosexuality in this novel, but they do seem intent on treating it as an aberration, a brief side note in Baldwin's otherwise illustrious career. Whereas most reviews make mention of *Go Tell It on the Mountain* and Baldwin's essays, almost none of them refer to *Giovanni's Room*. It is almost as if, by the time of *Another Country*'s publication, the popular press had erased *Giovanni's Room* from Baldwin's resume. *Giovanni's Room* was a reminder of those aspects of Baldwin's works readers and reviewers were unwilling or unable to make sense of. Recalling *Go Tell It on the Mountain* and "Stranger in a Village" instead allowed reviewers to assure readers that Baldwin was an important writer with great potential rather than a prurient writer wasting his potential.

In a second work published in 1963, Baldwin returned to the form in which reviewers felt he had the most potential, the essay. *The Fire Next Time* collected two previously published essays in one volume. Kyle Haselden's review in *Christian Century* offers a nice summary of *The Fire Next Time*.

> *The Fire Next Time* is not as it purports to be an essay on the Negro or on the racial turmoil which strangles the Negro so much as it is the candid confession of one man who, if he were writing as a white man, would deliver a substantially similar diatribe. It is not insignificant that Baldwin is an angry young *Negro* man; but, race apart, he would still be an angry young man. If in Baldwin's unrestrained yet beautiful shrieks of protests, his shameless confession of shame, the wasteful excessiveness of his language one thinks he sees hints of latent paranoia, he must remember that what he confronts is not *the* Negro but a man. (582–83)

That many readers were uncomfortable with these "beautiful shrieks" is evident in the reviews.

First there are those reviewers who chastise Baldwin for his lack of objectivity and emotional detachment. The *Economist* reviewer asks "how does it help to denigrate America as joyless and soulless" in response to the arguments presented in *The Fire Next Time*:

> To indulge in wishful thinking such as that blacks are better than whites and do not want to imitate white people; to write psychological clap-trap about whites needing Negroes as a race in which they can project the burden of white fears and inadequacies (particularly sexual inadequacies)? ... [W]ith a little more [sense of proportion] Mr. Baldwin might have done his race a greater service. That he is incapable of objectivity is part of the price now being paid by a country of white callousness toward his race. ("Too Much Fire?" 444)

And while Andrew Greely in *Critic* concedes that Baldwin "is what white men have made him," he asserts that "if anger can be the beginning of a fight for justice, it cannot be the end of it. One hopes that ultimately saner voices than Barnett or Byrd, or Malcolm X will be heard" (72). The popular image of Baldwin as an angry black man that emerges from these reviews is one that informs criticism of this period (as critics will debate the authenticity and justification of his anger).

The second essay in *The Fire Next Time*, "Down at the Cross: Letter from a Region in My Mind," in particular troubled reviewers. While the critic in *The Times Literary Supplement* states that "*The Fire Next Time* has few, if any equals," in its expression of the "dilemma" of the American Negro "in all its inescapable intricacies," and pronounces Baldwin "one of the great journalists of all time" for not completely rejecting the Black Muslim movement, but rather describing "its ethics and its personalities with sympathy" ("State of the Negro?"), other reviewers do not take so kindly to Baldwin's meeting with the Black Muslim leader Elijah Muhammad. John Cross in *The New Statesman* reads *The Fire Next Time* cynically, stating that "'Letter' is an intensely personal document, but it was also perfectly timed as a manifesto for the new mood of militancy among American negroes." He goes on to say that Baldwin moves to "dubious ground" with his account of meeting Elijah Muhammad. "Why," Cross asks, "with all the current examples of individual and organized bravery in front of him, did Mr. Baldwin choose to complicate matters by dwelling almost exclusively on an extremist group like the Black Muslims?" (79). Implicit in this question, and in many reviews of *The Fire Next Time*, is the assumption that Baldwin must necessarily assist the cause of civil rights in the most comforting (for whites) way possible. No room is given for the possibility that discomfort is necessary in the struggle for racial reconciliation or that the inevitability of this discomfort, this pain, is exactly what *Fire Next Time* speaks to.

Gary Wills's review essay in *The National Review* tackles this issue head-on. The reason reviewers and readers find the essays in *The Fire Next Time* so discomforting, according to Wills, is because

> he makes no effort to soften the hard lines of inconsistency that extrude everywhere in his piece—saying, in one breath, that it is too late for us to convince the Negro of our good faith, since the growth of black power in the world makes any gesture on our part look like an effort to buy off our future conquerors; then, with a change of mood, but no answer to the former argument, singing that our nation is one of the best equipped to lead the world into a new era of racial love. (408)

According to Wills, Baldwin makes no attempt at resolution or reconciliation. He attacks the ideals and beliefs of the United States and then "stand[s] back and observ[es] that no one defends them" (410). Where in previous essays Baldwin seemed to hold out hope for himself and whites, including himself in the "we" of the nation, in *The Fire Next Time* Baldwin offers instead an apocalyptic vision.

While Wills seems to admire Baldwin's style and passion, he takes exception to many of Baldwin's assertions, particularly those about American ideals and Christianity. He writes that Baldwin "is asking for immediate secession from our civilization" (410). And in response, Wills argues, his (white) reading audience is patronizingly tolerant, acting out of guilt rather than real critical engagement. Wills's review stands out because of the stance he takes, for engaging Baldwin's ideas rather than the ideas he believes Baldwin stands in for. He argues that it

> is not enough for us to merely sympathize with Baldwin's unhappy childhood, felicitate him on his style and send him back to Paris with more scholarships and literary prizes. He deserves an answer; he deserves a fight. He is an adversary worth our best arguments, and one of the uses of the fight is that it may force us to remember what our best arguments are. Once we do that, we have won; and so has he. (417)

Wills isn't yet ready to give up on American ideals and culture and argues that Baldwin depends too heavily on hyperbole and exaggeration to score ideological points. In this, Wills implies, Baldwin risks being taken lightly, risks being merely a token "Negro spokesman" rather than an intellectual force to be reckoned with.

Finally, Jean Carey Bond, in her *Freedomways* review, has a different criticism of Baldwin aimed directly at his newfound popularity and his role as "Negro leader." Bond is unimpressed with Baldwin's "provocative, gifted, yet enormously self-conscious and affected style" (237) and finds the whole book to be a "vaguely hysterical piece of instant controversy" (235). This review, like others in black publications or by black writers, objects to Baldwin's insistence in "My Dungeon Shook" (the first essay in the book) that the "Negro must accept and love the white man" (236). "Superficiality is, in fact, this essay's biggest problem," writes Bond, "and its prevalence tends to support the frequent claim that Mr. Baldwin is primarily concerned with the white reading public and is covetous of their attention and praise" (236). Baldwin's canon, and its reviews, reveals a writer and a reading public often at ideological odds. Readers wanted a writer who wrote about race but did so without making white readers feel guilty; they wanted a writer who could translate black anger for white audiences without succumbing to that anger himself; they wanted a writer who could engage the contemporary political and social terrain, but do so from a comfortable aesthetic distance. That these five books survive to become Baldwin's canon demonstrate their ability to navigate these competing, sometimes conflicting, demands more or less successfully.

Essays

James Campbell, author of the Baldwin biography *Talking At the Gates* (1991), writes that Baldwin "didn't think of himself as an essayist, but as a novelist and playwright, and he seems to have made little or no conscious effort to refine his essay technique after his reviewing days" (92). It is a great irony, then, that the essay is what we remember him most for; there is almost universal agreement that he is best at this genre. If the number of reviews is any indication, there was always lots of anticipation surrounding a new essay collection from Baldwin. While everything he published garnered attention, it is almost certainly his essays that generated the most response.

Nobody Knows My Name (1961) collects the essays Baldwin writes after he returns to the United States in 1958 to be a "witness" to the civil rights movement. Traveling throughout the South and meeting and befriending many civil rights leaders (including King and Megdar Evers), Baldwin published reports for numerous high-profile, high-circulation mainstream publications like *The New York Times*, *Harper's*, *Esquire*, and *The New Yorker*. The book remained on the best-seller list for six months and is notable for essays on William Faulkner, Norman Mailer, and Richard Wright.

The reviews of this collection, unlike those of *The Fire Next Time*, are on the whole sympathetic and encouraging. What is interesting about these reviews is that they are almost the exact opposite of those of *The Fire Next Time*, the essay collection that follows *Nobody Knows My Name*. *Phylon* praises his "humanism" (F. Campbell, "More Notes," 96) and the clarity that he brings to America's race problems. The reviewer argues that Baldwin shows us that "[the essence of segregation and discrimination] lies within the racist emotions permeating national life. Baldwin implies that lying below the forms of racism is a national betrayal of America's promise" (97). Beyond that Baldwin is praised for transcending his Negro identity. "Baldwin in these essays forces us to recognize in the center of his dark anonymity a skillful artist, an imaginative intellectual, and most of all, a kaleidoscopic human being" (97). *Atlantic Monthly* echoes this sentiment, implying, though, that Baldwin can transcend this identity because he recognizes it for the racist construct it is: "One hears in Baldwin's pages the voice of a new generation of Negroes, fortified by the conviction that the white man's power to mold their identity and control their fate is rapidly crumbling" (Rolo, "Questions," 126). It is also clear from many of these reviews that these essays are valued precisely because they cause little discomfort. They don't seem to call anyone to any specific action. This lack of a specific action is okay, though, because "practical politics" is not the "arena" of these essays (128). Unlike *The Fire Next Time*, which reviewers read as damning of American whites, many seem to read *Nobody Knows My Name* as confirming Baldwin's ultimate faith in America's promise. Rather than the prophet of doom we see two years later in *The Fire Next Time*, in *Nobody Knows My Name* we have a "'witness' who seeks to convey in human terms the truth, as he sees it, about a terrible injustice" (128).

It should come as no shock that Irving Howe, anticipating the argument he will make in "Black Boys and Native Sons," sees "protest" in Baldwin's witnessing. He argues that despite Baldwin best efforts to avoid the pitfalls of Wright's naturalism, Baldwin has nevertheless developed a protest that is "nonpolitical in character, spoken more in the voice of anguish than revolt, and concerned less with melodrama of discrimination than the moral consequences of living under an irremovable stigma" ("Protest," 4). In other words, as discussed in chapter 1, Howe is glad of Baldwin's turn toward protest, but, on the whole, is not terribly impressed with the effort.

The effort is marred by Baldwin's reliance on autobiography, on explicating the "anguish" and "stigma" that comes from living as a black man in America. Other reviewers, too, take up this issue of Baldwin's reliance on the personal in his essays. Julian Mayfield in *The New Republic* praises the eloquence of Baldwin's style, yet finds that Baldwin's "honesty and irreverence are his most maddening qualities as a writer and a human being" (25). He writes, "Baldwin reveals so much about himself that the embarrassed reader cannot help feeling he has stumbled upon a person performing a private act" (25). J. Saunders Redding, writing in *The New York Herald Tribune*, however, sees promise in Baldwin's autobiographical impulse. It is his *intellectual* impulse in *Nobody Knows My*

Name that gives Redding pause. "The intellectual quality" of the essays in part 1 of the collection (which Redding describes as "glittering with a verbal brilliance that, as when one looks too long at the sun, blinds one to all else") "does not match the emotional quality of the others. One remarks of them, here is the mind; but one says of the others, here is the man. And the suspicion grows that James Baldwin the man, agonized by his own superb equipment—and honest, unafraid, extravagant—is overwhelmingly more interesting than the mind" ("In His Native Land," 36). Both Mayfield and Redding desire the same thing from Baldwin: cogent analysis of the issues he raises, issues of race, history, national identity, and love. And both come to the same conclusion: Baldwin shows great intellectual promise, but his own "personality" may be getting in the way of that promise. Given that in two years time a great majority of the popular and critical conversation about Baldwin will concern his celebrity and its effect on his craft, Mayfield's and Redding's reviews of *Nobody Knows My Name* are quite prescient.

By the time of the publication of *No Name in the Street* (1972), however, Baldwin's popularity is in decline and he is becoming increasingly irrelevant in America's race drama. The two essays and epilogue function as a kind of coda on the civil rights movement, and is notable for the essay "Take Me to the Water," in which Baldwin recounts his attempt to attend King's funeral. Though the collection is eagerly anticipated as his first major work since *The Fire Next Time*, it garnered, at best, mixed reviews.

Considering the prophetic tone of *The Fire Next Time* and Baldwin's personal growing frustration with American race relations, not to mention the actual state of American race relations in 1972, it is somewhat surprising to find reviews lamenting Baldwin's lack of optimism or hopeful tone. For instance, *Atlantic Monthly's* reviewer objects to Baldwin's damning tone and laments that Baldwin doesn't acknowledge the "millions of thoughtful white Americans intent that reconciliation shall work" (Weeks, 110). *The Christian Science Monitor* counsels that "readers who yearn to be insulted, infuriated, and simultaneously informed will discover here more than enough to please their intellectual palates" (Haney, 11). *Choice* finds the collection "self-serving and pompous" (Review of *The Fire Next Time*, 1209), whereas *Newsweek* finds the collection "embarrassing" (Prescott, 85). The *Newsweek* reviewer goes on to state, "I am sure that this ramble toward digressions, self-pitying asides and truculent belligerence will presently become embarrassing to Baldwin, too, because he must soon realize that one who calls himself a 'public witness to the situation of black people' need not clutch so uneasily at the rigid postures of a younger generation" (85–86).

This notion that Baldwin tries too hard in this collection to mimic the anger of the "younger generation," by which they mean, of course, black nationalists, is another strain that runs through these reviews.

Library Journal states that "Baldwin has always written from inside the black movement. In this collection, however, his age and literary frame seem to have separated him from the experiences of the rising generation of black leaders" (Freedman, 1453). And *Time* laments that "Indeed, the sad irony of Baldwin's success is that it is based on terms laid down by white society before many black leaders had redefined the terms of success with their blood" ("Ashes," 83).

Baldwin's next book seems to confirm for reviewers that he is out of touch with contemporary American race politics. *The Devil Finds Work* (1976) is a long essay of film criticism mixed with autobiography and social commentary. While *Choice* praises the book's "controlled moral fervor" (Review of *The Devil Finds Work*, *Choice*, 804) and *Village Voice* appreciates its "passionate attack on racial images as depicted and fortified in the movies" (Review of *The Devil Finds Work*, *Village Voice*, 43), for most reviewers, Baldwin is a ghost from the past. For some, this is not a problem. The *Progressive* review claims that Baldwin's "life in France has diluted neither his skill nor his insight" and, as a result, his "blackness is the glue of the book, and the reader finds that his view from the mountaintop, in exile, is a clear and important one. Baldwin reminds us, again, that being black is different from being white, even at the movies" (Review of *The Devil Finds Work*, *Progressive*, 44). Others, like *The New York Times* reviewer, however, find this revelation "unfashionable" (Lehmann-Haupt, C23) and not actually a revelation. In fact, for this reviewer, *The Devil Finds Work* does little more than offer a glimpse of "James Baldwin testifying honestly to his own experience" (C23). There seems to be some concession, though, that Baldwin's staleness as a writer is not entirely his fault. The reviewer in *The Nation* concludes, "I am disappointed in this essay. I think it fails as a coherent piece. But that is almost like saying that the aging bear has failed, caught finally in a trap it always knew was there, contemplating its wound and, in extraordinary patience, waiting for its fate" (Bryant, 27). And the *New Leader* review asserts that Baldwin "has succeeded in raising expectations so high that scrutiny of his work and demands in his excellence grow more rigorous and merciless with each new book he writes" (Anderson, 19). The reviews of *The Devil Finds Work* provide a nice example of Baldwin's popular reputation at war with itself. Because he makes himself so available, both as a personality and on the page, the public seems to assume a great deal of ownership of him and comes to expect a certain kind of literary output—essays that speak eloquently and transcendentally of his experiences as a black man. Any deviation from these expectations, as in *No Name in the Street* or *The Devil Finds Work*, is met with pronouncements of his betrayal and his irrelevancy. What is important, though, is that these same readers continue to read him. Baldwin goes in and out of fashion and favor, but he is never out of sight.

Baldwin's final two essay collections were both published in 1985 and were often reviewed together. *Evidence of Things Not Seen* is an expansion of a *Playboy* article on the "Atlanta child murders" that took place from the summer of 1979 to the spring of 1981. The career-spanning *Price of the Ticket* collects Baldwin's nonfiction and is his last publication before his death. The juxtaposition of these books, especially at the end of Baldwin's career, demonstrates for reviewers a great talent wasted.

Evidence purports to be about the Atlanta Child murders but spends a great deal of time discussing contemporary race relations. *The New York Times Book Review* wants to be kind to Baldwin when reviewing *Evidence*: "There is far too much sermonizing here on the overall state of race relations in America and not enough digging into specific facts of the Atlanta murders. Nonetheless, when Mr. Baldwin steps down from the pulpit he can still bring passionate intensity to reportage" (Fleming, 25). *The Christian Science Monitor* is less kind: "The writing often rambles, and the book lacks a focus, failing to convey an understanding of what occurred before and during Williams's trial. Occasionally, the writing is so subjective and opinionated that the reader may be unsure that Baldwin knows what he is talking about" (Cornish, 40).

Reviewers generally perceived *Price* as the better book, allowing, as it did, a glimpse back at Baldwin's brilliance. The reviewer for *The New York Times Book Review* wrote, "Perhaps this collection will spur a new assessment of Mr. Baldwin's roles as a kind of cultural therapist, an artist who straddles two worlds—one black, the other white—possessing terrible and beautiful insights into both" (Muwakkil, 35). For some, though, that brilliance had been overstated. The reviewer in *Commentary* writes, "To revisit James Baldwin's nonfiction is to understand the full extent to which the trivializing claims of radical politics undermined [his] artistic career" (Teachout, 80). And *Kirkus* concludes with a sort of half compliment: "It is a stunning achievement, violently personal, gifted, distilled from a lifelong mediation on race, sometimes less intelligent than given to big generalizations and intellectual grandiosity, yet ever a whiplash on the national conscience, if steadily remote in its fury" (Review of *Price of the Ticket*, 833).

That Baldwin ends his career with the essay, particularly a collection that allows readers to consider the whole of his career, solidifies his reputation as that of an essayist who also wrote other things (despite Baldwin's desire to be a novelist who also wrote essays). While reviewers are often frustrated with and conflicted about Baldwin the essayist, they continue to find his voice and his insight compelling. The intense honesty and soul-baring nature of his prose, for most reviewers, is enough to overcome the deficiencies in his craft. The brilliance of his great essays—"Notes of a Native Son," "Stranger in a Village," "Take Me to the Water"—more than make up for the failings of the others. When it comes to Baldwin's novels, however, readers are not so forgiving.

Novels

Early in his career, Baldwin had this to say about his fiction:

> I wanted my people to be people first, Negroes almost incidentally. That is, I hoped by refusing to take a special, embattled tone, to involve the reader in their lives, and this to such an extent that he would close the book knowing more about himself, and therefore more about Negroes, than he had known before. (quoted in Brunn, "About People," 13)

Reviewers take Baldwin at his word and come to his novels always with the expectation that some truth about people and, more particularly, black people, will be revealed.

Tell Me How Long the Train's Been Gone (1968), the story of actor Leo Proudhammer, has the dubious distinction of being both the follow-up to *Another Country*, Baldwin's best-selling controversial novel, and of coming at the height of his career as a public witness, when his status as an artist is most in question. By 1968 Baldwin has a reputation for writing bad, if promising, books, a reputation seemingly confirmed here. The reviewer in *National Review* writes that once "he learns to design a novel (or abandons the novel for a more congenial form), Mr. Baldwin will be one of the most impressive writers of our time. His understanding of humanity is deeper than he gives himself credit" (Davenport, 701). *The Nation* objects to the autobiographical strain in this book: "Since Leo bears a certain resemblance to Baldwin himself, one feels that psychological strategies and fantasies are being acted out.... In the end, ego reduces the novel to a work of self-indulgence" (Long, 770).

The backdrop for this book is the growing protest movements of the 1960s and the increasingly violent reaction to them. Whereas most reviewers are finding Baldwin irrelevant to the current discussions of race, at least one reviewer believes he still has truths to tell. The review in *Commentary* reads,

> But as I understand it, Baldwin's story tells me that white society has forced black men to withdraw into impotent rage, like Leo's father; or into a totally-armored religiosity, like his brother Caleb; into crime; into irresponsibility; or very often it has simply and literally murdered them.... Now it is easier to understand, now that our own sons and daughters are being assaulted by the blackjacks and clubs of these same police. (Thompson, 68)

(Note that Baldwin's truth only becomes clear and relevant when "our" [white] kids begin suffering the abuses of an unjust state.) Despite the truths to be gleaned from Baldwin's fiction, however, his talent as a novelist will ever after remain in doubt. Mario Puzo, reviewing for *The*

New York Times Book Review, writes that this is "a simpleminded, one-dimensional novel with mostly cardboard characters, a polemical rather than narrative tone, weak invention, and poor selection of incident.... [It] becomes clearer with each book he publishes that Baldwin's reputation is justified by his essays rather than his fiction" (5).

Baldwin's next novel, *If Beale Street Could Talk* (1974), tells the tragic love story of fifteen-year-old Tish and her boyfriend Fonny. Reviewers seem to like this novel because of its old-fashioned feel, though Baldwin's irrelevancy to contemporary politics is still central to the reviewers' assessment; some question whether Baldwin's work is worth the effort. (It is important to note that no one ever questions whether reading Baldwin's essays is worth the effort.) For instance, the *Saturday Review* states,

> The absolute rightness of his cause coupled with his self-righteousness in proselytizing for it have very effectively kept at bay many commentators who might otherwise have approached him with the critical skepticism they habitually bring to the work of his white contemporaries.... One can only wonder whether his other and, in some respects, more central subject, interracial sexuality and homosexuality, would be quite so effective as a silencer of opposition. (Aldridge, 20)

In other words, white guilt about race keeps Baldwin's reputation afloat and keeps readers from seeing the defects in his novels.

One defect of particular concern to female reviewers is the fact that Baldwin fails to adequately separate his thoughts and feelings from that of the story's female narrator, fifteen-year-old Tish. In *The National Observer*, Barbara Smith writes, "Tish often sounds less like a black girl painfully in love than she does like a less articulate Baldwin, shifting from conversation to rhetoric within a single passage" (37). June Jordan in *The Village Voice* argues, "And if you were not advised, as you are, that she's doing the talking, so to speak, you would swear it's the narrative of a rather famous, articulate man who entertains himself with bizarre women-hating ideas at every turn" (34). She offers Toni Cade Bambara's *Gorilla, My Love* (1972) as a more satisfying alternative.

Other reviewers, however, see in Tish the source of the novel's power. The *Freedomways* review finds that in spite of the inconsistency in voice, "through Tish we are able to see and feel a love that is not just that of two people, but of an entire family that is fiercely loyal, protective of each other, and unselfish. This takes on special significance especially now, when so many 'black films' and 'black books' depict only characters whose relationships are destructive, abrasive, or wounding, not to say violent beyond belief" (Flamer, 358–59). And Joyce Carol Oates finds that "Tish's voice comes to seem natural and we learn to know her from the inside out" (1). She concludes that the novel is "a quite moving and very traditional celebration of love. It affirms not only love between a man and a woman, but love of a type that is dealt with only rarely in contemporary fiction—that between members of a family, which may involve extremes of sacrifice" (1).

Baldwin's final novel finds him returning to fertile, familiar ground—the black Protestant church of his childhood. For a man who set out to become a novelist (rather than an essayist or witness or polemicist), the end of his fiction career must have been a better disappointment. *Just Above My Head* (1979) is greeted with near universal disdain. Perhaps most damning is Stanley Crouch's review in *The Village Voice*, in which Crouch not only argues that this novel is poorly written, but also that Baldwin squanders his talent by continuing to write about homosexuality:

> It is Baldwin's sentimental and poorly argued attempt to present homosexuality as some form of superior erotic enlightenment that continually slackens the power of *Just Above My Head*. The sentimentality results from a tendency to overstatement, pretension, and pomposity, as well as the creation of situations and responses the sole function of which is to prove the degradation of black people at the behest of racism and sexual convention. (39)

The book fails as well, according to reviewers, because Baldwin is no longer able to fulfill his mission as novelist, which is to tell us something true about black people. The reviewer in *Commentary* writes that the failure of the novel "arises from Baldwin's inability to decide exactly where he belongs in the black world today, and what role he has to fill" (P. Bell, 75). And *Maclean's*, in a typical complaint about black expatriate writers, concludes that it "may be that Baldwin's long sojourn in St. Paul de Vence near the French Riviera have [*sic*] distanced him from the truth about life in America" (Amiel, 55). The popular consensus that these novels fail as works of art account, in part, for their exclusion from the Baldwin canon.

Plays and Screenplays

Blues for Mr. Charlie (1964), Baldwin's first published and first produced play, is his response to the 1955 murder of Emmet Till. The play is told in flashback and tells the story of the murder of black Richard Henry by a white shopkeeper. It was workshopped by the Actor's Studio and opened on Broadway with Rip Torn playing the white lead and Burgess Meredith directing.

Most of the reviews of the text (rather than the production) echo Howe in "Black Boys and Native Sons." The reviews assume Baldwin's importance, the necessity of his voice in the public discourse, even as they concede that his art is not very good. Granville Hicks asks,

Is the play propaganda? I suppose that it is, to the extent that Baldwin hopes to have a specific effect on an audience of Mister Charlies—to make them change, to make them see that the present crisis makes change imperative. But it is not propaganda if one means by that distortion of the truth for a political purpose. Is it a major piece of literature? I doubt it, though I believe that it should be very moving on the stage. Its weaknesses, however, do not seem to arise out of Baldwin's preoccupation with a cause but out of the limitations of his medium, or, perhaps, his unfamiliarity with it. ("Gun," 28)

Bookweek agrees, though its reviewer doesn't see the same importance that Hicks does: "It is not subtle and not meant to be; and it is not art, though perhaps it is meant to be. And if, after three relentless acts, it is finally moving, it is not because of Baldwin's skill as a playwright but because the kind of people who will sit for *Blues for Mister Charlie* want to be moved by what he is saying" (Kluger, 5). Again, white guilt is offered as an explanation for Baldwin's success.

Philip Roth, reviewing both *Blues for Mister Charlie* and Amiri Baraka's *Dutchman* in *The New York Review of Books,* finds that Baldwin has lost his way in this play and shows signs of the of black nationalist fervor taking over large parts of black America: "If there is ever a Black Muslim nation, and if there is television in that nation, then something like Acts Two and Three of *Blues for Mr. Charlie* will probably be the kind of thing the housewives will watch on afternoon TV. It is soap opera designed to illustrate the superiority of blacks over whites" (11).

Baldwin's second play, *Amen Corner* (1968), tells the story of Sister Margaret and her storefront church. It was performed on Broadway in 1965. As with *Beale Street* (though it comes six years later), and in contrast to *Blues for Mister Charlie*, reviewers like the old-fashioned feel of the play and the perceived absence of polemic. *Library Journal* describes it as "a play that reveals a religion of beautiful desperation, a seeking out of a heavenly life to justify an earthly death" (Wortis, 2428). *Choice* agrees, stating that in "that remarkable way that Baldwin has of personalizing in the service of the universal, he puts this early play into an autobiographical framework, helping us to view the play as a result of a man's/artist's agony" (Review of *Amen Corner*, 382). Despite this kind of praise, however, the play is not widely reviewed as a text.

Finally, Baldwin worked for several years on a film adaptation of Alex Haley's *Autobiography of Malcolm X*. Ultimately the film project fell apart, but Baldwin published his screenplay, *One Day When I Was Lost: A Scenario Based on Alex Haley's "The Autobiography of Malcolm X"* (1972). Reviews of this work are slight, the general agreement being that Baldwin and Malcolm X's story are not suited to the screenplay. The *Commonweal* critic, however, is not so generous, writing, "Unfortunately, it is not much worth reading at all, except for those who have a special interest in Baldwin's career and its curious downward spiral during the last years" (Cook, 47). While this screenplay garnered little attention at the time of its publication, it would go on to serve as the basis for Spike Lee's popular 1992 biopic *Malcolm X*.[1]

Short Stories, Poetry, and Children's Literature

Going to Meet the Man (1965) collects Baldwin's published short fiction to date. There is almost universal acclaim for "Sonny's Blues," though people are torn about the title story. Many reviewers forgo assessment of the collection to instead discuss Baldwin's celebrity status, which is at its height, and whether all the attention is ruining his art. The general conclusion is that this collection is an opportunistic move "scraping the past in response to an author's present popularity" (Kauffmann, 5). Other reviewers are clearer about their disdain for Baldwin's celebrity. The *Newsweek* review reads, "James Baldwin is an angry man, and his anger, in its justness and virulence, has intimidated a great deal of opinion into becoming a hallelujah chorus for his anti-white jeremiads" ("Tortured Voice," 114). (White guilt rears its head again.) And then there are the typical homophobic reviews that plague Baldwin's career. The reviewer in *Saturday Review* argues that the homosexual can't, like the black, be used "as an emblematic figure for the revolt against bourgeois compromise." And since this seems to be Baldwin's project in these short stories, the reviewer concludes, "what a ludicrous choice the homosexual is for this role. He is a clinical case, and therefore unable to represent more than himself and his own infantilism" (Stern, 32).

Little Man, Little Man (1976), Baldwin's only children's book, was promoted by the publisher as a children's story for adults. The lovingly illustrated story is told in the black idiom of five-year-old TJ and is primarily a series of scenes from his life in Harlem. Very few reviewers took note of this anomalous entry in Baldwin's oeuvre. When they did it was to comment on the oddity of the book. *Book World* describes *Little Man* as an "exciting, perhaps an important book, but a book with an inherent flaw: its concept of audience is skewed" (Haskell, E6); and *Publishers Weekly* wonders if "this a manifesto to establish a separatist language structure, one speech pattern for blacks, another for whites?" (Mercier, 78).

Notably, Julius Lester, a black nationalist-inspired author of children's books and a fan of Baldwin's, reviewed *Little Man* for *The New York Times Book Review*. He concludes that this "is a slight book, and that it was written by a man I will always honor cannot alter this assessment. Children's literature is a province of its own, a fact which the literati do not take seriously enough" (22). For most reviewers, Baldwin is quite out of his element in this form.

Reviewers also agree that Baldwin steps out of his comfort zone when he attempts poetry. The reviews of Baldwin's only collection of poetry, *Jimmy's Blues* (1983), are few and far between. And where they are found, they are not very flattering. Whereas the reviewer in *Library Journal* praises Baldwin's "streetwise yet visionary poetic voice" (Review of *Jimmy's Blues, Library Journal,* 153), *Virginia Quarterly* laments that one "would expect a prose stylist as intense and sophisticated as James Baldwin to turn out a dense, fiercely ironic, unfailingly elegant lyric poetry. Instead, his verses are discursive, loosely cumulative in structure, and haunted by the rhetorical ghosts of Black Power" (Review of *Jimmy's Blues, Virginia Quarterly,* 99). As D. Quentin Miller demonstrates in his essay on *Jimmy's Blues* in *Re-Viewing James Baldwin*, this is the least written about, least acknowledged of all Baldwin's works, and the reviews bear this out.

Dialogues and Collaborations

Nothing Personal (1964) is a collaboration between Baldwin and his high-school friend Richard Avedon. The coffee-table book combines Avedon's photographs of the famous and near famous with text by Baldwin. The book was widely seen as a vanity project for both authors, though *Newsweek* does praise it as demonstrating "an intense sensitivity to the masks and gestures, the public charades, which mask the private person" (Review of *Nothing Personal,* 122). More common, though, is the opinion expressed in *Library Journal*: "an exploitative work with photographer and author collaborating in their own exploitation, while in turn they exploit the stupidities, miseries and sorrows of the world" (Cooley, 4925). And *The New York Review of Books* clearly expected more of Baldwin (though, apparently, not of Avedon). "The author of *Notes of a Native Son* was a highly aware and complicated individual; the author of *Nothing Personal,* and the rest of his recent writings, is merely a self-constituted Symbol, bucking hard for the rank of Legend" (Brustein, 10).

In 1971 Baldwin had a series of three conversations with the celebrated anthropologist Margaret Mead. Those conversations were transcribed and published as *Rap on Race*. The reviews cast Mead as the reasonable teacher to Baldwin's overemotional pupil. Though the book made quite an impression, based primarily on the celebrity of the participants, the consensus seems to be that the "rap" amounts to very little. *The Virginia Quarterly Review* concludes that it "is not a book that contributes much to our understanding of race, or to racial understanding. Very early in the dialogue it becomes evident that neither Baldwin nor Mead represents any considerable intellectual constituency" (Donald, 619). And *The New York Times Book Review* finds that "You must either be a world-famous white liberal anthropologist, or a brilliant black writer, or else there isn't much of an audience for this sort of thing except among your friends, or in taverns and bars where people generally call it baloney" (Elman, 5).

A Dialogue (1973) transcribes a PBS telecast of a conversation between Nikki Giovanni and Baldwin. This book seems to have made little impact, though the few notices it did receive were favorable. *Library Journal* recommends the book, stating, "This book, then, not only serves as a vehicle for presenting issues, but becomes a stage on which the issues are dramatized in a confrontation between man and woman, between established and new writer, and between two generations of black experience" (Maginnis, 771).

I hope I have demonstrated the importance of the popular reviews in Baldwin criticism. Far from being marginal to the critical conversation, the reviews, in fact, provide many of the contours of that conversation. Many of our critical assumptions about Baldwin—that he is at his best in the essay, that white guilt fueled his popularity, that he never lived up to the promise of his early career—have their roots in assessments made by reviewers in the popular press. Despite the increasingly lukewarm, even hostile, reviews Baldwin received as his career wore on, that major mainstream publications saw fit to review even his most obscure work testifies to the importance and influence of James Baldwin as a writer. While the critics would debate his relevancy to questions of race and sexuality and politics, the reading public continued to think of him as a writer who mattered, even when they felt he was a disappointment. While literary criticism would move away from questions of biography and authorial intent, the popular reviews continued to judge whether Baldwin lived up to the goals he set for himself: to be an honest man and a good writer.

Notes

[1] The screenplay of Lee's 1992 film credits James Baldwin as one of the writers. See Brian Norman, "Reading a 'Closet Screenplay': Hollywood, James Baldwin's Malcolms, and the Threat of Historical Irrelevance," for an interesting history of the Baldwin's screenplay.

Part III

6: Baldwin Studies Now

Brian Norman, a prolific scholar of African American and multiethnic literature, provides a useful glimpse into contemporary Baldwin studies. Since 2005 Norman has published no fewer than five essays on Baldwin's work, and has included Baldwin in a book-length study of the American protest essay. Norman writes about *Blues for Mister Charlie* in the collection *Emmett Till in Literary Memory and Imagination* (2008). He argues that, rather than shy away from difference and division, Baldwin used the play to address it head-on. The "power of the polemics of *Blues for Mister Charlie*, and its moral challenge to its audience to claim reasonability for racial violence, resides in Baldwin's consistent demand that we address the complexities of religion, violence, and class *within* each side *and across* the ditch separating the two races" ("James Baldwin's Unifying Polemic," 95, original emphasis). In "Crossing Identitarian Lines: Women's Liberation and James Baldwin's Early Essays" (2006), he reconsiders Baldwin's early essays in light of reconsiderations of second-wave feminism. Taking seriously scholarly assertions that Baldwin's early work was "proto-feminist" offers us a "productively blurry genealogy of a feminism that arises out of the experiences of African-Americans, including men" (252). Baldwin's early essays, argues Norman, effectively model building a "we" (so important to second-wave feminism) through a speaking "I." In "Reading a 'Closet Screenplay': Hollywood, James Baldwin's Malcolms, and the Threat of Historical Irrelevance" (2005), Norman offers a reading of Baldwin's unproduced screenplay for a film about Malcolm X in which he characterizes Baldwin's "scenario" as "presenting a transformative disorienting history with multiple Malcolms existing at once in the same location in opposition to [Alex] Haley's or [Spike] Lee's versions" (113). And finally, Norman also contributed a piece to *James Baldwin's Go Tell It on the Mountain: Historical and Critical Essays* (2006). In it he argues that the novel "deserves a central status as a pretext for the successful emergence of the American Civil Rights Movement" (13) and that the "simultaneous embrace and harsh critique of religion and the status of the Black Church in the novel is a site at which to bring together previously competing strands of critical debate in Baldwin studies: Baldwin as a novelist and Baldwin as political figure" (14).

What makes Norman's Baldwin scholarship refreshing, and why I begin this chapter with his work, is his willingness to take the time to work methodically through Baldwin's texts, offering new readings in conversation with old ones, putting Baldwin in conversation with other American writers and literary movements, and drawing our attention to neglected works. Norman does not use Baldwin as a synecdoche. Baldwin and his work do not stand in for a particular literary movement or intellectual stance or moment in time. Instead, Norman holds Baldwin and his work up to the scrutiny of close reading and sustained critical attention. In this way, he very much reflects the current field of Baldwin scholars.

Twenty-first century Baldwin scholars explore and engage in the rich possibilities that come from understanding Baldwin and his work as belonging to multiple traditions, sometimes contradictorily, but always simultaneously. There is a great deal of work on Baldwin being published right now, creating a rich critical field in which to work. The collections edited by Quentin Miller and Dwight McBride at the close of the twentieth century ushered Baldwin studies into the twenty-first century and set the stage for a Baldwin renaissance. The works discussed in this chapter, all published within the last ten years, give evidence of the enduring critical interest in Baldwin and his work. More important, these works suggest the direction Baldwin studies will take in the future—gone are articles that refute or reclaim Baldwin's blackness, that assert the importance of his homosexuality, that defend or deride his spirituality, that celebrate him as an essayist and disparage him as a novelist. Since 2001, critics have written about Baldwin in the contexts of American literature, queer literature, the civil rights movement, the Beat movement, the protest movement, the American essay tradition, and the blues tradition. We see in this period an outward expansion of black queer studies, with Baldwin at the center, as critics attempt to construct a usable past. There are more monographs than ever specifically on Baldwin and his work, but also an increasing number of works in which Baldwin is merely one of many players in a critical conversation. He is being considered alongside his literary peers and progeny with greater regularity. And this consideration is happening within black and ethnic studies, but also women's and gender studies, queer studies, and American studies, to name but a few critical arenas for Baldwin's work. Further evidence of this Baldwin renaissance can be found in the recent conferences held to consider his work and legacy: the James Baldwin Conference in 2009 at Suffolk University, and the James Baldwin's Global Imagination conference held in 2011 at New York University. In addition, nearly twenty-five dissertations published in the last decade feature Baldwin as their focus; many more feature Baldwin as a secondary focus or employ him as part of the project's critical apparatus.

While paying special attention to those critics who are extending conversations discussed in previous chapters, in this chapter I will also highlight those critics new to the conversation who are reshaping what we think of as Baldwin studies. What follows, I hope, is a useful introduction to Baldwin scholarship as it stands in the twenty-first century.

Not surprisingly, Baldwin continues to play a central role in the extension and continued theorizing of black queer studies. His work provides a space for the further development of black queer studies and the investigation of how black studies and queer studies intersect and inform each other. Scholars working with Baldwin in the context of black queer studies are both reexamining his most famous works and using him as a jumping-off point to theorize black queer studies more broadly.

Michael J. Cobb's 2001 essay "Pulpitic Publicity: James Baldwin and the Queer Uses of Religious Words" is a good example of the former critical move. Examining religious rhetoric in *Go Tell It on the Mountain*, Cobb's essay seeks to provide a counternarrative to several overly simplistic arguments in black studies and queer studies. He wants to complicate two commonplace critical notions. First, that African American religious rhetoric provides black culture a haven from a hostile world and, second, that religion offers little to our understanding of queer sexuality. Baldwin's use of religious rhetoric, as well as his discussions of race and sexuality, are always more complicated than this, Cobb argues.

Through a reading of John's conversion in *Go Tell It on the Mountain*, highlighting John's religious awakening as well as his imagining of the "violence and anguish of religion," Cobb argues convincingly for an understanding of "religious rhetoric that is not so much therapeutic as it is strategic." Characters like John, Cobb asserts, "learn to inflect, queerly, the normal religious rhetoric of Baldwin's world. They showcase the particular ways religious words can equip queers with a language that possesses enough 'normal' authority to provide the kinds of safety Baldwin attributed to religious words. The queer's use of the heterosexually dominant language, however, is not a gesture of accepting tenets of the resisting black church or even an appropriation of a white religious language for black use but, rather, an oblique deployment of the closest language of authority at hand" (287). Cobb encourages us to look beyond the oft-posited queer sexuality and religious rhetoric binary to see the accomplishment of *Go Tell It on the Mountain* more clearly. Baldwin doesn't give us the story of a religious conversion in order to avoid the story of a queer awakening, nor does he attempt to subvert the spiritual awakening of a queer character. Instead, and here is Cobb's point, Baldwin uses religious rhetoric to facilitate the queer narrative. "Queerness becomes the ambiguous 'It' of religion, of *Go Tell 'It' on the Mountain*, the It that must be told, however indirectly and violently. That is, 'our queer love is God'" (299). John doesn't convert to heterosexuality. Despite his use of religious rhetoric and his entrance into a very specific spiritual community, he remains a queer character. The seeming violence of his conversion, both physical and emotional, serves as a mask for his voice.

Cobb concludes, "When queers assume the safety of religious experience, although at the level of representation it might seem like violence, religious words actually endorse the queer's ability to be public" (302). I think Cobb quite usefully provides a space for discussions of religion *and* sex in Baldwin as mutually generative.

Douglas Field's 2004 essay, "Looking for Jimmy Baldwin: Sex, Privacy, and Black Nationalist Fervor," comes at the question of Baldwin and sexuality from a different angle. Acknowledging that Baldwin serves, for many writers and critics, as the most significant black gay American writer of the twentieth century, Field asks, "What happens when we go looking for Jimmy?" What happens if we challenge the taken-for-granted notions that Baldwin's sexuality has never been in question, that he is a direct descendant of gay writers like Wallace Thurman and Countee Cullen? For Field, "a closer examination of [Baldwin's] work reveals a myriad [of] ambiguities, contradictions and uncertainties that sit uneasily with his increasingly iconic status" (457).

Field asserts that the complexity of Baldwin's views on homosexuality has been obscured as critics have anointed him the progenitor of black queer studies. He cites Baldwin's portrayal of homosexuality primarily through bisexual men in interracial couplings, his critical (Field is careful not to use the term "homophobic") remarks on gay subculture, and his reticence on homosexuality in his essays as reasons why we need to delve back into the matter of Baldwin and sexuality. Lest we think Field seeks to unseat Baldwin from his central role in black queer studies, he assures us that "it is crucial to explore how Baldwin's views operate along complex circuits of desire that make his work more challenging—and therefore more interesting—than is often assumed" (458–59).

Field attempts to tease out the complex and problematic distinctions Baldwin made between the public and private sphere. Baldwin asserted repeatedly, particularly in the 1985 Goldstein interview, that sexuality is a private matter, a matter between himself and God. As a result, seemingly, Baldwin reserved the public forums of his essays for discussions of race rather than (homo)sexuality. And yet, as Field points out, Baldwin's novels, which certainly can't be construed as private communication, contain numerous depictions of homosexual and bisexual desire. To what should we attribute this paradox?

Field argues convincingly, through a summary of Baldwin's involvement in the civil rights movement, and of civil rights and black nationalist activists' opinions of him, that Baldwin (commonly referred to as Martin Luther Queen at the time) failed miserably to embody the prevailing notions of black masculinity. Both the civil rights movement and the Black Power movement looked with suspicion on gay black men and saw homosexuality as a threat to their movements. "Baldwin's move away from the subject of homosexuality came directly out of the criticism that he received by African-American writers such as Eldridge Cleaver; this in turn led to Baldwin's increasing anxiety over his role as both an artist and a spokesman" (466). As a result, Baldwin's essays became more strident, more mindful of his role as spokesman, which is to say, more focused on race and silent on sexuality.

Field reminds us, though, that even when Baldwin seemed to capitulate to black nationalist politics in his essays, he nonetheless remained committed to his ethos of love. Baldwin published *Tell Me How Long the Train's Been Gone* in 1968, the same year Cleaver published *Soul on Ice*, which contains the deeply homophobic screed against Baldwin, "Notes on a Native Son." Field contends that in *Tell Me How Long*, which is as public a statement as any of his essays, Baldwin attempted to "reconcile his sexuality with black radical politics" by hinting "at the ideal of an erotic and revolutionary black companionship" (471). Acknowledging the current resurgence in Baldwin scholarship, Field cautions critics to embrace, rather than resist or elide, Baldwin's complexity, however vexing.

Seeking to do just that and to "interanimate both black studies and queer studies," the essay collection *Black Queer Studies* (2005), "stages a dialogic and dialectic encounter between these two liberatory and interrogatory discourses" (Johnson and Henderson, 1). Growing out of the groundbreaking black queer studies conference held at UNC-Chapel Hill in 2000, the volume brings together leading scholars in black queer studies in an effort to make disciplinary and ideological boundaries more permeable. While Baldwin figures prominently in three of the collection's sixteen essays (the other two are by Mae G. Henderson and Maurice O. Wallace), I am most interested in Dwight A. McBride's contribution.

McBride's essay "Straight Black Studies: On African American Studies, James Baldwin, and Black Queer Studies" is both a criticism of African American Studies and an attempt to provide a "usable past" for black queer studies (68). The essay contains two assertions familiar to readers of McBride's work in volumes like *Why I Hate Abercrombie and Fitch* (2005). First, that cultural studies provides a particularly useful critical lens through which to view the complexity of Baldwin's work. This is the entire premise of *James Baldwin Now* (1999). Second, that the discipline of African American Studies, with its "limited embrace of race-centered bias, does so at the expense of other critical forms of difference that are also rightly constitutive of any inclusive understanding of black subjectivity" (72). As a result of this bias, McBride maintains, "the critical legacy regarding Baldwin's work has been relatively sparse when viewed in proportion to his voluminous contributions to African American letters" (73). While it is true that Baldwin occupies a surprisingly marginal role in African American literary criticism (though this is increasingly less true), I would hardly term his critical legacy "sparse." As I've demonstrated in the previous chapters, the critical center in Baldwin studies is difficult to find because the field is so disparate and diffuse. Baldwin belongs to many canons, as the criticism of his work suggests. Still, McBride does make an excellent point when he states that "cultural studies work and black queer studies work has shown that it is possible to think critically about African Americans and African American culture without simply essentializing the category of racial blackness, appealing to outmoded and problematic notions of an authentic blackness; or fixing, reifying, and/or separating race, gender, and/or sexuality in the name of their political serviceability to racial blackness" (74–75). What we see in this current period of Baldwin studies, particularly with those critics working with Baldwin as part of the African American literary canon, are deliberate efforts to avoid these missteps. The critics in this chapter seem to share with McBride the opinion that Baldwin and his work are especially useful in illuminating and teasing out these racial, sexual, gender, class, and cultural complexities.

Baldwin scholars are carrying this notion of the complexity of identities to their reframing of the Black Power movement and black nationalism. In *Black Manhood in James Baldwin, Ernest Gaines, and August Wilson* (2002), Keith Clark aims to counter the commonsense notion that "African-American men have been historically denied the power and privilege that should accrue to them based on their gender" (1), a central tenet of black nationalist thought in the 1960s and 1970s. Apart from the close readings of works he offers (of "Sonny's Blues" and *Just Above My Head*), Clark's overall project is important. In terms of Baldwin scholarship, Clark puts Baldwin in conversation with Gaines and Wilson, writers not often paired with Baldwin but whose work nonetheless offers compelling similarities and contrasts to Baldwin's. More generally, though, Clark's decidedly feminist approach to this period is refreshing not only because he is a male critic, but also because he has chosen to turn his critical attention to black male writers whose works are seemingly as interested in grappling with gender as they are with race.

Clark is interested in the ways works by "African-American male authors that thematically and narratologically foreground black men" grapple with "questions surrounding voice, gender, sexuality, community—in essence subjectivity" (3). Subjectivity is at the center of Clark's study, and Baldwin, Gaines, and Wilson are important because they can imagine a "subjectivity not exclusively tied to gender or gender privilege" (9). Here Clark attempts what McBride urges—a rearticulation of black subjectivity that doesn't depend on rigid notions of gender (or sex or race).

Rolland Murray is similarly interested in challenging black nationalist masculinist politics. *Our Living Manhood: Literature, Black Power, and Masculine Identity* (2007) looks at the work of writers like Baldwin, John Edgar Wideman, and John O. Killens, who in "fiction and essays written during the heyday of Black Power ... tracked the unevenness, political incoherence, and anxiety that beset nationalisms tethered to masculinist identity politics" (2). Like Robert Reid-Pharr (whose work, as noted below, continues to be important in Baldwin studies) and Philip Brian Harper, Murray reminds us that black nationalism was not a "cohesive totality but a set of identity claims that are always internally divided" (5).

Like a few critics during this period, Murray makes an effort to clarify Baldwin's post-1964 aesthetic and ideological positions. "Because critics have assumed Baldwin's alliance with the movement, neither his skepticism regarding nationalism nor his ambiguous ties to radical organizations such as the Black Panthers have been sufficiently examined" (13). Focusing his reading of Baldwin on *Just Above My Head*, Murray argues that "Baldwin allows us to begin telling an alternative story about the evolution of nationalism, one in which the instantiation of racial solidarity rooted in the masculine also produced its potential undoing" (39). Like Clark, Murray urges us to look to literature of the period, not just rhetoric, and to embrace rather than ignore competing and contradictory narratives. One of the major themes in current Baldwin scholarship is the usefulness of Baldwin's work in naming and working through complex notions of identity.

A trend I would like to see continue is critical interest in Baldwin's religious philosophy, or lack thereof. Contemporary criticism begins with a fairly conventional reading of religion and John's conversion in *Go Tell It on the Mountain*. Writing in *Christianity and Literature* in 2001, Miriam Sivan argues that though "John Grimes's commitment to Christ is representative of black assimilation into American (White) culture, this adoption of Christian beliefs not only helped the community forge a stronger connection to this country and society, but it also enabled slaves and then emancipated Africans to shore up their sense of self-worth and value" (30). There is nothing surprising in Sivan's article. Her reading of the black church and its role in the construction and maintenance of black identity is fairly conventional—that "African Americans found a way to blend their traditional form of worship with that of their new land" (31). Thus the Christian church became an empowering rather than assimilating institution for marginalized, disenfranchised black people. Baldwin's novel, according to Sivan, is a dramatized version of this "traditional American narrative of conversion and redemption" (31).

I offer Sivan's reading of *Go Tell It on the Mountain* not because I find it especially convincing, but because it is a good example of what McBride finds limiting in Baldwin studies, particularly where it intersects with African American Studies, and it stands in sharp contrast to the great strides Baldwin studies has taken in its reconsideration of religion. Rather than accepting as fact that Baldwin embraced an uncomplicated, empowering black church, critics currently focusing on Baldwin and religion ask us to think more broadly and more deeply about the nature of the religion Baldwin portrays in his work.

Both Clarence E. Hardy, III's *James Baldwin's God: Sex, Hope, and Crisis in Black Holiness Culture* (2003) and Douglas Field's article "Pentecostalism and All That Jazz: Tracing James Baldwin's Religion" (2008) try to get at the heart of Baldwin's theology by looking at the religion in his texts specifically rather than in the abstract. Hardy is intrigued by the "black holiness culture" represented in Baldwin's work because of the complexity there, and believes that unraveling that complexity will help in unraveling some of Baldwin's complexity. He argues that the ambiguous nature of Baldwin's relationship with Christian faith "represents the deepest methodological problems in interpreting the meaning(s) of Baldwin's connection to holiness culture" (9). Hardy seems to tackle this "methodological" problem by suggesting that the ambivalence Baldwin shows toward religion stems from the ambiguity of black holiness culture. Rather than the wholly liberatory institution that Sivan describes in her essay, Hardy reads this iteration of the "black church" as more compromised. He argues that the black Christian church has offered black people hope and strength in hard times, but it has also contributed to the "severe disfigurement of black people where many believed the lies about how 'ugly' it was to be black and wondered aloud whether our sufferings were divinely intended" (111). In other words, Baldwin's vexed relationship with the black church is perhaps inevitable considering the actual history of the church.

Douglas Field's superb article builds on Hardy's work by focusing specifically on Pentecostalism, the religion of Baldwin's childhood. Field does an excellent job of steering us away from the "black church," a term that works always to elide the historical and theological specificity and diversity of black religious institutions and their effects on black communities. He focuses our attention instead on the religious institution that played a significant role in shaping Baldwin's worldview, a worldview plainly evident in his work. Field wonders why, in this moment of intense critical energy around Baldwin and his work, so little attention is paid to religion. "In a critical era that is dominated on [*sic*] areas such as gender, masculinity and sexuality," he asks, "might it be that the sophistication of cultural studies is ill-equipped or simply unable to grapple with the religious?" (438). This is a question worth considering as cultural studies continues to be offered as the most useful critical lens through which to view Baldwin's multifaceted work, whereas religion continues to remain on the margins of Baldwin studies.

For his part Field rejects the notion that Baldwin rejected religion completely. Instead, Field argues, Baldwin works on developing a "notion of spirituality," defined here as Baldwin's "explorations of transcendence from outside the institution of the church. In Baldwin's writing transcendence or ecstasy frequently occurs outside of religious worship and is most likely to be formed in the communion of friends and lovers through playing or listening to music or making love" (438–39). (Field suggests here another gap in Baldwin studies: the influence of music in Baldwin's work, outside the short story "Sonny's Blues.") Field asserts that Baldwin's notion of spirituality stems directly from the tenets of his boyhood church, but ultimately cannot exist within its structures.

Field states that the defining feature of the Pentecostal church's identity and the identity of its members is exile. Its belief in the power of the holy spirit to heal the sick, its acceptance of untrained ministers and storefront churches, and the practice of speaking in tongues, all contributed to the Pentecostal church's exile from mainstream Protestantism. Field sees in Baldwin's work the influence of this identification with exile, as well as the church's efforts to "preserve or restate what was believed to be the oldtime religion" (442). In Field's reading of Baldwin, the less celebrated novels—*Just Above My Head, Tell Me How Long the Train's Been Gone,* and *If Beale Street Could Talk*—become important because they reveal Baldwin's development of an anti-institutional spirituality, particularly in the figure of the (gospel) musician. As Field states, "*Just Above My Head* is an important novel, not least because it suggests the ways in which Baldwin was becoming, not less secular, but more acutely aware of the need to distinguish between institutionalized religion and the spiritual authenticity, a point illustrated through the character of Florence," who doesn't go to church because the people there have lost their religion (449).

Field's essay is also notable because he foregrounds Baldwin's notion of love. Contemporary Baldwin studies pays scant attention to Baldwin's love ethic, but Field asserts that it is central to understanding Baldwin's spirituality. He reminds us that Baldwin did not confuse love with sentimentality; instead his definition of love is "explicitly active and political." Instead of salvation and redemption through God, Baldwin emphasizes salvation and redemption through "a love that is founded on the sharing of pain," which Baldwin often represents through physical and spiritual touch (450–51). According to Field, Baldwin is arguing that if we can stop insisting on our own and others' spiritual and physical purity, if we can live with our own pain and respect the pain of others, then and only then might we attain some redemption. With this essay, Field has set the stage for a retheorizing of love and religion that could yield new and compelling arguments about Baldwin's other less studied works.

Also hoping to carve out new critical space is Meredith M. Malburne in "No Blues for Mr. Henry: Locating Richard's Revolution" (2007). This essay is part of a collection edited by Trudier Harris and Jennifer Larson on contemporary African American drama. Malburne takes aim at Baldwin's 1964 play *Blues for Mister Charlie* and attempts to "save Richard Henry from literary oblivion, since he cannot, after all, be saved from death" (39). She argues for the importance of this critically neglected character, claiming that we "must see Richard as both the object of significant historical weight and the small but significant seed of potential revolution." He is more than a "stereotypical provocateur, a cardboard cut-out whose final telos is nothing more than a meaningless death at the hands of a white bigot" (39). In Richard Henry, Malburne says, Baldwin gives us a character who makes choices and pays the price for them, and in so doing influences a revolution. Rereadings like this one not only shed new light on Baldwin's work but also open up space for a reconsideration of African American literature generally, particularly African American literature of the so-called protest era. Whereas a critic like Kenneth W. Warren claims in *What Was African American Literature?* that African American literature during this era was written primarily in response to white racism and oppression, work like Malburne's reminds us that African American writing was never simply reactionary, was always much more than protest.

Critics are also attempting to reframe Baldwin's neglected work, particularly overlooked essays and short stories. As a new generation of critics takes for granted Baldwin's significance and his "canon," they are turning their attention to those aspects of Baldwin that have received little attention in the past.

Steven Weisenburger's "The Shudder and the Silence: James Baldwin on White Terror" (2002) offers a persuasive close reading of "Going to Meet the Man," a work that editors are increasingly choosing to represent Baldwin's short fiction in anthologies. Weisenburger reads the short story as a lynching story and positions his reading in dialogue with other treatments of "literary and testamentary representations of lynching" (3). He wishes to "use and to supplement" readings of lynching as "recuperative fantasmatic" and/or as "sacrificial rites" to offer a reading that considers lynching in its historical context (3). For Weisenburger this means considering the literal, physical facts of lynching (and other kinds of racial violence) and what those facts mean in the context of American racial thinking in the first half of the twentieth century. In short, he reads the "shudders" in the story, Jesse's physical reactions to the repugnance of blackness, as the impetus for racial violence. The monstrous blackness must be destroyed. These shudders, and their consequences, in turn, produce the silence and absence of blacks, as they attempt literally to remove themselves from the threat of that violence. I find this reading compelling because it takes care to attend to the bodies in Baldwin's work. Physical experiences are often as important as emotional and psychological experiences in Baldwin's fiction, and this essay provides a good model for reading those experiences.

James Miller, in a 2008 article, considers Baldwin's "Paris essays": "Encounter on the Seine: Black Meets Brown" (1950), "Stranger in the Village" (1953), "A Question of Identity" (1954), "Equal in Paris" (1955), "Princes and Powers" (1956), "The Discovery of What It Means to Be an American" (1959), and the "New Lost Generation" (1961). Miller asserts that previous criticism typically focused on Baldwin's relationship with Wright during the 1950s, and contemporary criticism seems most interested in queer identity and postmodern theory (a claim not entirely true, as this chapter indicates). He makes the claim that Baldwin's concepts of identity and citizenship are formed in these essays and in Europe and thus deserve more sustained critical attention. Taking seriously Baldwin's status as an expatriate and reading the Paris essays as articulations of Baldwin's experience of expatriation, Miller argues that Baldwin was able to "shed what he felt to be an oppressive and imposed 'Negro' identity and embrace a much more emancipated and individuated sense of himself as an American. Intrinsic to this new sense of himself was his realization that he shared an experience of alienation common to all Americans" (53). Notably, though Miller argues that looking at Baldwin's work as a whole "one can only conclude he is a deeply pessimistic writer," the Paris essays, written early in his career, are more hopeful. They represent Baldwin at his "most optimistic. He envisages an America transformed by recognition and inclusion of the African American citizen within the body politic" (66).

Magdalena J. Zaborowska, *James Baldwin's Turkish Decade: Erotics of Exile* (2009), continues with the theme of expatriation. It is also of fundamental biographical importance, as it offers new details and new photographs of Baldwin's life outside the United States. Zaborowska foregrounds the connections to and influences of Turkey in Baldwin's work: he revised and finished *Another Country* in Turkey and he wrote *No Name in the Street* and began the *Welcome Table* there. Indeed, Zaborowska claims that Baldwin's "engagements with his and his friends' interpretations of Turkish notions of sociability helped him not only to establish his art as his home and hearth in the world, but also to claim femininity and queer and transgender subjectivities as artistic inspirations" (xxiv). Given this reappraisal of Baldwin's expatriation, Zaborowska urges a reevaluation of neglected works.

Lynn Orilla Scott attempts this task in *Witness to the Journey: James Baldwin's Later Fiction* (2002). Scott takes up where Miller leaves off, that period in which Baldwin's tone seems to shift. Her book looks at three novels—*Tell Me How Long the Train's Been Gone, If Beale Street Could Talk*, and *Just Above My Head*. She argues that "Baldwin's later writing is of particular interest because of the way it traverses the cultural divide between the fifties and the sixties. Baldwin's writing is a much more sophisticated negotiation of the rapidly changing politics of 'difference' than has previously been acknowledged" (xiv). Perhaps this new sophistication accounts for the pessimism that Miller reads in Baldwin's work after the Paris essays. The three themes connecting these novels are "the role of family in sustaining the artist; the price of success in American society; and the struggle of the black artist to change the ways race and sex are represented in American culture" (xxiii). Scott's argument connects nicely back to earlier criticism that privileged the artist as the central figure in Baldwin's work. In addition it maintains a critical space for close readings for Baldwin as novelist, even as contemporary scholarship works to place him in multiple intellectual traditions.

In addition to charting new territory in Baldwin studies, contemporary critics are also revisiting key ideas in Baldwin scholarship. Michael Nowlin, "Ralph Ellison, James Baldwin, and the Liberal Imagination" (2004) attempts to foreground the very specific ideological and aesthetic milieu in which Ellison and Baldwin began their careers. He cites the first essay of Lionel Trilling's *The Liberal Imagination*, "Reality in America" (1950), as a succinct articulation of the aesthetic judgment driving the (white) audience in its praise of Baldwin and Ellison. Basically, Trilling dismisses left-wing naturalist fiction like that of Theodore Dresier, cites Henry James as a writer of significantly better quality, and, according to Nowlin, sets the stage for a "loose community of white, largely Jewish, New York-based intellectuals" to lavish uncritical praise on Ellison and Baldwin (117). In this context, Nowlin goes on to read Irving Howe's "Black Boys and Native Sons" (1963), which argued that Wright and *Native Son* "brought out into the open, as no one ever had before, the hatred, fear and violence that have crippled and may yet destroy our culture" (Howe, "Black Boys and Native Sons," 256) as an essay on the "politics of canon formation" (Nowlin, 117). Howe's essay becomes, then, not just a defense of Wright in the face of Baldwin and Ellison's growing popularity with leftist intellectuals. For Nowlin, the essay is also a critique of a "seemingly widespread willingness on the part of adversarial intellectuals to embrace the possibilities of Americanism" (117).

Aside from the reframing of Howe's seminal essay and a reconsideration of the real influence Henry James had on both Ellison and Baldwin (Nowlin, 124), Nowlin's article stands out for its insistence on contextualizing the work of these two writers in the larger American intellectual tradition. For while we often pay lip service to the fact that Baldwin (and Ellison) were published early in their careers in leftist magazines and that they were championed by leftist intellectuals, Nowlin is correct when he states that "this political and aesthetic milieu is too generally downplayed and unobserved. This owes something, on the one hand, to critical paradigms committed to creating and explicating a specifically African American literary tradition (with a concomitant emphasis on difference and strategies of critical subversion) and, on the other hand, to a critical preoccupation with the Jewishness and/or left-of-center political movement of the New York intellectuals" (134, note

4). Nowlin urges a reconsideration of the critical reception of African American intellectual thought and expressive culture, and of how that reception continues to influence, for good or ill, contemporary criticism. Critics like Nowlin, McBride, and others discussed in this chapter not only read Baldwin as belonging to multiple traditions, but they also find him a useful vehicle through which to argue against limited notions of African American literature.

In "Three Lean Cats in a Hall of Mirrors: James Baldwin, Norman Mailer, and Eldridge Cleaver on Race and Masculinity" (2010), Douglas Taylor revisits several instances of call and response between these three writers. More specifically, he is interested in Baldwin's responses to Mailer's "The White Negro" and Cleaver's *Soul on Ice*, responses found explicitly in "The Black Boy Looks at the White Boy" and, less explicitly, in *Another Country*. Ultimately Taylor concludes that Baldwin fails in "The Black Boy Looks at the White Boy" because the essay fails to "disentangle itself from the masculinist presuppositions it attempts to critique.... *Another Country*, on the other hand, can be read as both a highly effective response to Mailer's 'White Negro' and a more complex rendering of the racial and sexual dimensions of the same US social imaginary that Cleaver attempts to map six years later in *Soul on Ice*" (97).

Taylor's excellent piece stands out not just because of what it argues, but also for the way Taylor constructs his argument. Like Rolland Murray and Keith Clark, Taylor's interest in Baldwin lies in part in his interest in reframing black masculinity as an identity that "acquires meaning within a social-relational framework, a semiotic grid in which white masculinities and black and white femininity also feature prominently" (98). Baldwin can be used in this way by Taylor and other critics because of the familiarity with Baldwin that Baldwin critics assume readers have. Taylor doesn't remind his reader of the plot of *Another Country* or offer long passages from the novel. He assumes you've read enough Baldwin to keep up. (In contrast, he quotes extensively from Mailer and Cleaver, presumably because he assumes the reader is less familiar with these works.) In addition, by treating Mailer's and Cleaver's work as theoretical texts defining masculinity rather than (simply) racist and homophobic polemics, Baldwin's work becomes something more than simply "protest" in response. Taylor's work is indicative of the way contemporary critics no longer write to a variety of skeptical audiences that need convincing of Baldwin's importance. Critics are now confident of being received by a community of Baldwin scholars for whom Baldwin's theoretical and aesthetic significance is a given.

This is very much the case with *Once You Go Black: Choice, Desire, and the Black American Intellectual* (2007). From the provocative picture of a young, shirtless Huey P. Newton gracing the book cover, to the opening chapter in which the author Robert Reid-Pharr coyly refers to himself in the third person, *Once You Go Black* promises more of the provocative and intensely theoretical criticism he is known for. Part autobiography, part literary history, part critical theory, *Once You Go Black* takes aim at commonsense notions about the tradition of black cultural production. The project, Reid-Pharr writes, "resists notions of a profound black tradition that not only underwrites but dictates contemporary black cultural production" precisely because these "same ideas underwrite logics of segregation and apartheid" (14). Reid-Pharr wants to assert the idea of blackness as choice rather than birthright or burden.

He gets there, primarily, by looking at the work of the triumvirate so central to Baldwin studies: Baldwin, Ellison, and Wright. Their work, he argues, rejects "the notion of the black as innocent and instead insist[s] upon his modernity and thus responsibility within modern society. In so doing they challenge notions of an already decided black identity." They "suggest in their works that black identity, if it is to exist at all, must be chosen by contemporary generations of Americans" and that, if blackness is to have any future, black intellectuals "must create models of black articulation that do not turn on the erroneous assumptions of profound racial distinction" (33).

In focusing on Wright, Baldwin, Ellison, and, later, Newton and Melvin Van Peebles, Reid-Pharr acknowledges that his study "partakes in a suspect, if not altogether outmoded, literary historical method built around great men and their great books" (37). That said, his treatment of Baldwin is really a treatment of the reception of Baldwin, particularly the familiar "perplexing notion of the artist in decline" (99). Taking up *Just Above My Head*, a novel that has quickly, if belatedly, become a favorite with Baldwin critics, Reid-Pharr acknowledges, but challenges, the almost universal assessment of it as a failed novel because it rehashes old, worn themes. He argues that in this novel Baldwin plays a "trick" on the reader by "reestablishing early themes in this late novel even as he insists that those themes can no longer sustain either the artist or the communities that produced the artist" (101). Reid-Pharr rejects the already assumed connection between the black intellectual and the black community (and, thus, challenges much of the work of this Baldwin renaissance, particularly the work establishing a black queer intellectual tradition). If the black intellectual does not have a "real option to reject the other (because he is not distinct from the other), then he also has no real option to embrace" (101).

And for Reid-Pharr this notion of choice is key. In reading *Just Above My Head* as engaging in the American birthright of "forgetting," he argues that Baldwin highlights "an active relationship to one's history, an agency established on the ability to start from scratch, as it were, to re-member, in the fullest sense of the word, to maintain a consciousness of self and community that allows one to survive with one's neighbor whether that neighbor stinks of hate or not. This is perhaps the primary manner in which Black American persons can be said to be engaged in a constant process of choosing blackness, choosing a relationship to American history that privileges critique without insisting upon the destruction of either state or society" (104). Baldwin is useful to Reid-Pharr, as he is for McBride and Taylor, as a model of critical engagement with the world around us. Reid-Pharr and others like him are attempting to map the intellectual path Baldwin laid out more than half a century ago.

James Darsey, in "James Baldwin's Topoi" (2004), states that a "cosmopolitan rhetoric would be a rhetoric created by those ... who have 'left home,' who have been alienated, sometimes multiply alienated, who have lost, left, or forgotten their place yet who somehow found new, transcendent places or struggled toward such places, and from these new places served as compelling moral spokespersons on significant public issues—rhetors who found a way, despite their displacement, to take a position" (9). I can think of no better description of James Baldwin the artist or contemporary Baldwin studies. In many ways, twenty-first century Baldwin criticism, so far, abandons most efforts to "place" Baldwin in favor of efforts to better engage his "cosmopolitan rhetoric," that is, engage the multiple positions he takes and occupies without insisting on their fixity. This impulse in Baldwin scholars promises to yield a body of criticism rich and complex for many years to come.

Conclusion

Even in this current moment of Baldwin scholarship, in which many critics find Baldwin useful in exploring, expanding, and revising ideas in a wide variety of intellectual traditions, I still find him most helpful in thinking through questions of race. Perhaps that is no surprise—I am a scholar of African American literature and spend most of my intellectual life grappling with writers who have themselves grappled with the persistent and perplexing conundrum of race. It is also, though, the fact that Baldwin's words continue to resonate. A decade into the twenty-first century, the old hurts and fears remain, and Baldwin's thoughts on race are as relevant now as they were sixty years ago.

In 1956 Baldwin penned an essay in response to William Faulkner's plea to civil rights activists to "Go slow now. Stop now for a time, a moment" (Faulkner, 51). Writing in *Partisan Review*, Baldwin begins, "Any real change implies the breakup of the world as one has always known it, the loss of all that gave one an identity, the end of safety. And at such a moment, unable to see and not daring to imagine what the future will now bring forth, one clings to what one knew, or thought one knew; to what one possessed or dreamed that one possessed" (209). That essay is nearly sixty years old now, and was Baldwin's attempt to explain the "minds and hearts of white Southerners" as they violently resisted the call for integration. It could easily have been written today, just weeks after the United States reelected its first black president, an event that caused many pundits to lament that the "white establishment is now the minority" (Weinger, "Bill O'Reilly").

When I first began this book, the United States was in the middle of a historic political campaign. Barack Obama and Hillary Clinton were competing for the Democratic nomination for the 2008 presidential race. Before the contest was even decided, Americans agreed that this political season told us a lot about who we were as a nation and who we hoped to become. We congratulated ourselves for a presidential race that didn't default to two white men, for getting all kinds of Americans excited about the democratic process once again. We already remember this campaign as one that moved the country a little further down the path of racial reconciliation. But, perhaps paradoxically, we will also remember this campaign for revealing the continued racial tensions that still lay just below the surface of the American political and social fabric.

One of the most (though certainly not the only) powerful instances of this racial tension were tapes of Reverend Jeremiah Wright, former pastor of Trinity United Church of Christ in Chicago and Barack Obama's spiritual adviser, which began to make the news cycle in spring 2008. In them, Wright stands at the pulpit on various Sundays, delivering fiery jeremiad after jeremiad accusing America of neglect of the poor and brown in this country, claiming that the 9/11 attacks were "American chickens come home to roost," and exhorting that the continued legacy of racism should have us shouting "God Damn America" rather than "God Bless America." Given the twenty-four-hour news networks' constant need for controversy and the lull between the Texas and Ohio primaries and the primary in Pennsylvania, it is easy to understand why and how this story got so much play. Wright was quickly labeled a racist and unpatriotic, and Obama, the pundits maintained, would almost certainly suffer by association. How could Obama's campaign, the success of which seemed to hinge on his racial transcendence and the multiracial coalition gathered around him, possibly survive this debacle, the pundits asked. Wasn't he, by association with Wright, participating in exactly the kind of racial animosity that the very existence of his campaign told us was in the past?

The Wright controversy was one more in a long line of racially charged skirmishes in the Democratic primary race. And on March 18, 2008 Obama gave the speech he seemed to be inevitably working toward since his Iowa caucus win, the speech many hoped would be his response to King's "I Have a Dream" speech. Taking to the stage in Philadelphia to explain his relationship to Rev. Wright, but also to talk to Americans about race, Obama urged us toward "A More Perfect Union." He urged us to think of America as a place that rewards the "audacity of hope," to understand that a single moment of recognition between any one black person and any one white person by itself is not enough, but it is, nonetheless, "where the perfection begins" (Obama).

It seemed natural to turn to Baldwin's words in the wake of the fallout, as Obama severed his relationship with Wright, as he kept his eyes on the prize of the White House. In my attempts to process what until that moment had been an impossibility (a viable black presidential candidacy), I found myself doing what so many other critics and academics have done—using Baldwin as a theoretical frame, as a means of organizing my own ideas. I found myself going back to "Notes of a Native Son." One can imagine that Baldwin spent many Sundays listening to sermons, delivered by his father, steeped in the same black jeremiad tradition as Rev. Wright's. No doubt many of those sermons expressed similar themes of black frustration and anger and deep suspicion about America's goodwill. No doubt Baldwin delivered such sermons himself as a child preacher. What relationship does Baldwin the writer have to that tradition?

In "Notes" Baldwin expresses a deep, troubled, complicated affection for his father. He comes to some clarity about why his father always seemed so angry, but he can't come to the same conclusions about America and the human condition as his father. In other words, Baldwin understands exactly why his father is bitter and miserable and mean, he sees how American racism has beat him down; Baldwin experienced that same racism himself, but he couldn't give in to that same bitterness. The relationship between black and white Americans is far too complicated for that. Baldwin writes,

> In order to really hate white people, one has to blot so much out of the mind—and the heart—that this hatred itself becomes an exhausting and self-destructive pose. But this does not mean, on the other hand, that love comes easily: the white world is too powerful, too complacent, too ready with gratuitous humiliation, and, above all, too ignorant and too innocent for that. One is absolutely forced to make perpetual qualifications and one's own reactions are always canceling each other out. It is this, really, which has driven so many people mad, both white and black. One is always in the position of having to decide between amputation and gangrene. Amputation is swift but time may prove that amputation was not necessary—or one may delay the amputation too long. Gangrene is slow, but it is impossible to be sure that one is reading one's symptoms right. The idea of going through life as a cripple is more than one can bear, and equally unbearable is the risk of swelling up slowly, in agony, with poison. And the trouble, finally, is that the risks are real even if the choices do not exist. ("Notes," 82–83)

Baldwin emerged from his father's tradition not as a nationalist, but as a man committed to a fully integrated nation, all the while acknowledging the painful process necessary to get there. At every turn he urged his readers, all of them, to change the nature of the American conversation on race. He doesn't want us to forget the anger or hide the pain or pretend that the tensions didn't exist. Rather, we are to recognize that we all must ultimately move forward from the anger. And I would argue that Baldwin can come to this conclusion precisely because he spent his childhood and young adulthood (about the same number of years Obama spent in Wright's church) watching his father recede further and further into his own anger. Ultimately, it "was necessary to hold on to the things that mattered. [His father] mattered, [the new baby] mattered; blackness and whiteness did not matter; to believe they did was to acquiesce in one's own destruction. Hatred, which could destroy so much, never failed to destroy the man who hated and this was an immutable law" ("Notes," 83–84).

I also went back to the two long essays published together as *The Fire Next Time*. In the second Baldwin writes about meeting with the Nation of Islam just as it is gaining national notoriety. Baldwin expresses great sympathy for their ideas, ideas that are quite similar to Rev. Wright's. He writes, "Things are as bad as the Muslims say they are—in fact, they are worse, and the Muslims do not help matters—but there is no reason that black men should be expected to be more patient, more forbearing, more farseeing than whites; indeed, quite the contrary" ("Down at the Cross," 320–21). Baldwin understands, as I believe Obama does, why black people (or poor people or women or Muslims or any group of marginalized people in this country) would be angry, would regularly refer to this country as "God Damn America," would not see themselves as, or desire to be, part of the larger culture. Yet, again, that knowledge doesn't bring Baldwin, or Obama, to the same place as the Nation of Islam.

> Yet I could have hoped that the Muslim movement had been able to inculcate in the demoralized Negro population a truer and more individual sense of its own worth, so that Negroes in the Northern ghettoes could begin, in concrete terms, and at whatever price, to change their situation. But in order to change a situation one has first to see it for what it is: in the present case, to accept the fact, whatever one does with it thereafter, that the Negro has been formed by this nation, for better or for worse, and does not belong to any other—not to Africa, and certainly not to Islam. The paradox—and a fearful paradox it is—is that the American Negro can have no future anywhere, on any continent, as long as he is unwilling to accept his past. To accept one's past—one's history—is not the same thing as drowning in it; it is learning how to use it. An invented past can never be used; it cracks and crumbles under the pressure of life like clay in a season of drought. ("Down at the Cross," 333)

Baldwin ultimately determines that only a full accounting of America's past and a clear-eyed understanding of America's present can move us hopefully into America's future. In the first essay in *Fire Next Time*, a letter to his nephew, Baldwin writes, "if the word integration means anything, this is what it means: that we, with love, shall force our brothers to see themselves as they are, to cease fleeing from reality and begin to change it. For this is your home, my friend, do not be driven from it; great men have done great things here, and will again, and we can make American what America must become" ("Dungeon," 294).

I don't offer this reading of Baldwin and Obama to argue that Obama is an inheritor of Baldwin's legacy, or to argue that we subscribe to either man's vision of America. I offer this reading as a reminder of what can get lost in a project like this: the man himself, and his work. Any rereading of Baldwin, even now, nearly thirty years after his death, makes one thing abundantly clear. Baldwin is always talking about *us*: blacks, Americans, writers, the marginalized, ex-pats, readers, sons and daughters, brothers and sisters, lovers. His words resonate with us still because of the honesty he brought to bear on his own work and life. In the "Autobiographical Notes" of *Notes of Native Son* he writes that part of the "business of the writer is to ... examine attitudes, to go beneath the surface, to tap the source" (7). His unflinching, uncompromising efforts to tap the source—of himself, of the Negro problem, of the American myth, of human dignity and love—are as relevant today as they were when first published.

Baldwin, particularly in those early essays when he seems the most lucid, the most in control of his craft, the most committed to thinking through American race relations in public, offers us an understanding of American history and culture that can help move us out of our current racial stalemate. It would be wrong to reduce Baldwin to a writer who wrote only or simply about race. Indeed, any field that aims to articulate the complexities of social identities and the societies they exist in—feminist studies, disability studies, human rights advocacy, queer theory—will find an intellectual comrade in Baldwin. Yet because our country is still full of people more comfortable with evasion and amnesia than they are with one another, and because we, in many ways, are a country still choosing between gangrene and amputation, the honesty and clarity with which Baldwin addresses these issues still resonate. Critics and readers and teachers will continue to come back to him, will continue to read and reread him because he asks the questions we can't quite articulate, mines the places we find too dark and scary and painful.

Full-Length Works by James Baldwin

Go Tell It on the Mountain (1953).
Notes of a Native Son (1955).
Giovanni's Room (1956).
Nobody Knows My Name: More Notes of a Native Son (1961).
Another Country (1962).
The Fire Next Time (1963).
Blues for Mister Charlie (1964).
Nothing Personal (with photographs by Richard Avedon) (1964).
Going to Meet the Man (1965).
The Amen Corner (1968).
Tell Me How Long the Train's Been Gone (1968).
A Rap on Race (with Margaret Mead) (1971).
No Name in the Street (1972).
One Day When I Was Lost: A Scenario Based on Alex Haley's "The Autobiography of Malcolm X" (1972).
A Dialogue (with Nikki Giovanni) (1973).
If Beale Street Could Talk (1974).
The Devil Finds Work (1976).
Little Man, Little Man: A Story of Childhood (1976).
Just Above My Head (1979).
Jimmy's Blues: Selected Poems (1983).
The Evidence of Things Not Seen (1985).
The Price of the Ticket: Collected Nonfiction, 1948–1985 (1985).

Works Cited

Abram, M. H. *A Glossary of Literary Terms.* Boston: Thomson Wadsworth, 2005.
Albert, Richard N. "The Jazz-Blues Motif in James Baldwin's 'Sonny's Blues.'" *College Literature* 11 (1984): 178–85.
Aldridge, John W. "The Fire Next Time?" Review of *If Beale Street Could Talk* by James Baldwin. *Saturday Review,* June 15, 1974, 20+.
Allen, Shirley S. "Religious Symbolism and Psychic Reality in Baldwin's *Go Tell It on the Mountain.*" *College Language Association Journal* 19 (1975): 173–99.
Amiel, Barbara. "A 597-Page Doom." Review of *Just Above My Head* by James Baldwin. *Maclean's,* October 1, 1979, 54–55.
Anderson, Jervis. "Blurred Reflections on Hollywood." Review of *The Devil Finds Work* by James Baldwin. *New Leader,* May 24, 1976, 18–19.
Andrews, William L., Frances Smith Foster, and Trudier Harris, eds. *Oxford Companion to African American Literature.* New York: Oxford University Press, 1997.
"Ashes." Review of *No Name in the Street* by James Baldwin. *Time,* May 29, 1972, 83–84.
Baker, Houston. *Blues, Ideology, and Afro-American Literature: A Vernacular Theory.* Chicago: University of Chicago Press, 1987.
Baldwin, James. *James Baldwin: Collected Essays.* New York: Library of America, 1998.
―――. *James Baldwin: Early Novels and Stories.* New York: Library of America, 1998.
Barksdale, Richard K. "Temple of the Fire Baptized." Review of *Go Tell It on the Mountain* by James Baldwin. *Phylon* 14 (1953): 326–27.
Beam, Joseph, ed. *In the Life: A Black Gay Anthology,* 2nd ed. Washington, DC: RedBone Press, 2008.
Bell, George E. "The Dilemma of Love in *Go Tell It on the Mountain* and *Giovanni's Room.*" *College Language Association Journal* 17 (1974): 397–406.
Bell, Pearl K. "Roth and Baldwin Coming Home." Review of *Just Above My Head* by James Baldwin. *Commentary,* December 1979, 72–75.
Bigsby, C. W. *The Black American Writer: Volume 1: Fiction.* Baltimore: Penguin, 1969.
Bloom, Harold, ed. *James Baldwin.* New York: Chelsea House, 1986.
Blount, Marcellus, and George P. Cunningham, eds. *Representing Black Men.* New York: Routledge, 1996.

Bobia, Rosa. *The Critical Reception of James Baldwin in France*. New York: Peter Lang, 1997.
Bond, Jean Carey. "Grand Themes Sparingly Touched." Review of *The Fire Next Time* by James Baldwin. *Freedomways* (Spring 1963): 235–37.
Bone, Robert. *The Negro Novel in America*. 1958. Revised edition, New Haven: Yale University Press, 1965.
Breit, Harvey. "James Baldwin and Two Footnotes." In *The Creative Present: Notes on Contemporary American Fiction*, edited by Nona Balakian and Charles Simmons, 5–23. New York: Doubleday, 1963.
Bruck, Peter. "Dungeon and Salvation: Biblical Rhetoric in James Baldwin's *Just Above My Head*." In *History and Tradition in Afro-American Culture*, edited by Gunter H. Lenz, 130–46. Frankfurt: Campus, 1984.
———. "Protest, Universality, Blackness: Patterns of Argumentation in the Criticism of the Contemporary Afro-American Novel." In *The Afro-American Novel since 1960*, edited by Peter Bruck, 130–46. Amsterdam: Gruner, 1982.
Brunn, Robert. "About People—Who Are Also Negroes." Review of *Go Tell It on the Mountain* by James Baldwin. *The Christian Science Monitor*, May 28, 1953, 13.
———. "In a Negro's Shoes." Review of *Notes of a Native Son* by James Baldwin. *Christian Science Monitor*, December 16, 1955, 13.
Brustein, Robert. "Everybody Knows My Name." Review of *Nothing Personal* by James Baldwin and Richard Avedon. *New York Review of Books*, December 17, 1964, 10–11.
Bryant, Jerry H. Review of *The Devil Finds Work* by James Baldwin. *The Nation*, July 3, 1976, 25–27.
———. "Wright, Ellison, Baldwin—Exorcising the Demon." *Phylon* 37, no. 1 (1976): 174–88.
Burks, Mary Fair. "James Baldwin's Protest Novel: *If Beale Street Could Talk*." *Negro American Literature Forum* 10 (1976): 83–95.
Butler, Judith. *Bodies That Matter*. New York: Routledge, 1993.
Byam, Milton S. Review of *Notes of a Native Son* by James Baldwin. *Library Journal*, November 15, 1955, 2602.
Byerman, Keith E. "Words and Music: Narrative Ambiguity in 'Sonny's Blues.'" *Studies in Short Fiction* 19 (1982): 367–72.
Campbell, Finley. "More Notes of a Native Son." Review of *Nobody Knows My Name* by James Baldwin. *Phylon* 23, no. 1 (1962): 96–97.
Campbell, James. *Talking at the Gates: A Life of James Baldwin*. Berkeley: University of California Press, 1991.
Cederstrom, Lorelei. "Love, Race, and Sex in the Novels of James Baldwin." *Mosaic* 17, no. 2 (1984): 175–88.
Chametzky, Jules. *Black Writers Redefine the Struggle: A Tribute to James Baldwin: Proceedings from a Conference at the University of Massachusetts, Amherst, April 22–23, 1989*. Amherst, Mass: Institute for Advanced Study in the Humanities, 1989.

Champion, Ernest. "James Baldwin and the Challenge of Ethnic Literature in the Eighties." *MELUS* 8, no. 2 (1981): 61–64.
Charney, Maurice. "James Baldwin's Quarrel with Richard Wright." *American Quarterly* 15 (1963): 65–75.
Clark, Keith. *Black Manhood in James Baldwin, Ernest J. Gaines, and August Wilson*. Urbana: University of Illinois Press, 2002.
Clark, Michael. "James Baldwin's 'Sonny Blues': Childhood, Light, and Art." *College Language Association Journal* 29 (1985): 197–205.
Cleaver, Eldridge. *Soul on Ice*. New York: McGraw-Hill, 1968.
Cobb, M. L. "Pulpitic Publicity: James Baldwin and the Queer Uses of Religious Words." *GLQ: A Journal of Lesbian and Gay Studies* 7, no. 2 (2001): 285–312.
Coles, Robert. "Baldwin's Burden." *Partisan Review* 31 (1964): 409–16.
Collins, Lisa Gail, and Margo Natalie Crawford, eds. *New Thoughts on the Black Arts Movement*. New Brunswick: Rutgers University Press, 2006.
Cook, Bruce. Review of *One Day When I Was Lost: A Scenario Based on Alex Haley's "The Autobiography of Malcolm X"* by James Baldwin. *Commonweal*, October 12, 1973, 46–47.
Cooley, Margaret. Review of *Nothing Personal* by James Baldwin and Richard Avedon. *Library Journal*, December 15, 1964, 4925.
Cornish, Sam. "Baldwin Books Take Provocative Look at Blacks in America." Review of *Evidence of Things Not Seen* and *The Price of the Ticket* by James Baldwin. *Christian Science Monitor* [Boston], December 6, 1985, 40.
Crenshaw, Kimberle. "Demarginalizing the Intersection of Race and Sex: A Black Feminist Critique of Antidiscrimination Doctrine, Feminist Theory, and Antiracist Politics." In *Living with Contradictions Controversies in Feminist Social Ethics*, edited by Alison M. Jaggar, 39–52. Boulder, CO: Westview Press, 1994.
Cross, John. "Day of Wrath." *The New Statesman*, July 19, 1963, 79.
Crouch, Stanley. "Clichés of Degradation." Review of *Just Above My Head* by James Baldwin. *The Village Voice*, October 29, 1979, 39.
Dance, Daryl. "James Baldwin." In *Black American Writers: Bibliographical Essays*, vol 2, *Richard Wright, Ralph Ellison, James Baldwin, and Amiri Baraka*, edited by M. Thomas Inge, Maurice Duke, Jackson R. Bryer, 73–120. New York: St. Martin Press, 1978.
Darsey, James. "James Baldwin's Topoi." In *New Approaches to Rhetoric*, edited by Steven R. Goldzwig and Patricia Ann Sullivan, 5–29. Thousand Oaks, CA: Sage, 2004.
Davenport, Guy. "If These Wings Should Fail Me, Lord!" Review of *Tell Me How Long the Train's Been Gone* by James Baldwin. *National Review*, July 16, 1968, 701.
DeGout, Yasmin Y. "Dividing the Mind: Contradictory Portraits of Homoerotic Love in *Giovanni's Room*." *African American Review* 26 (1992): 425–35.
Dickson-Carr, Daryl. *The Columbia Guide to Contemporary African American Fiction*. New York: Columbia University Press, 2005.

Dickstein, Morris. "Wright, Baldwin, Cleaver." *New Letters* 38, no. 2 (1971): 117–24.
Diedrich, Maria. "James A. Baldwin—Obituaries for a Black Ishmael." In *James Baldwin: His Place in American Literary History and His Reception in Europe*, edited by Jakob Kollhofer, 129–32. Frankfurt: Peter Lang, 1991.
Donald, David. "A Fascinating Book." Review of *A Rap on Race* by James Baldwin and Margaret Mead. *The Virginia Quarterly Review* 47, no. 4 (1971): 619–22.
Dyson, Michael Eric. *Know What I Mean?: Reflections on Hip Hop*. New York: Basic Civitas, 2007.
Eagleton, Terry. *Literary Theory: An Introduction*, 2nd ed. Minneapolis: University of Minnesota Press, 1996.
Ellison Ralph. "Richard Wright's Blues." In *The Collected Essays of Ralph Ellison*, edited by John F. Callahan, 128–44. New York: Modern Library, 2003.
Elman, Richard. Review of *A Rap on Race* by James Baldwin and Margaret Mead. *New York Times Book Review*, June 27, 1971, 5.
Esty, William. "The Cities of the Plain." Review of *Giovanni's Room* by James Baldwin. *The New Republic*, December 17, 1956, 26.
Faulkner, William. "A Letter to the North." *Life*, March 5, 1956, 51–52.
Field, Douglas. "Looking for Jimmy Baldwin: Sex, Privacy, and Black Nationalist Fervor." *Callaloo* 27, no. 2 (2004): 457–80.
———. "Pentecostalism and All That Jazz: Tracing James Baldwin's Religion." *Literature and Theology* 22, no. 4 (2008): 436–57.
Finn, James. "A Gifted Native Son: The Identity of James Baldwin." *Commonweal*, October 30, 1962, 113–16.
Flamer, Merrianne. "Another Good Book by Man of Letters." Review of *If Beale Street Could Talk* by James Baldwin. *Freedomways* (Fourth Quarter 1974): 356–59.
Fleming, John. Review of *Evidence of Things Not Seen* by James Baldwin. *The New York Times Book Review*, November 24, 1985, 25.
Flint, Robert W. "Not Ideas but Life." Review of *Notes of a Native Son* by James Baldwin. *Commentary: A Jewish Newsletter* 21 (1956): 494–95.
Freedman, Janet. Review of *No Name in the Street* by James Baldwin. *Library Journal*, April 15, 1972, 1453.
Frontain, Raymond-Jean. "James Baldwin's *Giovanni's Room* and the Biblical Myth of David." *CEA Critic* 57 (1995): 41–58.
Fryer, Sarah Beebe. "Retreat From Experience: Despair and Suicide in James Baldwin's Novels." *The Journal of the Midwest Modern Language Association* 19 (1986): 21–28.
Gates, Henry Louis, Jr. "Preface to Blackness: Text and Pretext." In *Afro-American Literature: The Reconstruction of Instruction*, edited by Dexter Fisher and Robert B. Stepto, 58–68. New York: Modern Language Association of America, 1979.

Gayle, Addison, Jr. "A Defense of James Baldwin." *College Language Association Journal* 10 (1967): 201–8.

———. "The Dialectic of *The Fire Next Time*." *Negro History Bulletin* 30 (1967): 15–16.

George, Nelson. *Post-Soul Nation: The Explosive, Contradictory, Triumphant, and Tragic 1980s as Experienced by African Americans (Previously Known as Blacks and Before That Negroes)*. New York: Viking, 2004.

Gibson, Donald B. "Wright's Invisible Native Son." *American Quarterly* 21 (1969): 728–38.

Godsell, Geoffrey. "Old and New Novels on Racial Themes." Review of *Another Country* by James Baldwin. *Christian Science Monitor*, July 19, 1962, 11.

Goldstein, Richard. "'Go the Way Your Blood Beats': An Interview with James Baldwin." In *James Baldwin: The Legacy*, edited by Quincy Troupe, 173–85. New York: Simon & Schuster, 1989.

Greeley, Andrew M. Review of *The Fire Next Time* by James Baldwin. *Critic*, April 1963, 72.

Gross, John. "Day of Wrath." Review of *The Fire Next Time* by James Baldwin. *New Statesman*, July 19, 1963, 79–80.

Gross, Theodore. "The World of James Baldwin." *Critique: Studies in Modern Fiction* 7 (1965): 139–49.

Haney, Robert W. "James Baldwin in Search of Self." Review of *No Name in the Street* by James Baldwin. *The Christian Science Monitor*, June 21, 1972, 11.

Hardy, Clarence E. *James Baldwin's God: Sex, Hope, and Crisis in Black Holiness Culture*. Knoxville: University of Tennessee Press, 2003.

Harris, Trudier. "The Eyes as Weapon in *If Beale Street Could Talk*." *MELUS* 5 (1978): 54–66.

———. "Introduction." In *Black Women in the Fiction of James Baldwin*, by Trudier Harris, 3–11. Knoxville: University of Tennessee Press, 1985.

———, ed. *New Essays on "Go Tell It on the Mountain."* New York: Cambridge University Press, 1996.

———. "The South as Woman: Chimeric Images of Emasculation in *Just Above My Head*." In *Studies in Black American Literature Volume I: Black American Prose Theory*, edited by Chester B. Fontenot, 89–109. Greenwood, FL: Penkevill, 1984.

Haselden, Kyle. "Reverberating Explosion." Review of *The Fire Next Time* by James Baldwin. *Christian Century*, May 1, 1963, 582–83.

Haskell, Ann S. "Baldwin: Harlem on His Mind." Review of *Little Man, Little Man: A Story of Childhood* by James Baldwin. *Book World*, September 11, 1997, E6.

Hemphill, Essex, ed. *Brother to Brother: New Writings by Gay Black Men*. Washington, DC: RedBone Press, 2007.

Henderson, Carol E. *James Baldwin's Go Tell It on the Mountain: Historical and Critical Essays*. New York: Peter Lang, 2006.

Hicks, Granville. "A Gun in the Hand of a Hater." Review of *Blues for Mister Charlie* by James Baldwin. *Saturday Review*, May 2, 1964, 27–28.

———. "Tormented Triangle." Review of *Giovanni's Room* by James Baldwin. *The New York Times Book Review*, October 14, 1956, 5.

Hogan, William. "Baldwin's Comment on a 'Sub-Culture.'" Review of *Another Country* by James Baldwin. *San Francisco Chronicle*, June 28, 1962, 35.

Howe, Irving. "Black Boys and Native Sons." In *Five Black Writers: Essays on Wright, Ellison, Baldwin, Hughes, and LeRoi Jones*, edited by Donald Gibson, 254–70. New York: New York University Press, 1970.

———. "A Protest of His Own." Review of *Nobody Knows My Name* by James Baldwin. *The New York Times Book Review*, July 2, 1961, 4.

Hughes, Langston. "From Harlem to Paris." Review of *Notes of a Native Son* by James Baldwin. *The New York Times Book Review*, February 26, 1956, 26.

"In the Castle of My Skin." Review of *Notes of a Native Son* by James Baldwin. *Time*, December 15, 1955, 112+.

Jacoby, Jay Bruce. "The Music Is the Message: Teaching Baldwin's 'Sonny's Blues.'" *The English Record* 29 (1978): 2–4.

Johnson, E. Patrick, and Mae Henderson. *Black Queer Studies: A Critical Anthology*. Durham: Duke University Press, 2005.

———. "Introduction." In Johnson and Henderson, *Black Queer Studies*, 1–17.

Jones, Jacqueline C. "Finding a Way to Listen: The Emergence of the Hero as an Artist in James Baldwin's 'Sonny's Blues.'" *College Language Association Journal* 42 (1999): 462–82.

Jones, Leroi. "Black Art." In *Black Poets*, edited by Dudley Randall, 223. Toronto: Bantam, 1971.

Jordan, June. Review of *If Beale Street Could Talk* by James Baldwin. *The Village Voice*, June 20, 1974, 33–34.

Joseph, Peniel E. *Black Power Movement: Rethinking the Civil Rights-Black Power Era*. New York: Routledge, 2006.

———. *Waiting 'Til the Midnight Hour: A Narrative History of Black Power in America*. New York: Holt Paperbacks, 2007.

Karp, David. "A Squalid World." Review of *Giovanni's Room* by James Baldwin. *Saturday Review*, December 1, 1956, 34.

Kauffmann, Stanley. "Another Baldwin." Review of *Going to Meet the Man* by James Baldwin. *The New York Times Book Review*, December 12, 1965, 5.

Kent, George E. "Baldwin and the Problem of Being." *College Language Association Journal* 7 (1964): 202–14.

Kim, Kichung. "Wright, the Protest Novel, and Baldwin's Faith." *College Language Association Journal* 17 (1974): 387–96.

Kinnamon, Keneth, ed. *James Baldwin: A Collection of Critical Essays*. Englewood Cliffs, NJ: Prentice-Hall, 1974.

Kluger, Richard. "Shame May Scorch What Fury Singes." Review of *Blues for Mister Charlie* by James Baldwin. *Book Week*, May 31, 1964, 5.

Köllhofer, Jakob, ed. *James Baldwin: His Place in American Literary History and His Reception in Europe*. Frankfurt: Peter Lang, 1991.
Leeming, David Adams. *James Baldwin: A Biography*. New York: Knopf, 1994.
Lehmann-Haupt, Christopher. Review of *The Devil Finds Work* by James Baldwin. *The New York Times*, June 4, 1976, C23.
Leitch, Vincent B. *American Literary Criticism since the 1930s*, 2nd ed. London: Routledge, 2009.
Leitch, Vincent R., ed. *Oxford Companion to African American Literature, American Literary Criticism: 1930s–1980s*.
Lester, Julius. Review of *Little Man, Little Man: A Story of Childhood* by James Baldwin. *The New York Times Book Review*, September 4, 1977, 22.
Lobb, Edward. "James Baldwin's Blues and the Function of Art." *The International Fiction Review* 6 (1979): 143–48.
Locke, Alain. "New Negro." In *The New Negro*, edited by Alain Locke. 1925. Reprint, New York: Touchstone, 1992.
Long, Robert Emmet. "From Elegant to Hip." Review of *Tell Me How Long the Train's Been Gone* by James Baldwin. *The Nation*, June 10, 1968, 770.
"Lord, Hold My Hand." Review of *Go Tell It on the Mountain* by James Baldwin. *Time*, May 18, 1953, 126.
Lubiano, Wahneema, ed. *The House That Race Built: Original Essays by Toni Morrison, Angela Y. Davis, Cornel West, and Others on Black Americans and Politics in America Today*. New York: Vintage, 1998.
Lynch, Michael F. "*Just Above My Head*: James Baldwin's Quest for Belief." *Literature and Theology* 11 (1997): 284–98.
Macebuh, Stanley. *James Baldwin: A Critical Study*. New York: The Third Press, 1973.
MacInnes, Colin. "Dark Angel: The Writings of James Baldwin." *Encounter* 21 (1963): 22–33.
Maginnis, Ruth. Review of *A Dialogue* by James Baldwin and Nikki Giovanni. *Library Journal*, November 15, 1973, 3476.
Malburne, Meredith M. "No Blues for Mr. Henry: Locating Richard's Revolution." In *Reading Contemporary African American Drama: Fragments of History, Fragments of Self*, edited by Trudier Harris and Jennifer Larson, 39–57. New York: Peter Lang, 2007.
Malcolm, David. "Wrong Pulpit." Review of *Another Country* by James Baldwin. *The New Yorker*, August 4, 1962, 69–70.
Maloff, Saul. "The Two Baldwins." Review of *Another Country* by James Baldwin. *The Nation*, July 14, 1962, 15–16.
Marable, Manning. *Let Nobody Turn Us Around: Voices on Resistance, Reform, and Renewal*. Lanham, MD: Rowan and Littlefield, 2003.
Marcus, Steven. "The American Negro in Search of Identity." Review of *Go Tell It on the Mountain* by James Baldwin. *Commentary: A Jewish Review* 16 (1953): 456–63.

Mayfield, Julian. "A Love Affair with the United States." Review of *Nobody Knows My Name* by James Baldwin. *The New Republic*, August 7, 1961, 25.

McBride, Dwight A, ed. *James Baldwin Now*. New York: New York University Press, 1999.

———. "Straight Black Studies: On African American Studies, James Baldwin, and Black Queer Studies." In Johnson and Henderson. *Black Queer Studies*, 68–89.

Mengay, Donald H. "The Failed Copy: *Giovanni's Room* and the (Re)Contextualization of Difference." *Genders* 17 (1993): 59–70.

Mercier, Jean. Review of *Little Man, Little Man: A Story of Childhood* by James Baldwin. *Publishers Weekly*, March 21, 1977, 78.

Miller, D. Quentin, ed. *Re-Viewing James Baldwin: Things Not Seen*. Philadelphia: Temple University Press, 2000.

Miller, James. "What Does It Mean to Be an American?: The Dialectics of Self-Discovery in Baldwin's 'Paris Essays' (1950–1961)." *Journal of American Studies* 42, no. 1 (2008): 51–66.

Mitra, B. K. "The Wright-Baldwin Controversy." *The Indian Journal of American Studies* 1 (1969): 101–5.

Moon, Eric. Review of *Another Country* by James Baldwin. *Library Journal*, June 1, 1962, 2154.

Morland, Iain, and Annabelle Willox, eds. *Queer Theory*. Houndmills: Palgrave Macmillan, 2005.

Murray, Albert. "Something Different, Something More." In *Anger and Beyond: The Negro Writer in the United States*, edited by Herbert Hill, 112–37. New York: Harper & Row, 1966.

Murray, Rolland. *Our Living Manhood: Literature, Black Power, and Masculine Ideology*. Philadelphia: University of Pennsylvania Press, 2007.

Muwakkil, Salim. Review of *The Price of the Ticket* by James Baldwin. *The New York Times Book Review*, October 20, 1985, 35.

Neal, Larry. "The Black Writer's Role, III: James Baldwin," in *Visions of a Liberated Future: Black Arts Movement Writings*, edited by Michael Schwartz. New York: Thunder's Mouth Press, 1989.

Nelson, Emmanuel S. "Critical Deviance: Homophobia and the Reception of James Baldwin's Fiction." *Journal of American Culture* 14 (1991): 91–96.

———. "James Baldwin's Vision of Otherness and Community." *MELUS* 10 (1983): 27–31.

Nordell, Roderick. "Old and New Novels on Racial Themes." *Christian Science Monitor*, July 19, 1962, 11.

Norman, Brian. "Crossing Identitarian Lines: Women's Liberation and James Baldwin's Early Essays." *Women's Studies* 35, no. 3 (2006): 241–64.

———. "Duplicity, Purity, and Politicized Morality: *Go Tell It on the Mountain* and the Emergence of the Civil Rights Movement." In Henderson, *James Baldwin's Go Tell It on the Mountain: Historical and Critical Essays*, 13–27.

———. "James Baldwin's Unifying Polemic: Racial Segregation, Moral Integration, and the Polarizing Figure of Emmett Till." In Pollack and Metress, *Emmett Till in Literary Memory and Imagination*, 75–97.

———. "Reading a 'Closet Screenplay': Hollywood, James Baldwin's Malcolms, and the Threat of Historical Irrelevance." *African American Review*, nos. 1–2 (2005): 103–18.

Nowlin, Michael. "Ralph Ellison, James Baldwin, and the Liberal Imagination." *Arizona Quarterly* 60, no. 2 (2004): 117–40.

Oates, Joyce Carol. "A Quite Moving and Very Traditional Celebration of Love." Review of *If Beale Street Could Talk* by James Baldwin. *The New York Times Book Review*, May 19, 1974, sec. 7, 1–2.

Obama, Barack. "A More Perfect Union." Speech. *Wall Street Journal*, March 18, 2008, http://blogs.wsj.com/washwire/2008/03/18/text-of-obamas-speech-a-more-perfect-union/.

O'Daniel, Therman B. "James Baldwin: An Interpretive Study." *College Language Association Journal* 7 (1963): 37–47.

Olson, Barbara K. "'Come-to-Jesus Stuff' in James Baldwin's *Go Tell It on the Mountain* and *The Amen Corner*." *African American Review* 31, no. 2 (1997): 295–301.

Pickering, James H., ed. *Fiction 100: An Anthology of Short Fiction*, 9th ed. Upper Saddle River, NJ: Prentice Hall, 2001.

Pollack, Harriet, and Christopher Metress, eds. *Emmett Till in Literary Memory and Imagination*. Baton Rouge: Louisiana State University Press, 2008.

Porter, Horace A. *Stealing the Fire: The Art and Protest of James Baldwin*. New York: Wesleyan University Press, 1989.

Pratt, Louis. *James Baldwin*. Boston: Twayne Publishers, 1978.

———. "James Baldwin and 'The Literary Ghetto.'" *College Language Journal* 20 (1976): 262–72.

Prescott, Peter S. "This Train's Long Gone." Review of *No Name in the Street* by James Baldwin. *Newsweek*, May 29, 1972, 85–87.

Puzo, Mario. Review of *Tell Me How Long the Train's Been Gone* by James Baldwin. *The New York Times Book Review*, June 23, 1968, 5.

Rainer, Dachine. "Rage into Order." Review of *Notes of a Native Son* by James Baldwin. *Commonweal*, January 13, 1956, 384–86.

Raleigh, John Henry. "Messages and Sagas." Review of *Go Tell It on the Mountain* by James Baldwin. *The New Republic*, June 22, 1953, 21.

Redding, Saunders. "In His Native Land." Review of *Nobody Knows My Name* by James Baldwin. *The New York Herald Tribune*, June 25, 1961, 36.

———. "James Baldwin Miscellany." Review of *Notes of a Native Son* by James Baldwin. *The New York Herald Tribune Book Review*, February 26, 1956, 4.

———. "Sensitive Portrait of a Lovely Boy." Review of *Go Tell It on the Mountain* by James Baldwin. *The New York Herald Tribune Book Review*, May 17, 1953, 5.

———. "Since Richard Wright." *African Forum* 1 (1966): 21–31.
Reid-Pharr, Robert F. *Once You Go Black: Choice, Desire, and the Black American Intellectual*. New York: New York University Press, 2007.
———. "Tearing the Goat's Flesh: Homosexuality, Abjection, and the Production of Late Twentieth-Century Black Masculinity." *Studies in the Novel* 28, no. 3 (1996): 372–94.
Reilly, John M. "'Sonny's Blues': James Baldwin's Image of Black Community." *Negro American Literature Forum* 4 (1970): 56–60.
Review of *The Amen Corner* by James Baldwin. *Choice*, May 1969, 382.
Review of *The Devil Finds Work* by James Baldwin. *Choice*, September 1976, 804.
Review of *The Devil Finds Work* by James Baldwin. *Progressive*, August 1976, 44.
Review of *The Devil Finds Work* by James Baldwin. *The Village Voice*, March 29, 1976, 43.
Review of *Go Tell It on the Mountain* by James Baldwin. *The Nation*, January 5, 1953, 488.
Review of *Jimmy's Blues* by James Baldwin. *Library Journal*, April 1, 1986, 153.
Review of *Jimmy's Blues* by James Baldwin. *Virginia Quarterly Review* 62 (1986): 99.
Review of *No Name in the Street* by James Baldwin. *Choice*, November 1972, 1209.
Review of "Notes of a Native Son" by James Baldwin. *United States Quarterly Book Review* (March 1956): 35–36.
Review of *Nothing Personal* by James Baldwin and Richard Avedon. *Newsweek*, October 26, 1964, 122.
Review of *The Price of the Ticket* by James Baldwin. *Kirkus Reviews*, August 15, 195, 833–34.
Robbins, Susan. "Anguish and Anger." *Virginia English Bulletin* 36 (1986): 59–61.
Robertson, Patricia K. "Baldwin's 'Sonny's Blues': The Scapegoat Metaphor." *The University of Mississippi Studies in English* 9 (1991): 189–98.
Rolo, Charles. "Questions of Color." Review of *Nobody Knows My Name* by James Baldwin. *Atlantic Monthly*, July 1961, 126–28.
———. Review of *Giovanni's Room* by James Baldwin. *Atlantic Monthly*, December 1956, 98.
Roth, Philip. "Channel X: Two Plays on the Race Conflict." Review of *Blues for Mister Charlie* by James Baldwin. *The New York Review of Books*, May 28, 1964, 10–13.
Salaam, Kalamu ya. "Black Arts Movement." In *The Oxford Companion to African American Literature*, edited by William L. Andrews, Frances Smith Foster, and Trudier Harris, 70–74. New York: Oxford University Press, 1997.
Sanderson, Jim. "Grace in 'Sonny's Blues.'" *Short Story* 6 (1998): 85–95.

Savery, Pancho. "Baldwin, Bebop, and 'Sonny's Blues.'" In *Understanding Others: Cultural and Cross-cultural Studies and the Teaching of Literature*, edited by Joseph F. Trimmer and Tilly Warnock, 165–76. Urbana, IL: National Council of Teachers of English, 1992.

Schraufnagel, Noel. *From Apology to Protest: The Black American Novel*. Deland, FL: Everett/Edwards, 1973.

Scott, Lynn Orilla. *Witness to the Journey: James Baldwin's Later Fiction*. East Lansing: Michigan State University Press, 2002.

Scott, Nathan O., Jr. "Judgment Marked by a Cellar: The American Negro Writer and the Dialectic of Despair." *Denver Quarterly* 2 (1967): 5–35.

Sedgwick, Eve Kosofsky, ed. *Novel Gazing: Queer Readings in Fiction*. Durham: Duke University Press, 1997.

Shawcross, John T. "Joy and Sadness, James Baldwin, Novelist." *Callaloo* 18 (1983): 100–11.

Sheppard, R. Z. "Ashes." Review of *No Name in the Street* by James Baldwin. *Time*, May 29, 1972, 83–84.

Sherard, Tracey. "Sonny's Bebop: Baldwin's 'Blues text' as Intracultural Critique." *African American Review* 32 (1998): 691–704.

Sivan, Miriam. "Out of and Back to Africa: James's Baldwin's *Go Tell It on the Mountain*." *Christianity and Literature* 51, no. 1 (2001): 29–41.

Smethurst, James Edward. *The Black Arts Movement: Literary Nationalism in the 1960s and 1970s*. Chapel Hill: The University of North Carolina Press, 2005.

Smith, Barbara. "Banked Fires on 'Beale Street.'" Review of *If Beale Street Could Talk* by James Baldwin. *The National Observer*, July 20, 1974, 37.

"Sorry Lives." Review of *Go Tell It on the Mountain* by James Baldwin. *The New Yorker*, June 20, 1953, 93.

Spurlin, William J. "Transgressing Boundaries: James Baldwin and the Identity Politics of Race and Sexuality." In *Fissions and Fusions: Proceedings of the First Conference of the Cape American Studies Association*, edited by Lesley Marx, Loes Nas, and Lara Dunwell, 46–55. Cape Town: University of the Western Cape Press, 1997.

Standley, Fred L. "'... Farther and Farther Apart': Richard Wright and James Baldwin." In *Critical Essays on Richard Wright*, edited by Yoshinobu Hakutani, 91–103. Boston: G. K. Hall, 1982.

———. "James Baldwin: The Artist as Incorrigible Disturber of the Peace." *Southern Humanities Review* 4 (1970): 18–30.

———. "James Baldwin: The Crucial Situation." *The South Atlantic Quarterly* 65 (1966): 371–81.

Standley, Fred L., and Nancy V. Burt, eds. *Critical Essays on James Baldwin*. Boston: G. K. Hall, 1988.

———. *James Baldwin: A Reference Guide*. Boston: G. K. Hall, 1980.

"State of the Negro." Review of *The Fire Next Time* by James Baldwin. *The Times Literary Supplement*, July 26, 1963.

Stern, Daniel. "A Special Corner on Truth." Review of *Going to Meet the Man* by James Baldwin. *Saturday Review*, November 6, 1965, 32.

Strong, Augusta. Review of *Another Country* by James Baldwin. *Freedomways* (Fall 1962): 500–503.
Tate, Greg. *Flyboy in the Buttermilk*. New York: Simon & Schuster, 1992.
Taubman, Robert. "Early Sartre." Review of *Another Country* by James Baldwin. *The New Statesman*, July 13, 1962, 53.
Taylor, Douglas. "Three Lean Cats in a Hall of Mirrors: James Baldwin, Norman Mailer, and Eldridge Cleaver on Race and Masculinity." *Texas Studies in Literature and Language* 52, no. 1 (2010): 70–101.
T. D. J. "Search for Identity." Review of *Notes of a Native Son* by James Baldwin. *Phylon* 17 (1956): 87–88.
Teachout, Terry. "Tragic Decline." Review of *The Price of the Ticket* by James Baldwin. *Commentary*, December 1985, 76–80.
Tedesco, John L. "*Blues for Mister Charlie*: The Rhetorical Dimension." *Players: Magazine of American Theatre* 50 (1975): 20–23.
Thomas, Kendall. "'Ain't Nothin' Like the Real Thing': Black Masculinity, Gay Sexuality, and the Jargon of Authenticity." In Blount and Cunningham, *Representing Black Men*, 55–69.
Thompson, John. "Baldwin: The Prophet as Artist." Review of *Tell Me How Long the Train's Been Gone* by James Baldwin. *Commentary*, June 1968, 68.
"Too Much Fire?" Review of *The Fire Next Time* by James Baldwin. *Economist*, August 3, 1963, 444.
"Tortured Voice." Review of *Going to Meet the Man* by James Baldwin. *Newsweek*, November 8, 1965, 114.
Troupe, Quincy. *James Baldwin: The Legacy*. New York: Simon & Schuster, 1989.
Waldrep, Shelton. "'Being Bridges': Cleaver/Baldwin/Lorde and African-American Sexism and Sexuality." In *Critical Essays Gay and Lesbian Writers of Color*, edited by Emmanuel S. Nelson, 167–80. New York: Haworth Press, 1994.
Warren, Kenneth W. *What Was African American Literature?* Cambridge: Harvard University Press, 2011.
Webster, Harvey Curtis. "Community of Pride." Review of *Go Tell It on the Mountain* by James Baldwin. *Saturday Review*, May 16, 1953, 14.
Weeks, Edward. Review of *No Name in the Street* by James Baldwin. *Atlantic Monthly*, June 1972, 108+.
Weinger, Mackenzie. "Bill O'Reilly: 'The White Establishment Is Now the Minority.'" *Politico.com*, November 6, 2012. http://www.politico.com/blogs/media/2012/11/bill-oreilly-the-white-establishment-is-now-the-minority-148705.html.
Weisenburger, Steven. "The Shudder and the Silence: James Baldwin on White Terror." *ANQ: A Quarterly Journal of Short Articles, Notes and Reviews* 15, no. 3 (2002): 3–12.
Werner, Craig. "The Economic Evolution of James Baldwin." *College Language Association Journal* 23 (1979): 12–31.

West, Anthony. Review of *Giovanni's Room* by James Baldwin. *The New Yorker*, November 10, 1956, 220.
Wills, Garry. "What Color Is God?" Review of *The Fire Next Time* by James Baldwin. *The National Review*, May 21, 1963, 408–17.
Wortis, Irving. Review of *The Amen Corner* by James Baldwin. *Library Journal*, June 15, 1967, 2428.
Wright, Richard. *Black Boy (American Hunger)*. 1945. New York: HarperPerennial, 1998.
Zaborowska, Magdalena J. *James Baldwin's Turkish Decade: Erotics of Exile*. Durham: Duke University Press, 2009.

Index

Abram, M. H., 78
Albert, Richard N., 87–88, 90
Allen, Shirley S., 47–48
Andrews, William, 57
Angelou, Maya, 60
Atlanta child murders, 2, 114
Atlantic Monthly, 105, 11, 112
Avedon, Richard, 76, 120

Baker, Houston A., 37, 84
Baker, Josephine, 35, 60
Baldwin, James, works by:
 "Alas, Poor Richard," 14
 The Amen Corner, 59, 70, 71, 118
 Another Country, 7, 12, 13, 16, 21–23, 37, 29, 50, 55, 74, 93, 97, 98, 105–7, 115, 135, 137
 Blues for Mister Charlie, 21–23, 46, 47, 55, 59, 94, 97, 118, 125, 133
 The Devil Finds Work, 113
 A Dialogue, 121
 "Down at the Cross," 28, 108, 142
 "Everybody's Protest Novel," 2, 10–11, 14, 52, 94, 102
 Evidence of Things Not Seen, 61, 114
 The Fire Next Time, 1, 7, 8, 11, 12, 14, 17, 21–24, 27, 28, 43, 55, 60, 70, 75, 76, 97, 98, 107–12, 142, 143
 "Freaks and the American Ideal of Manhood," 64
 Giovanni's Room, 7, 22, 27, 29, 42, 50, 52, 53, 62–65, 67–69, 74, 93, 97, 98, 103, 104, 105, 107
 Go Tell It on the Mountain, 7, 12, 22, 23, 27, 42, 47, 48, 50, 52, 53, 55, 56, 59, 61, 52, 63, 70, 71, 78, 93, 97, 98, 99, 100, 101, 103, 104, 105, 107, 125, 127, 131
 Going to Meet the Man, 81, 94, 119, 134
 "The Harlem Ghetto," 100
 If Beale Street Could Talk, 43–46, 54, 116, 118, 133, 135
 Jimmy's Blues, 76, 77, 120
 Just Above My Head, 53, 54, 61, 65, 70, 117, 130, 131, 133, 135, 138
 Little Man, Little Man, 119
 "The Male Prison," 64
 "Many Thousands Gone," 10, 14, 52
 "My Dungeon Shook," 28, 110, 143
 No Name in the Street, 40, 98, 112, 113, 135
 Nobody Knows My Name, 7, 40, 110, 11, 112
 "Northern Protestant," 1
 Notes of a Native Son, 1, 7, 10, 94, 97–98, 100, 101–4, 114, 120, 141
 Nothing Personal, 76, 120
 One Day When I Was Lost, 35, 41, 98, 118, 119, 121, 125
 "Previous Condition," 100
 The Price of the Ticket, 114
 Rap on Race, 120
 "Sonny's Blues," 1, 81–95, 130
 "Stranger in a Village," 94, 102, 107, 114
 Tell Me How Long the Train's Been Gone, 115, 129, 133, 135
 The Welcome Table, 35
Bambara, Toni Cade, 39, 116
Baraka, Amiri (Leroi Jones), 17, 28, 31, 36, 39, 60, 91, 92, 118

Baraka, Amiri, works by: *Dutchman*, 118
Beam, Joseph, works by: *In the Life: A Black Gay Anthology*, 62
bebop, 83–84, 91–92
Belafonte, Harry, 7
Bell, George E., 52–53
Berry, Edwin C., 7
Bigsby, C. W., 31
bisexuality, 74
black aesthetic, 31–33, 38, 56
Black Arts Movement, 57
black church, 2, 22, 45, 127, 131–32
black feminist theory, 67
black nationalism, 17, 24, 44, 99, 130, 131
Black Panthers, 15, 52, 131
Black Power, 17, 33, 36, 53, 120, 128, 130
black queer studies, 126–30
black studies, 33, 36, 37, 39, 51, 127, 129
Bloom, Harold, 54–55
Blount, Marcellus, works by: *Representing Black Men*, 62
blues, 9, 23, 74, 82, 83–85, 87–89, 91, 93, 94, 95, 126
Bobia, Rosa, 3, 78
Bone, Robert, 3, 9, 10, 18–23, 24–26, 29, 31, 33, 35, 41, 50, 52
BookWorld, 119
Bookweek, 118
Breit, Harvey, 24–25
Brooks, Gwendolyn, 8
Bruck, Peter, 53, 56
Brunn, Robert, 99, 102, 115
Bryant, Jerry H., 33, 51, 113
Burks, Mary Fair, 44–46
Burt, Nancy, 59
Byerman, Keith, 86–87, 90

Campbell, James, works by: *Talking at the Gates: A Life of James Baldwin*, 64, 66, 104, 110
Cederstrom, Lorelei, 49–50
Chametzky, Jules, 60
Champion, Ernest, 38–39, 53
Charney, Maurice, 14–15

Christian Science Monitor, 102, 106, 112, 114
Christianity, 23, 48, 59, 65, 71, 72, 102, 106, 107, 109, 112, 114, 131, 132
civil rights movement, 1, 8, 15, 38, 44, 102, 110, 112, 126, 128
Clark, Keith, 130–31, 137
Clark, Kenneth, 7
Clark, Michael, 88–89, 90
Cleaver, Eldridge, 3, 9, 10, 15–18, 24, 28, 29, 33, 35, 39, 50, 62, 67, 68, 70, 102, 129, 137
Cleaver, Eldridge, works by: "Notes on a Native Son," 9, 15–18, 29, 33, 70, 129
Clinton, Hillary, 140
Clotel, 19, 20
Cobb, Michael J., 127–28
Coles, Robert, 25
Collins, Lisa Gail, 57
Commentary, 100, 103, 114, 115, 117
Commonweal, 102, 106, 118
Congress of Racial Equality (CORE), 7
Crawford, Margo Natalie, 57
Crenshaw, Kimberle, 67
cultural studies, 56, 61, 64, 66, 70, 72–75, 77, 129, 130, 132
Cunningham, George P., works by: *Representing Black Men*, 62

DeGout, Yasmin, 63
Dickstein, Morris, 33
Diedrich, Maria, 60
Dorsey, James, 139
Dr. Dre, 66
Dreiser, Theodore, 136
Dyson, Michael Eric, 78

Eagleton, Terry, 78
Ellison, Ralph, 2, 8, 9–12, 14, 20, 33, 36, 51–52, 56, 77, 99, 100–101, 136, 138
Ellison, Ralph, works by: *Invisible Man*, 8, 20, 47, 56, 99, 100, 101; "The World and the Jug," 14

eroticism, 71
Evers, Medgar, 8, 110
expatriation, 61, 67, 135

Farrakhan, Louis, 66
Faulkner, William, 110, 139
feminism, 49, 50, 125
feminist theory, 2, 4, 50, 61, 70, 77, 130, 143
Field, Douglas, 128–29, 132–33
France, 3, 35, 78, 113
Franklin, Aretha, 74
Freedomways, 107, 109, 116
Frontain, Raymond-Jean, 64–65
Fryer, Sarah Beebe, 51

Gaines, Ernest, 130
Garies and Their Friends, The, 19
Gates, Henry Louis, 1, 35, 37–38, 56, 60
Gayle, Addison, 27–30, 37, 70, 97
gender, 2, 49, 50, 68, 69, 75, 126, 130, 132
George, Nelson, 95
Gibson, Donald B., 33
Goldstein, Richard, 60, 64, 128
Gross, Theodore, 25–26

Hansberry, Lorraine, 7
Happersberger, Lucien, 65, 74
Hardy, Clarence, 78, 132
Harlem, 11, 12, 23, 36, 45, 48, 82, 86, 93, 100, 119
Harper, Philip Brian, 131
Harris, Trudier, 1, 54, 55, 78, 133
Hemphill, Essex, works by: *Brother to Brother: New Writing by Black Gay Men*, 62
Henderson, Mae G., 129
Henderson, Stephen, 37
Hicks, Granville, 106, 117–18
Himes, Chester, 22
Hole, Jeffrey, W., 75
homoeroticism, 42, 70, 97
homosexuality, 2, 17, 23, 29, 42, 45, 49, 50, 60, 62–66, 73, 78, 104, 105, 107, 116, 117, 126, 128
Horne, Lena, 7

Howe, Irving, 3, 8, 9–15, 20, 22, 24, 29, 31, 33, 35, 39, 41, 111, 117, 136
Howe, Irving, works by: "Black Boys and Native Sons," 8, 9–15, 111, 117, 136
Hurston, Zora Neale, 2

Ice Cube, 66
Ice T, 66
identity, black, 49, 66, 131, 138
identity, gay, 49, 60, 62, 63, 67, 74

Jacoby, Jay Bruce, 84–85
James, Henry, 61, 78, 136
jazz, 74, 88, 93
Jones, Clarence B., 7
Jones, Jacqueline, 82, 92–93
Joseph, Peniel, 33
Julien, Isaac, works by: *Looking for Langston*, 62

Kenan, Randall, 75
Kennedy, John F., 7, 8
Kennedy, Robert F., 7
Kent, George, 26–27, 35, 40, 94, 106
Killen, John O., 130
Kim, Kichung, 51
King, Martin Luther, Jr., 28, 36, 110, 112, 140
Kinnamon, Keith, 3, 35
Kirkus, 114
Kun, Josh, 74–75

Larson, Jennifer, 133
Leeming, David, works by: *James Baldwin: A Biography*, 35, 64
Leitch, Vincent R., 57
Library Journal, 101, 107, 11, 118, 120, 121
Lobb, Edward, 85–86
Lorde, Audre, 67–69
love, 4, 25, 27, 28, 36, 41, 50, 52–54, 60, 63, 65, 67–68, 70–72, 74, 77, 105, 112, 117, 129, 133, 141, 143
Lubiano, Wahneema, 56
Lynch, Michael F., 70–71, 72, 76

Macebuh, Stanley, 32
MacInnes, Colin, 23–24
Maclean's, 117
Madonna, 62
Mailer, Norman, 22, 110, 137
Malburne, Meredith M., 133–34
Mapplethorpe, Robert, 62
Marable, Manning, 1
Marxist criticism, 4, 43
masculinity, 16, 36, 50, 66, 78, 128, 132, 137
McBride, Dwight A., 3, 72–73, 126, 129–31, 137, 139
McCarthy, Mary, 60, 61
Mengay, Donald, 67, 68–69
Miller, D. Quentin, 72, 75, 76–77, 120, 126
Miller, James, 134–35
Miller, Joshua L., 76
Millet, Kate, 50
Million Man March, 66
Mitra, B. K., 33
Morgenthau, Harry, 7
Morrison, Toni, 2, 36, 39, 56, 60
Muhammad, Elijah, 7, 28, 108
Murray, Albert, 33
Murray, Rolland, 130–31, 137
music, 74, 82–89, 91–93, 133

Napier, Winston, 78
Nation, The, 100, 106, 113, 115
Nation of Islam (Black Muslims), 28, 66, 108, 142
National Observer, 116
National Review, The, 109, 115
Neal, Larry, 17–18, 36, 91, 92
Nelson, Emmanuel, 48–49, 50, 62–63, 69
neo-black nationalism, 66
New Leader, 113
New Republic, 101, 104, 11
New Statesman, 107, 108
New York Herald Tribune, 111
New York Review of Books, 118, 120
New York Times, 110, 113
New York Times Book Review, 103, 105, 114, 116, 119, 120
New Yorker, 101, 104, 105, 106, 110

Newsweek, 112, 119, 120
Newton, Huey P., 137, 138
Norman, Brian, 121, 125–26
Nowlin, Michael, 136–37
NWA (Niggaz with Attitude), 66

Obama, Barack, 140–43
Olson, Barbara K., 70, 71–72, 76
O'Reilly, Bill, 140

Parker, Charlie, 91
Petry, Ann, 8, 22
Phylon, 99, 102, 110
Playboy, 114
Porter, Horace A., 78
postmodern theory, 61, 66, 67, 70, 77, 135
Pratt, Louis H., 39–42, 44
Public Enemy, 66
Publishers Weekly, 119

queer theory, 2, 3, 4, 15, 33, 61–63, 67, 70, 72, 77, 105, 143

Redding, J. Saunders, 18, 33, 99, 103, 111, 112
Reed, Ishmael, 39
Reid-Pharr, Robert, 69–70, 78, 131, 137–39
Reilly, John M., 83–86, 88
religion, 54, 68, 70–72, 77, 78, 99, 100, 102, 118, 125, 127–28, 131, 132–33
Riggs, Marlon, works by: *Tongues Untied*, 62
Robbins, Susan, 89
Robertson, Patricia K., 90
Ross, Marlon, 73–74, 76
RuPaul, 62

Salaam, Kalamu ya, 36
San Francisco Chronicle, 106
Saturday Review Magazine, 99, 104, 116, 119
Savery, Pancho, 82, 84, 91–93
Schraufnagel, Noel, 8
Scott, Lynn Orilla, 135–36
Scott, Nathan, 33

Sedgwick, Eve Kosofsky, 78
sexuality, 2, 23, 41, 48, 49, 51, 54, 62, 64, 66–70, 72–75, 85, 92, 93, 95, 116, 121, 127–30, 132
Shawcross, John T., 42
Sherard, Tracey, 93–94
Sivan, Miriam, 131–32
Smethurst, James, 57
Smith, Bessie, 74–75
Smith, Jerome, 7
Snoop Dogg, 66
Spurlin, William J., 62
St. Paul-de-Vence, 35, 117
Standley, Fred, 3, 30, 31, 52, 54, 59
Standley, Nancy, 54
Stowe, Harriet Beecher, 78
Student Nonviolent Coordinating Committee (SNCC), 7

Tate, Greg, 95
Taylor, Douglas, 137, 139
Tedesco, John L., 46–47
Thelwell, Michael, 66
theology, 70–71, 132
Thomas, Kendall, 65–67
Time (magazine), 7, 8, 35, 44, 101, 102, 113
Times Literary Supplement, 108
Torn, Rip, 7, 117
Trilling, Lionel, 136
Troupe, Quincy, 60
Turkey, 135

Van Peebles, Melvin, 138
Village Voice, 64, 113, 116, 117
Virginia Quarterly, 120

Waldrep, Shelton, 67–68, 70
Walker, Alice, 39
Walker, Margaret, 8
Wallace, Maurice O., 129
Warren, Kenneth W., 134
Weisenburger, Steven, 134
Werner, Craig, 1, 43–44
West, Cornel, 56, 66
West, Dorothy, 8
Wideman, John Edgar, 39, 130
Williams, John A., 39
Wills, Gary, 109
Wilson, August, 130
Wright, Jeremiah, 140–42
Wright, Richard, 1, 2, 3, 8, 9–30, 31, 33, 36, 39, 51, 52, 56, 78, 100, 102, 11, 135, 136, 138
Wright, Richard, works by: *Black Boy*, 9; *Native Son*, 8–11, 13, 14, 19, 20, 47, 52, 56, 136; *The Outsider*, 99–100
Wright-Baldwin debate, 14–15, 33, 36

X, Malcolm, 36, 98, 108, 118–19, 125

Yerby, Frank, 22

Zaborowska, Magdalena, 135

www.ingramcontent.com/pod-product-compliance
Lightning Source LLC
Chambersburg PA
CBHW030656230426
43665CB00011B/1116